The Last Leopard

THE LAST LEOPARD

A Life of Giuseppe di Lampedusa

DAVID GILMOUR

Pantheon Books, New York

Library of Congress Cataloging-in-Publication Data

Gilmour, David, 1952-
The last leopard: a life of Giuseppe di Lampedusa / David
Gilmour.
p.   cm.
Originally published: London; New York: Quartet Books, 1988.
Includes bibliographical references and index.
1. Tomasi di Lampedusa, Giuseppe, 1896–1957—Biography.
2. Authors, Italian—20th century—Biography.   I. Title.
PQ4843.053Z68 1991   853'.912—dc20   90-53408
[B]   ISBN 0-679-40183-0

Manufactured in the United States of America
First American Edition

To Gioacchino and Nicoletta

Contents

Note on Translations

I am grateful to Collins Harvill for permission to quote from Archibald Colquhoun's fine translations of *The Leopard* and *Two Stories and a Memory*. Occasionally I have amended them, partly because (in the case of the memoir) he was given an imperfect text to work from, and partly because he himself made a number of minor mistakes in his translations. All other quotations from Lampedusa's published and unpublished works, his letters, diaries and other documents, have been translated by me. So have all the quotations from other people, except in those cases where reference is made to an English source in the notes.

GENEALOGICAL TABLE OF THE LAMPEDUSAS
AND SOME OF THEIR DESCENDANTS

(N.B. People not mentioned in the book have usually been omitted)

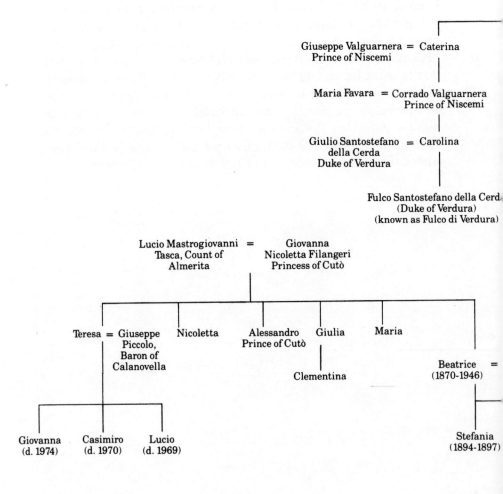

Giuseppe Valguarnera = Caterina
Prince of Niscemi

Maria Favara = Corrado Valguarnera
Prince of Niscemi

Giulio Santostefano = Carolina
della Cerda
Duke of Verdura

Fulco Santostefano della Cerda
(Duke of Verdura)
(known as Fulco di Verdura)

Lucio Mastrogiovanni = Giovanna
Tasca, Count of Nicoletta Filangeri
Almerita Princess of Cutò

Teresa = Giuseppe   Nicoletta   Alessandro   Giulia   Maria
Piccolo,   Prince of Cutò
Baron of
Calanovella   Beatrice =
                                                                 (1870-1946)
                                  Clementina

Giovanna   Casimiro   Lucio   Stefania
(d. 1974)   (d. 1970)   (d. 1969)   (1894-1897)

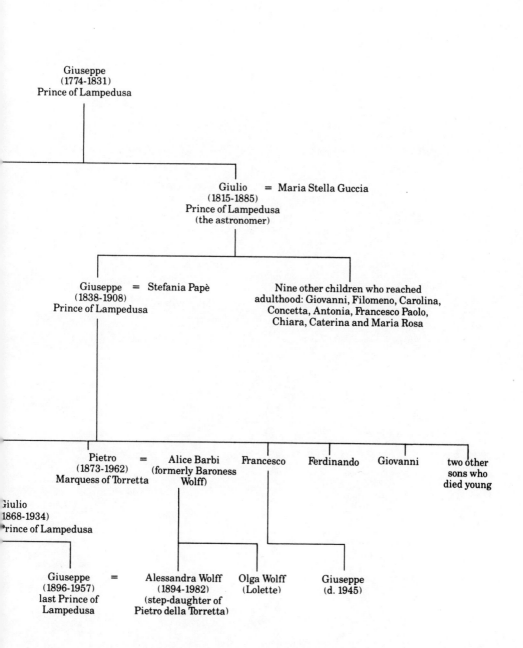

Giuseppe
(1774-1831)
Prince of Lampedusa

Giulio = Maria Stella Guccia
(1815-1885)
Prince of Lampedusa
(the astronomer)

Giuseppe = Stefania Papè
(1838-1908)
Prince of Lampedusa

Nine other children who reached
adulthood: Giovanni, Filomeno, Carolina,
Concetta, Antonia, Francesco Paolo,
Chiara, Caterina and Maria Rosa

Pietro = Alice Barbi   Francesco   Ferdinando   Giovanni   two other
(1873-1962)   (formerly Baroness   sons who
Marquess of Torretta   Wolff)   died young

Giulio
1868-1934)
Prince of Lampedusa

Giuseppe = Alessandra Wolff   Olga Wolff   Giuseppe
(1896-1957)   (1894-1982)   (Lolette)   (d. 1945)
last Prince of (step-daughter of
Lampedusa   Pietro della Torretta)

Our life is bounded by two silences: the silence of stars and that of graves.

Thomas Carlyle
(from the commonplace book
of Giuseppe di Lampedusa)

Foreword

In Search of Lampedusa

In the courtyard of the Villa Lampedusa, a few miles from Palermo, Frisian cows pick their way carefully through the rubble. Their home is a wasteland of defunct objects: broken boxes, squashed petrol cans, a clutter of old bathtubs. The villa itself is deserted, its broken shutters creaking with languor in the hot afternoon breeze. The facade is cracked and pockmarked, and the stucco has faded to a mild ochre; only the ceilings are intact, delicate, highly-wrought arrangements of fruit and flowers.

Most of the family homes recalled in the memoirs of Giuseppe Tomasi, last Prince of Lampedusa, are in similar stages of advanced ruin: the others have been destroyed altogether. The palace at Palma di Montechiaro, feudal base of the Lampedusas in southern Sicily, stands gaunt and derelict; their house at Torretta, in the hills west of Palermo, has been demolished and replaced by a monstrous orange school. The places of his mother's family have fared no better: at Bagheria the Villa Cutò is now a squalid tenement forming part of the station yard. More dismal still is the state of the Palazzo Cutò at Santa Margherita, most beautiful of all the palaces and inspiration for Donnafugata in *The Leopard*. Stricken by an earthquake twenty years ago, its wreckage remains undisturbed, the courtyards filled with beams and ruined masonry, the palm trees knocked sideways, some of them half buried. The front slumps down one side of the town's piazza, displaying broken balustrades and twisted balconies: all that remains of the internal decoration is a primitive fresco of the Castel Sant'Angelo in Rome. Behind the devastation, the garden which Lampedusa described as 'a paradise of parched scents' has become a wilderness infested by giant thistles. In its integrity he

described the house as 'a kind of eighteenth-century Pompeii, all
miraculously preserved intact'; in its desolation it symbolizes the
death of the Sicily to which he had belonged.

Biographers who travel 'in the footsteps' of their subjects invite
delusion and disappointment: amid buildings decayed and
gardens neglected, in once-peaceful places desecrated by
highways and concrete, it is often difficult to imagine the
inspiration of the writer or the poet. But if it is hard to conceive
of nightingales in north London, it is harder still to picture the
myrtles and fountains of Donnafugata. Sicily, wrote Lampedusa,
is 'the most destructive of countries', over-burdened by a past for
which it has little respect. Yet even he, disillusioned by his island
and pessimistic of the future though he was, would have been
surprised by the rapidity and extent of this decay.

In the course of a recent journey through Sicily I visited each of
the Cutò and Lampedusa houses in turn. Amid all the other
spectres of decadence, all the other evidence of feudal and island
decline, one sight stood out in a special, abject category of its
own. The old Palazzo Lampedusa in Palermo, birthplace and
home of the prince, was destroyed in the American bombing of
1943: more than forty years later it was still there, in the heart of
the old city, gutted and plundered; the 'repugnant ruins', which
had so distressed its last owner, remained untouched. I tried to
photograph the derelict outer wall, the only part visible from the
street, but three *carabinieri* approached, shaking their heads and
wagging their fingers. They were charming and polite, explaining
that photography was forbidden in that area because of the
proximity of the police station. It was useless to claim that my
sole interest was the remains of the Palazzo Lampedusa: no one,
they laughed incredulously, could be interested in a ruined wall.

As I retreated along the Via Lampedusa, I noticed a loose plank
in the padlocked gates of the palace. The next day was Sunday
and I rose before dawn, reached the building in the grey half-light,
and squeezed through the gap in the gate. The front courtyard
was full of rubble but I remembered the layout of the palace from
Lampedusa's memoirs and knew which way to climb. As the light
improved I could recognize some of the rooms: his mother's
boudoir with its domed ceiling in gold and shades of blue, her
dressing room overlooking the Oratory of Santa Zita, the place of
Giuseppe's earliest childhood memory. Perhaps the most pathetic

sight in the place was the wreck of the old library. Tattered shreds
of green velvet lay among splinters of cornice and large chunks of
plaster; from a pile of rusty chair springs stuck a faded parasol.
Underneath the rubble, scattered pages of Lampedusa's favourite
authors mixed with the remains of his library catalogue, burnt and
insect-eaten cards bearing the names of Shakespeare, Dickens
and others. Buried among them, I found a number of more
personal documents: photographs, ancestral correspondence,
papers in his own handwriting, letters from his mother which
testified to the closeness of their relationship.

It was after a visit to Sicily in 1985 that I decided to write a
book about Lampedusa, but I had little idea then of the form it
would eventually take. I had been to Palma di Montechiaro to see
Andrea Vitello, a medical doctor who had been doing research
on Lampedusa and his ancestors for many years, and had shown
him my discoveries. I knew he was working on a biography, but I
did not realize that the widowed Princess of Lampedusa had
denied him access to all the material she had in her home in
Palermo; nor did I realize, until I saw it later, how much
documentary evidence of Lampedusa's life had survived there.

I did not consider attempting a biography myself until after I
met Gioacchino Lanza Tomasi, Lampedusa's adopted son,
during a visit to London at the beginning of 1987. I became a
friend of him and his second wife Nicoletta, and they invited my
wife and myself to stay at their home in Palermo, the house in Via
Butera where Lampedusa had spent the last ten years of his life
and in which his wife had lived out her widowhood. It is a
commonplace for a writer to declare that 'without the help of so-
and-so, this book could not have been written', but in my case it is
the exact truth. Without Gioacchino's help I would never have
come near to an understanding of Lampedusa. During the days
he allowed me to search his house for documents; in the evenings
he answered innumerable questions and told countless anecdotes.
At breakfast he would direct me to a disused room and suggest I
might find something in an old cupboard: I would go there, force
it open with difficulty, and encounter a cascade of Lampedusa's
letters. One evening, after Gioacchino had gone to Rome, I went
down to the basement and noticed an old cardboard box in a
corner. Inside were documents which had not been seen since
Lampedusa's death: the diaries of his last years, the files of his

time in the Red Cross, letters, unpublished essays, a commonplace book, some photograph albums of the 1920s. To take these upstairs to Lampedusa's own library and work through them in the small hours was a memorable experience.

I stayed in the Via Butera at different periods during the summer and autumn of 1987, studying these and other documents, notably the thousand-page survey of English literature which Lampedusa had written for a small group of pupils near the end of his life. Although I grew accustomed to his difficult handwriting, I would not have been able to decipher the most illegible passages without the help of Nicoletta Lanza Tomasi.

The hospitality of Gioacchino and Nicoletta also brought me into contact with other people who had known Lampedusa. I am particularly grateful to Giuseppe Biancheri, a nephew of the Princess of Lampedusa, who answered questions and sent me important material, including extracts from his grandmother's diary and information on Lampedusa's experiences in the First World War. His brother Boris Biancheri, now Italian ambassador to London, was also very helpful, and I learnt much too from conversations with Francesco Agnello and with Vences and Giuseppe Lanza. Several other people have related personal memories of the prince including Derek Hill, Sir Steven Runciman, Giuseppe di Sarzana and Lady Hermione della Grazia; all of these have been extremely valuable. I am also grateful for the assistance, in different ways, of Giovanni Tadini, Andrea Vitello, Elizabetta and Bernard Giraud, Lotti and Franco Persico, Gaia Servadio, Geraldine Zalapi, Elisa di Cataldo, Caroline and Pierre de Cabarrus, and the custodian of the Fondazione Piccolo at Capo d'Orlando. I owe a special debt to Francesco Orlando, author of a beautiful memoir of Lampedusa, and to Caterina Cardona, the author of a study of the prince's correspondence with his wife.

Denis Mack Smith, Christopher Duggan, Robert Swann, my father Ian Gilmour and other members of my family have read all or parts of the manuscript. I am grateful to each of them for many helpful suggestions.

Lastly I would like to thank Cristina Celestini, who checked all my translations, and Zelfa Hourani of Quartet Books, for her customary diligence and efficiency.

East Lothian, June 1988

1

The Inheritance

Giuseppe Tomasi was born in Palermo on 23 December 1896, son of the Duke of Palma and grandson of the Prince of Lampedusa. His father Don Giulio was one of five married brothers who between them managed to produce only three children, none of whom had offspring of their own. Two weeks after his birth, Giuseppe's sister Stefania died of diphtheria at the age of two; many years later, the solitary first cousin on his father's side died in his youth. On Giuseppe's own death in 1957, the only surviving Lampedusa was his childless uncle Pietro.

The family's extinction had been preceded by its economic ruin. Like many Sicilian aristocrats, the Lampedusas had been in financial difficulties since the abolition of feudalism in 1812 and subsequent changes in the system of primogeniture. These were greatly exacerbated towards the end of the century when Giuseppe's great-grandfather, Prince Giulio, died of cholera in Florence without making a will. Disagreements between his nine children, followed by a series of legal disputes, led to a court order blocking the distribution of his property. When the division was finally made in 1945, long after all the original claimants were dead, the number of heirs had multiplied (through the female line) while the value of the estate had declined. Giuseppe's share of the family patrimony was thus an insignificant fraction of his great-grandfather's wealth.

Nearly all the later members of the Lampedusa family combined financial incompetence with a total lack of interest in even attempting to make money. Giuseppe's uncle Pietro, who as Marquess of Torretta pursued a successful diplomatic career, used to boast that he was the first Lampedusa to work.[1] He was also the last. It does not seem to have occurred to his brothers, or to his nephew Giuseppe, that they should earn a living, although their only alternative was an impoverished existence on the margins of aristocratic society. And even that life was made harsher for them by the uncharitable attitude of Giuseppe's father: in Don Giulio's eyes, his three youngest brothers had married so far beneath them that they could not be allowed to live in the Palazzo Lampedusa.*[2]

The destruction of the great house in Palermo during the Second World War, followed rapidly by the ruin or demolition of every other Lampedusa property in Sicily, was the dramatic culmination of the family's decline. In *The Leopard* Giuseppe described his protagonist Don Fabrizio 'watching the ruin of his own class and his own inheritance without ever making, still less wanting to make, any move towards saving it'. Yet Fabrizio did care, as did Giuseppe, about that inheritance, not because of what it brought in material benefits but because of what it represented in the form of tradition and family history. The decadence of the Lampedusas was resented by Giuseppe because it consigned his family to historical obscurity; but he did not attempt to halt it. On his deathbed Don Fabrizio reflects that 'the significance of a noble family lies entirely in its traditions, that is in its vital memories; and he was the last to have any unusual memories, anything different from other families'. Giuseppe di Lampedusa also had those memories: it was his need to preserve them, before they disappeared for ever, that compelled him to start writing in the last years of his life.

The origins of the Tomasi di Lampedusa are obscure and have not been clarified by genealogists eager to provide them with an exotic ancestry. Attempts have been made to trace the family back to the Emperor Titus, to a follower of Constantine, and to the sixth-century Byzantine emperor Tiberius. A modern historian of the family has produced a genealogical table based on heraldic evidence which he warns should not be taken too literally.[4] According to this, the founder of the family was

---

*Giuseppe di Lampedusa used to refer to this palace in conversation and in his memoirs as Casa Lampedusa because he felt the word *palazzo* had been 'debased' by its application to modern blocks of flats. One of his cousins, however, has since explained that people called their own palace a *casa* because 'it was supposed to be common' to refer to it as a *palazzo*.[3]

Thomaso 'the Leopard', commander of the Imperial Guard and husband of Tiberius's daughter Irene, and the Tomasi are descendants of one of their sons who returned to Italy and settled in Ancona. Irene, however, is not mentioned in any Byzantine text and some of her descendants seem equally mythical. The genealogists refer to Peter as 'sovereign count' of Cyprus in the tenth century, when no such title existed, and to his father Basil as 'sovereign baron' of Lepanto, when again there was no such position and the place was a half-ruined village called Naupakton in a province overrun by Slav brigands. Some of the exploits of Thomaso's other descendants also sound improbable: two brothers are alleged to have taken part in the First Crusade although their father had been born 120 years earlier.[5]

Little is known of the family's existence in Ancona, but a branch seems to have remained there until the twelfth century when it moved to Tuscany. In Siena the Tomasi revealed that powerful and single-minded religious vocation which later made them famous in Sicily. One went to England as papal legate and tried to settle the dispute between Henry II and Thomas à Becket, while another became Bishop of Famagusta and Patriarch of Constantinople. From Siena a Ludovico Tomasi travelled south to Naples and it is from the branch he established at Capua that the family reached Sicily in the sixteenth century.[6] In about 1580 Mario Tomasi, a military officer in Spanish service at Licata, married a local heiress who brought him the barony of Montechiaro, and over the following two generations the Tomasi established themselves as landed nobility on Sicily's southern coast. In 1638 they became dukes of Palma, after a town they founded south east of Agrigento, and in 1667 princes of Lampedusa, a largely barren and usually deserted island nearer Africa than Sicily. Like the Tomasi families on the mainland, however, they retained a rampant leopard on their coat of arms and the motto *Spes mea in Deo est*.[7]

The Lampedusas were not typical of the Sicilian nobility which in the sixteenth and seventeenth centuries formed one of the least distinguished aristocracies in Europe. The island's Spanish rulers complained that the feudal lords were of no use either for the army or for public service and that they spent much of their time quarrelling over precedence or competing in fashionable extravagance. Yet they could keep the province under control for

Spain if their vanity was sufficiently flattered by the concession of enough titles and privileges. In 1563 the first prince was created and by the end of the following century there were 102 princedoms in a population of about a million.[8] There was little merit attached to these awards, most of which were sold to raise money for Spain, but the Lampedusas were evidently an exception. One of the family's most notable characteristics in the seventeenth century was its aversion to traditional forms of vanity and worldly recognition.

A recurring hazard for the Lampedusas between the end of the sixteenth and the beginning of the eighteenth centuries was their near-extinction: in three generations their survival depended on the health of a single small child. This dearth of descendants can be ascribed largely to religious fervour. It was the custom in Sicily for younger sons and daughters to enter the Church, but in the Tomasi family the eldest boys were anxious to do so as well. This happened both in the Capuan branch, where in a single generation six out of eight children became priests or nuns, and in Sicily. In two consecutive generations at Palma the eldest sons renounced their titles and left them to brothers who also had religious ambitions. All the adult children of the first Prince of Lampedusa took holy orders except his youngest son Ferdinando. Yet even he wished to abandon the world after his wife died in childbirth, and he was planning to join the Capuchin monks at Milazzo when he died at the age of twenty-one.[9]

The first dukes of Palma were the twins Carlo and Giulio Tomasi. Carlo gave up his dukedom shortly after founding the town and became a distinguished theologian. Giulio, who extended the family's estates through marriage and later became the first prince, was a more powerful religious figure. Known as the 'saint-duke', he turned his palace at Palma into a Benedictine convent and built himself a new one nearby. He also founded numerous churches as well as the cathedral, an impressive baroque building by Angelo Italia reached by a massive stone staircase from the main square.[10] The saint-duke's life was ascetic and bordering on the fanatical, a life devoted to prayer, looking after the poor, and daily bouts of self-inflicted flagellation. In *The Leopard* his descendant described the saint-duke: he 'scourged himself alone, in sight of his God and his estates, and it must have seemed to him that the drops of his blood were about to rain down on the land and redeem it; in his holy exaltation it must have seemed that only through this expiatory baptism could that earth really become his, blood of his blood, flesh of his flesh ...'

The most remarkable of the saint-duke's daughters to enter the Benedictine convent at Palma was Isabella, who was officially venerated a century after her death by Pius VI. As the only game she enjoyed as a child was 'playing nuns', it was almost inevitable that she should enter the convent at an early age. Her life was as disciplined and self-critical as her father's – like him she regularly lacerated herself with whips – but was further complicated by a lengthy campaign of torments and temptations by the devil. Once she described to her confessor how a rock hurled at her by the devil was warded off by St Catherine of Siena. [11] Although plainly obsessed with her own problems, Isabella was nevertheless a talented woman and in her works, published in the eighteenth and nineteenth centuries, there are echoes of the mysticism of St Teresa of Avila.

Isabella's austerity and asceticism were shared by her brother Giuseppe, who renounced his titles and estates in order to pursue a career as a liturgical scholar. His reforms were aimed at simplifying the Roman breviary, removing its 'liturgical embroideries' and returning to the Scriptures. He was so obsessed by the need for austerity that, as a later admirer admitted, he 'sacrificed nearly all that was picturesque and attractive in the old breviary ... solely from a desire to return to antiquity'.[12] In 1700 Giuseppe was one of four theologians who advised Clement XI that he would be committing a grievous sin unless he accepted his election as Pope. Twelve years later, Clement placed Giuseppe in a similar situation by making him a cardinal: the ascetic Tomasi, for whom religious titles were almost as unwelcome as noble ones, refused to accept until a papal order reminded him of the grievous sin he might commit. The following year he died and a process of canonization was begun immediately, much encouraged, apparently, by the Jacobite Old Pretender and his mother, the former Queen Mary.[13] The process, however, subsequently slowed down. Cardinal Tomasi was beatified in 1803 but did not become a saint until 1986.

Giuseppe di Lampedusa, the writer-prince, was proud of being the descendant of 'a family of ascetics and mystics' and believed that this made him uncharacteristically 'sympathetic to all fanatics'.[14] But in the eighteenth century the Lampedusas lost some of their religious vigour and moved to Palermo to play more administrative roles under the Bourbon regime. Although several members of the family entered the Church, they do not seem to have had that spiritual intensity which characterized 'the race of saints' from Palma. The dominant figure of the period, and indeed the most powerful member the dynasty produced, was Prince Ferdinando II. A learned man and a patron of the arts, he was three times mayor of Palermo, a deputy of the kingdom and 'vicar-general' appointed to deal with the Messina plague in 1743.[15] It is recorded that, as mayor in 1746, he spent so much of Palermo's budget on fireworks to celebrate its escape from the plague that he completely upset the city's accounts.[16]

In the course of the seventeenth and eighteenth centuries nearly all Sicilian nobles moved into the cities, especially Palermo which had a privileged tax status and great social prestige. Absentee landlords had long been a problem in Sicily but now they seemed to repudiate all interest in the land, refusing to invest in their estates or even to visit them. Their agricultural rents were spent on their households in Palermo and in constructing summer villas a few miles outside the walls, at Bagheria to the east of the city and at Piana dei Colli a few miles to the north west. Once again the Lampedusas were perhaps untypical of their class because there are continuous references to visits to their estates at Palma and Torretta. Nevertheless, they did settle in Palermo and remained there, in the Palazzo Lampedusa beside the Oratory of Santa Zita. A massive palace constructed around three courtyards, the white and yellow facade seventy yards long, it had been built in 1620 and much altered in the following century. Before becoming the home of the Lampedusas, the building had been a seminary.[17]

After Ferdinando II's death, his descendants continued for a time to play a role in public life. In 1800–1 his grandson Giulio was mayor of Palermo and a damaged letter from the ruins of the Palazzo Lampedusa indicates some of his more unusual duties: the document is from one of Lampedusa's officials sent to Tunis with a large amount of money to buy wheat from the Bey, to bribe his chief minister and to ransom six Sicilian slaves.[18] After Giulio's death in 1812, however, the family withdrew almost completely from public affairs and tried to deal with the new economic situation created by the abolition of feudalism and the change in the inheritance laws. The author of *The Leopard* later wrote that 'for centuries [the Salina family] had been incapable even of adding up their own expenditure and subtracting their own debts', a description that could apply to almost every member of the Lampedusa family during its last five generations. Certainly they were quite unable to cope with the Neapolitan law on entails which aimed at dividing up the larger and more unproductive estates and making agriculture more efficient. Laws which permitted the sale of feudal property or its distribution to younger children were crucial to the development of the Sicilian economy, and their inevitable consequence was the decline of the landowning aristocracy.

The chaotic state of the properties at Palma, Torretta and elsewhere, and the demands of numerous creditors, forced Prince Giuseppe III to sell some land before his death. But the energy and tenacity of his young half-German widow, Carolina Wochinger, preserved the bulk of the patrimony for their son Giulio. Two surviving but often illegible letters from Giulio to his mother give a good indication of their preoccupations in the middle of the century. Apart from some family news, they are wholly concerned with business matters: the sale of some property, the repayment of a loan, difficulties with rents, a problem with the administrator, and endless legal disputes – Carolina even took the Benedictine convent at Palma to court, and won.[19]

The widow's most spectacular success was the sale of the island of Lampedusa. This useless property had belonged to the family for over 250 years and, in spite of various attempts at colonization, possessed only twenty-four Maltese inhabitants. In about 1840 Princess Carolina tried to sell the island to Queen Victoria, a move that so alarmed the Neapolitan king, Ferdinand II, that he insisted on buying it himself for the considerable sum of 12,000 ducats.[20] Unfortunately, this windfall was not invested profitably but used by Giulio to acquire yet more property in Palermo: another palace in Via Butera, where he gave firework displays during the Santa Rosalia festivities, and a villa at San Lorenzo, a fashionable area in the shadow of Monte Fellegrino where aristrocratic families used to retreat in August. At the villa, a beautiful mellow house constructed around a courtyard in the previous century, the prince built himself a tower with an astronomical observatory.

Prince Giulio was the historical model for *The Leopard*'s Don Fabrizio, with whom he shares certain characteristics. Giulio was also an enthusiastic astronomer, prepared to travel long distances to see an eclipse, and the possessor of a small scientific library. But he was not a distinguished astronomer, and the claim that he discovered two secondary planets and won a prize at the Sorbonne appears insubstantial.[21] Perhaps Giulio had some of the despotic qualities of his fictional counterpart: Giuseppe di Lampedusa used to recount how his great-grandfather changed the date of Easter for his household when the prescribed day was inconvenient for him.[22] Yet on the whole he appears a milder, weaker and more insignificant person than Don Fabrizio. He was not interested in politics, although like almost all his fellow peers he signed the proclamation deposing the Bourbons in 1848 and had to beg Ferdinand's forgiveness the following year. In 1859–60 his sister Princess Niscemi helped the anti-Bourbon forces and her son fought for Garibaldi, but Prince Giulio appears to have remained neutral, merely allowing the palace in Via Butera to be used as an observation post by British naval officers.[23]

During the Risorgimento the British consul in Palermo described the 'idle, objectless lives' of the Sicilian aristocrats and claimed that 'two only of the nobles are men of fortune, none of them are men of energy, and none enjoy the public confidence'.[24] Aims and energy were certainly lacking in the lives of the Lampedusas in this period, but they still retained much of their fortune and were able to live comfortably in their villas and palaces in Palermo. It was only after Prince Giulio died in 1885 without leaving a will that the collapse took place. In Sicily it is considered unlucky to make a will, but for a man of seventy who cared deeply about his inheritance, this is unlikely to have been the reason for his failure. Possibly he did make a will which was destroyed by his widow, but it is more probable that he forgot all about it. In any case, the omission was disastrous for his estate and for his family.

During his lifetime Prince Giulio granted annual sums to his married children, but after his death the property had to be divided evenly between all his sons and daughters. The position was so complicated, and the discord between his nine children so strong, that the entire estate was placed under the control of a 'judicial administration'. On only one matter was there agreement: in 1886 all his brothers and sisters (except one sister who refused to ratify it for another forty years) ceded their rights to the Palermo home to the new prince Giuseppe.[25] Various attempts were made to distribute the rest of the estate – the matter was dealt with by a civil court in Palermo in 1891 and in subsequent years by the Court of Appeal, the Court of Cassation and then the Court of Appeal again – but without success.[26] Its division frustrated by squabbling relations, the estate remained under the 'judicial administration' for another sixty years. The houses could be lived in but the estate could not be exploited, invested in or otherwise improved, and so its real value declined while the number of interested parties increased. A document drawn up by Giuseppe di Lampedusa in 1938 listed thirty-three adult heirs, almost half of them descendants of Prince Giulio's daughter Chiara.[27]

Apart from the Palazzo Lampedusa, Prince Giuseppe stood to inherit one-ninth of his family's property, which would later have to be divided between his five sons. His heir Don Giulio, father of *The Leopard*'s author, could thus expect barely two per cent of his grandfather's patrimony, a dismal prospect for a proud and quarrelsome prince determined to live in aristocratic style. But it was not one with which his uncles and aunts had much sympathy. There seems to have been little clan solidarity among these two generations of Lampedusas, and the wills of their childless members never benefited the head of the family. When Filomeno died in Dover in 1892 (like Giovanni in *The Leopard* he had gone to England to work as a clerk in a coal depot), he left his inheritance not to Prince Giuseppe but to his two other brothers.[28] When his unmarried sisters died later, their portions were left to a third unmarried sister Concetta.

Giuseppe di Lampedusa's spinster great-aunts lived the last decades of their lives much as he described them in his novel, amassing a collection of dubious religious relics at the Villa Spaccaforno. Perhaps he was too kind to Concetta, a bigoted and uncharitable woman who seemed to relish the financial difficulties of her married relations. After the deaths of her sisters, she owned a third of Prince Giulio's estate which she proposed to leave to her widowed sister-in-law Stella – in spite of the fact that Stella already possessed her husband's portion and part of Filomeno's, and in any case had no children. In his youth Giuseppe di Lampedusa was made to visit this fanatical great-aunt with his mother and send her postcards from abroad, but Concetta refused to change her mind. At her death in 1930 she left nothing to him or any of her nephews (whose impoverishment she was fully aware of: one of them lived in an attic in her house), but made Stella her sole heiress. Four months later Stella herself died, leaving her enlarged assets (now half of Prince Giulio's fortune) to a spendthrift nephew in Naples whom she had adopted on condition he spent a few days each year with her in Palermo.[29] At this stage Don Giulio contested Concetta's will, claiming she had lost her memory and mental faculties and that she had been dominated by Stella. But as there was no evidence to support him, he was unsuccessful. The Lampedusa fortune was now irrecoverable. Don Giulio's aristocratic lifestyle had long been maintained by his wife's money and the generosity of some of his friends, but these sources had now virtually dried up. When he died shortly afterwards, there was little for his son to inherit.

In *The Leopard* Lampedusa refrained from describing the last stages of the decline of the Salina family. But he gave Don Fabrizio the opportunity to speculate from his deathbed on the final generations. After him, he believed, there would be no more memories or traditions, and the possessions of centuries, the tapestries, the almond groves, even the statues, would disappear so that his heir could spend money on can-can girls and *foie gras*. And the family would go with them. 'He had said that the Salina would always remain the Salina. He had been wrong. The last Salina was himself. That fellow Garibaldi, that bearded Vulcan had won after all.'

The Lampedusas' decline was even more dramatic than that prophesied by Don Fabrizio for the Salina. But they did have one advantage over their fictional counterparts: at the end of the line there was one person who remembered and understood the traditions of his family and who was able, at the last moment, to transform them into literature.

2

A Sicilian Childhood

One of Giuseppe di Lampedusa's earliest memories can be dated to 30 July 1900 when he was three and a half. He was sitting on the floor while his mother was at her dressing table, brushing her hair with the help of her Piedmontese maid Teresa, when his father rushed excitedly into the room with some important news. Giuseppe remembered his mother dropping her long-handled silver brush, Teresa exclaiming 'Good Lord!' in Piedmontese, and the consternation in the room. Later he was told that Don Giulio had been announcing the assassination of King Umberto.[1]

From that same period Giuseppe recalled staying with the Florio family on the island of Favignana. One morning he was woken earlier than usual by his Sienese nanny, dressed up in smart clothes and taken out on to the veranda. Among a group of people in cane chairs 'sat a very old, very bent lady with an aquiline nose, enwrapped in widow's weeds which were waving wildly about in the wind'. She bent towards Giuseppe, said something which he did not understand, and kissed him on the forehead with the words *'Quel joli petit!'* In the afternoon it was explained that the old lady was Eugénie, the widow of Napoleon III, whose yacht was anchored close by. Having dined with the Florios the previous evening, the former empress had decided to pay them a farewell visit at seven the next morning, during which she had inconveniently asked to meet the children.[2]

Lampedusa recalled these incidents in the summer of 1955, two years before his death. He had been rereading Stendhal's autobiography, *Vie de Henry Brulard*, and was much impressed by its 'immediacy of feeling' and 'obvious sincerity'. It was 'a remarkable attempt to shovel away accumulated memories and reach the essence' and had a quality of memory Lampedusa regretted he could not match. Stendhal seemed to remember everything about his childhood, particularly the episodes when he was bullied and tyrannized, whereas for Lampedusa childhood was a period when everyone was good to him and he was 'king of the home'. Looking back at the age of fifty-eight past a life that had been vexatious, disappointing and often pathetic, he recalled his infancy as 'a lost Earthly Paradise'.[3]

Giuseppe's childhood was based at the Lampedusa home, that vast palace in the middle of Palermo in an area mostly 'crawling with hovels and wretchedness'. It was the main anchor to his life for nearly fifty years: shortly before its destruction in 1943 he was still sleeping in the bedroom in which he had been born. As the only child living in the palace, it was

> a real kingdom for a boy alone, a kingdom either empty or sparsely populated by figures unanimously well-disposed ... I was its absolute master and would run continually through its vast expanses, climbing the great staircase from the courtyard to the loggia on the roof, from which could be seen the sea and Monte Pellegrino and the whole city as far as Porta Nuova and Monreale.[4]

Lampedusa's memories of the palace were often sensual. He recalled forgotten smells, of his grandparents' kitchen or the violets in his mother's dressing room, felt again the polished leather in the saddle rooms, remembered the stuffiness of the stables. He could picture too the contrasting styles of the many rooms: the great hall flagged in white and grey marble, the ballroom frescoes of mythological scenes packed with 'all the deities of Olympus', or the ceiling of his mother's boudoir 'scattered with flowers and branches of old coloured stucco'. Lampedusa was always sensitive to the quality of light. Describing the 'perspective of drawing rooms extending one after the other for the length of the facade', he recalled

> the magic of light, which in a city with so intense a sun as Palermo is concentrated or variegated according to the weather, even in narrow streets. The light was sometimes diluted by the silk curtains hanging before balconies, or

heightened by beating on some gilt frame or yellow damask chair which reflected it back; sometimes, particularly in summer, these rooms were dark, yet through the closed blinds filtered a sense of the luminous power that was outside; or sometimes at certain hours a single ray would penetrate straight and clear as that of Sinai, populated with myriads of dust particles and going to vilify the colours of carpets, uniformly ruby-red throughout all the drawing rooms: a real sorcery of illumination and colour which entranced my mind for ever. Sometimes I rediscover this luminous quality in some old palace or church, and it would wrench at my heart were I not ready to brush it aside with some *wicked joke*.[5]*

Giuseppe grew up in a world populated by domestic servants and adult relations. In one wing of the *piano nobile* he lived with his parents; in the other were the apartments of his paternal grandparents. On the floor above lived his bachelor uncles until their quarrels with his father Giulio forced them to leave. In the memoirs of his childhood Giuseppe recalled little of his grandparents except that until his schooldays he spent the afternoons reading in their apartments. 'At five o'clock my grandfather would call me into his study to give me my afternoon refreshment – a hunk of hard bread and a large glass of cold water.' The elderly Prince Giuseppe seems to have been a dull, conventional man, though he had the un-Sicilian habit of keeping a diary. Unluckily, one of the few things recorded of him is that he had malodorous feet and on that account was known to some people as *'Piedifitusi'*.[6] His ten-volume diaries reveal that he lived a dreary life, based on undeviating routines in which horse-riding and religious services played major parts.[7] In *The Leopard* there is a strong hint of his dullness in the character of Don Fabrizio's eldest son Paolo. His wife Stefania, however, was a more interesting and sympathetic person who used to read poetry and sometimes even wrote it. She evidently got on well with her grandson and one of her letters, thanking him for writing and for not forgetting her in old age, survives.

Giuseppe seems to have had little real affection for any of the male members of his father's family except for his uncle Pietro, who spent nearly all of these years at the Italian embassy in St

*Italicized words in English in the original.

Petersburg. His other uncles were familiar but not important
figures in his life. One made a rash marriage, left the palace and
was ostracized by most of the family. Another had tuberculosis
and went to live on the family estate at Torretta where *mafioso*
elements forced him to marry a sheepfarmer's daughter. The
third, Francesco, had a brief military career followed by a more
glamorous one on the fringes of the Belle Epoque society in
which, according to one observer, he 'flitted from one flirtation to
another without attaching himself closely to anyone'.[8] He formed
part of the circle around Vincenzo Florio, the millionaire pioneer
of motor-car racing in Sicily, and a rather absurd photograph
shows them both in semi-fancy dress, Francesco with cigar, tweed
cap and a bow-tie.[9] Like the other male Lampedusas of this
period, he had a moustache and large bulging eyes. Yet he was
evidently a fashionable man about Palermo: another photograph,
taken at La Favorita races, portrays him as a sort of Sicilian
Burlington Bertie with a straw boater and a carnation in his
button-hole.[10]

The most difficult member of the family was Giuseppe's father,
the Duke of Palma. He was more intelligent than his three
youngest brothers but led an equally wasted life. There was not
much in common between Don Giulio and his son, who recorded
little about him in his memoirs except that he had an 'infallible
eye' in matters of equestrianism and that he drove four-horse
teams 'with mastery to race-meetings at La Favorita'. He was a
man of fashion, a fine horseman and a regular attender at
Palermo's aristocratic club, the Circolo Bellini. Arrogant, sharp-
tongued and autocratic, he spent much of his life quarrelling with
relations over money. Embittered by his financial misfortune, he
retained a rather ridiculous sense of family and personal pride: in
spite of the impoverishment of the Lampedusas and his own
dependence on his wife's money, Don Giulio refused to forgive
his brothers for their 'low' marriages.

Giuseppe's mother was a very different character, although she
too could be domineering and caustic. Beatrice Mastrogiovanni
Tasca Filangeri di Cutò was one of five sisters brought up in a far
more enlightened and European way than the five Lampedusa
brothers. On her eleventh birthday her mother gave her a
number of large leather-bound volumes in which for several years
Beatrice conscientiously recorded her Palermitan childhood, days

divided into periods of study, play, music lessons and carriage drives that might have been modelled on the novels of Jane Austen.[11] Photographs of her as an adult depict an attractive, clever and strong-willed face. She impressed contemporaries with her intelligence, and long after her death it was rumoured in her family's country district that she was the real author of *The Leopard* and that her son had merely found and corrected the manuscript.[12] Yet she was also a highly fashionable woman, who shocked Giuseppe's great-aunts with her modish clothes, and her company and conversation were found exhilarating in society drawing rooms.[13]

Until her death in 1946, Beatrice Palma was the most important figure in Giuseppe's life. Their relationship was extraordinary and perhaps excessively close, even for Sicilian society where the bond between mother and son is unusually strong. She retained an overpowering, almost smothering influence over Giuseppe until long after his marriage at the age of thirty-five. It should be remembered that the birth of her only boy coincided with the death of her only daughter and that afterwards in her mind she might have conflated the two children. Giuseppe became the sole object of her adoration but in her eyes may have retained some of the characteristics of his sister. Perhaps that explains why sometimes she addressed him in her letters, even when he was a soldier in the First World War, in the feminine.[14]

The best of Giuseppe's childhood in Palermo was spent in the Palazzo Lampedusa with his dog, and that is the part that he later recalled. But he also had to endure a busy social life which he did not enjoy and tried to forget. A cousin, Fulco di Verdura, remembered him as 'fat and taciturn with big, sad eyes, ill at ease in the open air, timid with animals'.[15] Verdura was not always a reliable witness (judging from contemporary photographs, the adjective 'fat' is an exaggeration), but the impression of a shy, reticent child who did not play games with other children is correct. From an early age Giuseppe was happiest with books and later described himself as 'a boy who loved solitude, who liked the company of things more than of people'.[16]

Perhaps he was unlucky to grow up during the most fashionable decade of Palermo's history. At the turn of the century the city's exotic, partly oriental character appealed greatly to the royal

families of northern Europe, and a procession of princes and
grand-dukes turned up in their yachts. Among the regular visitors
were the Kaiser, King Victor Emmanuel, Edward VII and
Alexandra, as well as flocks of Balkan and Scandinavian royalty.
The power of the Sicilian nobility had been largely destroyed over
the previous eighty years but an aristocratic remnant in Palermo
survived to welcome the visitors. About twenty of the great
palaces were still inhabited by their owners (compared to two
hundred a century earlier)[17] such as the Mazzarino family in Via
Maqueda or the princes of Trabia at the Palazzo Butera. But
much of the glamour and magnificence were provided by a few
new families. The huge Florio fortune, amassed over the previous
two generations and based on shipping, sulphur and Marsala, was
squandered at a fantastic rate during these years: Ignazio and
Franca Florio (whose beauty was praised by almost everyone
from D'Annunzio to the Kaiser) built immense villas and
organized an endless series of balls and other entertainments.
Another fortune largely consumed during this period belonged to
the Whitakers, an English family whose wealth had been founded
on Marsala wine. One brother built himself the Villa Malfitano,
surrounded by a large garden of tropical plants, where he
entertained Edward VII. Another constructed a curious palace in
Venetian Gothic beside the Palazzo Lampedusa in which he
installed an unruly group of servants. Beatrice Palma complained
that they looked in through her windows and shouted
obscenities.[18]

The social and cultural lives of the Belle Epoque society
intermingled at theatres, balls and the new Excelsior cinema in
the Palazzo Rudinì, where Beatrice Palma was a regular
spectator.[19] It is a little strange now to read about the pastimes of
these people, to learn how much time was spent preparing fancy-
dress parties and amateur theatricals, to realize how seriously
such entirely frivolous pursuits were taken. Yet in its way it was a
brilliant society, above all in scale, and one that could attract the
talents of Puccini and Sarah Bernhardt. It was also short-lived,
beginning to go downhill after the Messina earthquake in 1908, so
that its style remained in the memory of its participants as part of
a transient golden age. Towards the end of his life Fulco di
Verdura recalled the garden parties of the epoch:

ladies in light colours with boas, veils under enormous straw
hats, gentlemen with their boaters under their arms and a few
cavalry officers thrown in. Lace parasols against a background
of palm trees and cypresses and long tables covered with white
cloths spread with pyramids of strawberries and every sort of
ice-cream.[20]

Palermo's society passed much of its time in carriages, whose
wheels were sometimes painted in 'livery' to assist recognition of
their owners.[21] Even ice-cream eating, which had long been one
of the Palermitans' favourite habits,* was done in carriages
parked outside a *gelateria* as it was 'unthinkable' to sit at one of
the tables on the pavement (it had to be a private carriage,
though, since it was considered 'in the worst possible taste' to eat
ice-cream in a hired cab).[23] A certain amount of shopping was
also conducted in this way – the shopkeeper bringing out his
articles for inspection – but the principal use for carriages was for
the evening drive on the Marina or along the new avenues in the
west of the city. This again was an historic pastime: a hundred
years earlier one of the most prominent social reformers had tried
to persuade noblemen to ride over their estates from time to time
instead of trundling up and down the seafront each day.[24] Special
carriage entertainments included the *Festa della zagara* (festival
of orange blossom) and the *Corso di Fiori* or 'Battle of the
Flowers', recently introduced from the carnival in Nice. The
Corso was a peculiar event, requiring Palermo's upper classes to
dress up and drive out to the Via della Libertà in carriages
covered in roses and other flowers. Once they had reached the
plane trees lining the avenue, 'they would parade around,
throwing little bouquets at each other'.[25] At the *Festa della zagara*
of 1906, Beatrice Palma drove in a landau decorated with white
freesias; a photograph of the event shows her in a white dress,
with Giuseppe sitting opposite in a straw hat.

Giuseppe probably associated some of the worst parts of his
childhood with sailor suits; there are several photographs of him
in different nautical costumes of blue and white. When he was
about six a fashionable Florentine photographer took a series of

---

*The Piedmontese king, Victor Amadeus, who briefly ruled Sicily in the early
eighteenth century, used to talk about Palermo's 'ice-cream parliament' because
eating ice-creams was its members' most conspicuous activity.[22]

pictures of Beatrice and her son together: Giuseppe is in a blue
sailor suit with his hair cut, unflatteringly, in fringe and pudding-
bowl style. Even more painful for him must have been the annual
round of children's fancy-dress parties. On one occasion his
Mazzarino cousins gave a party in which they were dressed up as
the children of Charles I painted by Van Dyck; on another there
were children's theatricals at the Hotel Excelsior where Giuseppe
at the age of nine had to play Cyrano de Bergerac.[26]

In spite of the penury of the Lampedusas, Giulio and Beatrice
Palma were able to participate and shine in this society partly
because she had some wealth of her own and partly because of
the generosity of their friends the Florios. Several books on this
era hint that Beatrice was the mistress of Ignazio Florio, and
although he was capable of disinterested acts of charity, it is
possible that this was the motive of his kindness. The suggestion,
however, seems to depend on malicious gossip of the time and on
one subsequent piece of written evidence.* Whatever the truth of
it, the Palmas saw a lot of their Florio friends, visiting them at
Favignana and staying with them in Paris. Lampedusa later
recalled several visits to France as a small child and declared that
he had learnt to speak French before he could write Italian. One
year he caught scarlet fever and passed an entire winter in Paris.[28]
On a later visit he is said to have spent his pocket money buying
books from the *bouquinistes* along the Seine.[29]

Most of Giuseppe's childhood travels, however, were in Sicily.
One of his earliest memories was of a hired carriage driven at
great speed to a small country house near Catania. Another was
of a visit to Sciacca, at the age of six or seven, to have lunch with
some friends of his parents. Later he remembered nothing of the
lunch or the people but, typically, retained a clear image of the
quality of the light: '... a very blue, almost black, sea glinting
furiously beneath the midday sun, in one of those skies of high
Sicilian summer which are misty with heat ...'[30] Then there were
regular visits to the country houses of his two families. Some of
the Lampedusa properties, disputed since his great-grandfather's
death, were avoided, although Giuseppe did go to the house at
Torretta in the hills west of Palermo. More often he stayed at

---

*Tina Whitaker's diary, 17 March 1906: 'I noticed that Bice [Beatrice Palma's
nickname] was wearing the bracelet that Ignazio Florio had given her. Poor
Franca!'[27]

houses belonging to his mother's family, the Villa Cutò at Bagheria and the beautiful palace at Santa Margherita. Occasional visits were also made to Capo d'Orlando, in the province of Messina, where Beatrice's sister Teresa lived with her children.

After the Palazzo Lampedusa, the most important place of Giuseppe's childhood was the Santa Margherita palace in the Belice district, about forty miles south west of Palermo, though much further by rail or track. The property had been inherited by Beatrice's mother, heiress of the Filangeri di Cutò, a distinguished family of Norman origins which had been in southern Italy for eight centuries. Around the walls of the entrance hall hung a large quantity of pictures of the Filangeri, recording their exploits from 1080 to the time of Giuseppe's great-grandfather. They seem to have been a more active family than the Tomasi di Lampedusa. During the thirteenth century they fought in Cyprus, took part in the Crusades and campaigned for the Hohenstaufen in central Italy.[31] Five hundred years later, they were solid upholders of the Bourbon regime. Two Filangeri princes of Cutò, one of whom had been wounded and captured at Bonaparte's first victory at Lodi, became governors of Sicily. This conservative political tradition was broken by their descendant, Giuseppe's uncle Alessandro, who became a socialist member of parliament and was known as 'the red prince'.

Santa Margherita was the place for summer holidays, but Beatrice loved it so much that sometimes she and Giuseppe spent parts of the winter there as well. Years later Lampedusa described the excitement of a small child leaving Palermo for the country in late June. This was a major expedition, lasting twelve hours and requiring a large number of vehicles. The family rose at half-past three and crossed the city at dawn in three carriages: one for Giuseppe, his parents and his governess (who was usually a German called Anna although at one time he had a French 'mademoiselle'); another for his mother's maid, his father's valet and the accountant (the cooks and other servants had travelled the day before); and a third for the luggage and hampers for lunch. By five o'clock they had reached the Lolli railway station and crowded into the train for Castelvetrano.

For hours then we crossed the lovely, desperately sad

landscape of western Sicily; it must have been I think just
exactly the same as Garibaldi's Thousand had found it on
landing – Carini, Cinisi, Zucco, Partinico; then the line went
along the sea, the rails seeming laid on the sand itself; the sun,
already hot, was broiling us in our iron box. There were no
thermoses in those days and no refreshments to be expected at
any station. The train next cut inland, among stony hills and
fields of mown corn, yellow as the manes of lions.[32]

It was an astonishingly slow train; Giuseppe later recalled that
it took nearly six hours to run the seventy-five miles to its
destination. Eventually they reached Castelvetrano, 'a dreary
plàce, with open drains and pigs walking in the main street', and
piled into two landaus. For an hour the road was level and easy
but from Partanna they needed an escort of three *carabinieri* on
horseback. 'The road became mountainous: around us unrolled
the immeasurable scenery of feudal Sicily, desolate, breathless,
oppressed by a leaden sun.' They had lunch in the shade of a
ruined peasant's hut and sent food and wine over to the waiting
policemen. At two o'clock, 'the truly ghastly hour of the Sicilian
countryside in summer', they were back in the carriages, moving
at walking pace down to the Belice river and up the slope on the
other side. They passed through Montevago with its 'wide
deserted streets, houses weighed down equally by poverty and by
the implacable sun, not a living soul, only a few pigs and some
cats' carcasses'. But after that both buildings and countryside
improved, and by five o'clock they were at the bridge of Santa
Margherita where the municipal band was waiting to play a
polka. Then they drove through the streets to the piazza and
swung into the gateway of their house. At the bottom of the
outside staircase stood 'a little group of retainers' headed by the
excellent administrator who had prepared crushed ice and lemon
drinks in one of the drawing rooms. Giuseppe was taken off and
plunged into a tepid bath while his parents stayed to welcome
their acquaintances.[33]

Santa Margherita and most of the Belice district were destroyed
by an earthquake in 1968 and it is difficult today to imagine the
charm it once had. The house, which to Giuseppe seemed 'a kind
of Vatican', enclosed and self-sufficient, was on a smaller scale
than the massive palace he later described as Donnafugata in *The*

Leopard. Its facade, which with the chapel formed one side of the town's piazza, was of two storeys and a basement, with nine windows on the first floor. Inside were three small courtyards and behind them stretched the gardens with their alleyways of myrtle hedges. Built in 1680 and restored by Prince Niccolò Filangeri in 1810, it was to Lampedusa 'a kind of eighteenth-century Pompeii, all miraculously preserved intact'. The restoration had taken place during the Napoleonic wars, shortly before the Bourbon Queen Maria Carolina stayed there, and had evidently been done well. According to his descendant, 'Prince Niccolò had had the good taste, almost unique for his time, not to ruin the eighteenth-century salons.' And afterwards 'it had not been abandoned as were all other houses in Sicily, but constantly looked after, restored and enriched ...' Searching later for the causes of its preservation, Lampedusa ascribed it to three factors: the internal exile imposed by the Bourbons on his great-grandfather for 'some indecencies committed on the seafront at Palermo'; the attitude of his grandmother Cutò who, 'having lived in France until the age of twenty, had not inherited the Sicilian aversion for country life'; and to the honesty of her administrator Don Nofrio, 'the only one who ... was not a thief'.[34]

As the roads were so bad, and the train journey took so long, there were few visitors to Santa Margherita apart from Giuseppe's aunt, Giulia Trigona, and her daughter Clementina. Fifty years later Lampedusa recalled that his first cousin 'was then, as she is now, a male in a skirt. Determined, rough and aggressive, she was (exactly for those qualities which later proved negative) a welcome games companion for a boy of six or seven.' He remembered breakfasts together at a metal table in the garden, a prank in a large cage designed for monkeys, and 'interminable tricycle races that took place not only in the garden but also in the house between the entrance hall and the Leopoldo salon ...'[35]*

---

*Clementina and her mother were both omitted from the published version of 'The places of my early childhood', prepared by the late Princess of Lampedusa after her husband's death. The editing of these memoirs was in several respects unfortunate. To begin with, the princess made a number of mistakes, sometimes misreading Lampedusa's handwriting and occasionally misunderstanding the sense of certain words. She even managed to transcribe wrongly a line from Keats's 'Ode to a Nightingale', producing 'provincial noise' instead of 'Provencal song' and thereby forcing the English translator to assume that

Social life at Santa Margherita revolved around local notables whom Beatrice invited to dine in turn (without their wives partly because 'women in the country did not pay visits' before the First World War, and partly because their menfolk did not 'consider them sufficiently presentable') and to play cards in the ballroom twice a week. To Giuseppe the guests seemed 'good people without exception', and he has left some moving descriptions of these sad old men, forced by impecuniosity to live in Santa Margherita where they passed the time reminiscing on younger days spent in Paris or Palermo. Other evenings were enlivened by groups of strolling players who performed in the palace theatre. They used to arrive in summer, rent the theatre at a nominal price from Beatrice, and stage different plays every night for a fortnight. Almost half a century later, Giuseppe recalled how a performance of *Hamlet* at Santa Margherita had 'made an audience, ninety per cent of whom were illiterate labourers, shudder with excitement'.[36]

Each Sunday the family 'heard High Mass sung without excessive fervour' in the chapel, but there seem to have been few

---

Lampedusa had intended a play on words.

The princess made a number of excisions from a sense of propriety. The 'indecencies committed' by Lampedusa's great-grandfather in Palermo (apparently he was driving his carriage naked) were removed, and a reference to 'high-priced girls' in Paris was changed to 'high-priced elegance'. Perhaps Giulia Trigona, who was later involved in a scandal (see below, pp.29–30), and Clementina, on account of her 'aggressive' masculinity, were excluded for these reasons, but other names and events seem to have been taken out quite pointlessly. A blameless individual who played Chopin nocturnes in the evenings was struck out, and the princess's obsession with the anonymity of dead, unlibelled characters made her even change the names of places they visited, in one case ruining a story by substituting Viterbo for Frascati. A number of amusing anecdotes, such as the story of Don Giulio's relations with the mayor of Santa Margherita, were removed for no reason, although they contained interesting information on Giuseppe's childhood. Even innocent descriptions of inanimate objects like a musical box or a locked cupboard received similar treatment.

Most puzzling of all was the princess's rearrangement of the sequence of passages. None of this makes the memoir easier to follow and sometimes it entirely distorts the author's meaning. In the published version Giuseppe shot two robins and then held out his 'oily hand' to his dog who looked at him in a 'reproachful way'. Dogs do not usually look reproachful when they see dead birds and Lampedusa's poodle was no exception. As the manuscript makes clear, the reproaches were directed at Giuseppe not after the shooting incident but when he stroked the dog after crushing the evil-smelling berries of some castor-oil shrubs.

other duties for Giuseppe at Santa Margherita. For much of the time he could lead the solitary life he so loved in Palermo, exploring with his dog Tom. He could roam in the large informal garden which 'in the furnace of summer ... was a paradise of parched scents', or he could wander about the house: 'one would open a door on a passage and glimpse a perspective of rooms dim in the shade of half-pulled shutters, their walls covered with French prints ...' He liked to visit his grandfather's gun room with its stuffed birds, photographs of gun dogs and racks of shotguns. At the age of ten his father persuaded him to take up shooting and, encouraged by a gamekeeper, he went into the garden and shot two robins. Horrified by the sight of blood on their feathers, he went straight to Don Giulio and told him he would never shoot again.[37]

Giuseppe learnt to read at Santa Margherita, he recalled later, at the surprisingly late age of eight. Before then he was read biblical stories three days a week and tales of classical mythology on the other three. But sometimes he was allowed boys' adventure stories as well and later he recalled his grandmother trying hard not to fall asleep while reading about pirates in the Caribbean. At the age of eight Donna Carmela from Santa Margherita was brought in to teach him how to read and write. Beatrice then taught him to write French, and later he remembered her at a desk writing clearly *le chien, le chat, le cheval* in the columns of an exercise book. From this he graduated quickly to the library, which contained a varied collection of books including almost every work of the Enlightenment, some fine editions of Cervantes and La Fontaine, and various modern writers such as Zola and Verga. One of Giuseppe's favourite books was 'a collection of Napoleonic bulletins and campaign reports which were my delight in the long silence-filled summer afternoons as I read them sprawled on one of those enormous "poufs" which occupied the centre of the ballroom'. It was probably this book which stimulated his great interest in the Napoleonic wars. Fifty years later he could still draw detailed maps of Napoleon's battlefields from memory.[38]

One of the features of life at Santa Margherita was organized afternoon walks, though presumably these did not take place in the middle of summer. The walks were usually four miles in length and the participants would walk either two miles in one direction and then back again, or else four miles in another direction with a carriage following behind to transport them home. In the autumn they sometimes went to a vineyard to eat grapes, though when it was raining they went no further than the town's public gardens, a place of 'quite infinite melancholy' planted with ilexes and cypresses. From these, however, there was an impressive view: 'opposite stretched a vast range of low mountains, all yellow from reaping, with blackish patches of burnt stubble, so that one had a vivid impression of a monstrous crouching beast'. Against this great backdrop a few villages could be distinguished, 'all weltering in poverty and dog-days, and in an ignorance against which they never reacted with the very faintest of flickers'.[39]

Twice a year a more serious expedition was organized to La Venaría, a Cutò shooting lodge about four miles from Santa Margherita. The cooks left the palace at seven in the morning to prepare the macaroni, the Lampedusas and their local guests following more leisurely a few hours later. Giuseppe, his mother and his governess were driven in a dog-cart, but it was traditional for the men to go on donkeys even if they owned a horse. At La Venaría two tables were laid outside on the terrace and the guests settled down to a huge meal of pasta, fish, stuffed turkey and iced cake. Wines, however, were not important. Although the men liked their glasses filled to the brim, recalled Giuseppe, they never drank more than one or two of them.[40]

It is easy to understand why Lampedusa looked back at his childhood as a lost paradise. The years divided between Palermo and Santa Margherita were happy and untroubled and, in the light of what happened later, must have seemed almost cloudless. The only real shadow in his life, he later recalled, was the castor oil he had to take for his stomach aches.

This state of innocence ended in Palermo in December 1908, a few days after Giuseppe's twelfth birthday. On noticing one morning that the grandfather clock had stopped, he was told by his uncle Ferdinando that there had been an earthquake in the night. News of the Messina tragedy, in which 77,000 people lost their lives, came slowly, and it was several days before Beatrice learned that her sister Lina and her brother-in-law had starved to death under the rubble. Their son Filippo survived and came to Palermo before going to his other cousins at Capo d'Orlando.

Giuseppe visited him there 'on a bleak rainy winter's day' and found him drawing battleships and talking about naval guns, behaviour 'criticized by the family but charitably attributed to "shock"'. At the end of his life Lampedusa could still picture his mother's grief and remember her 'sobbing on a big armchair in which no one ever sat in the green drawing room'.[41]

Two years later, Beatrice had to contend with another family tragedy. One of her younger sisters was Giulia Trigona, a close friend of Queen Elena and a lady-in-waiting at the court. Married before she was twenty to Count Romualdo Trigona di Sant' Elia, she was described by an uncharitable acquaintance in Palermo as 'a poor, pretty, refined, witty creature, one of those eminently frivolous and inconsequential things who are bound to bring their men ruin and despair, unless ruled with a firm hand from the start'.[42] This was perhaps unfair because her marriage survived for fifteen years without obvious problems until she received an anonymous letter informing her of Romualdo's liaison with an actress. Soon afterwards Giulia began an affair with a Silician cavalry officer, Baron Vincenzo Paternò del Cugno, a highly emotional man and an addicted gambler. The relationship soon became known in the 'hateful city' of Palermo which, she wrote to her sister, was making her life 'a hell'.[43] She tried to shake the baron off, but he followed her around Europe demanding that she should settle his gambling debts. The Florios and the Lampedusas* intervened without success, merely provoking Paternò del Cugno to challenge Don Giulio to a duel. Giuseppe's father, however, ignored the threats and persuaded his brother Pietro, now a senior official at the foreign ministry, to have the baron transferred from Palermo to Naples.[44] In January 1911 Giulia arrived in Rome to resign as lady-in-waiting, but the Queen, perhaps because she was not told all the details, refused to accept her resignation. The following month Giulia agreed both to separate from her husband and to break with her lover, but unfortunately at this point Paternò del Cugno turned up on leave with fresh financial demands. She agreed to meet him at a squalid hotel near the station, and there the baron stabbed her to death before shooting himself through the temple.

There was of course a tremendous scandal and a great deal of

---

*Giulio and Beatrice Palma became Prince and Princess of Lampedusa after his father's death in 1908.

publicity. Ignazio Florio, a close friend of the Trigonas, helped organize a press campaign against Paternò del Cugno in which Giulia was represented as a more or less innocent victim. The train carrying her remains to Sicily was greeted by huge crowds at Messina, Bagheria (where she had spent much of her childhood at the Villa Cutò) and Palermo. At Cefalù the train had to stop so that local dignitaries could board it to present their condolences to Giulia's brother, the parliamentary deputy Alessandro Tasca.[45]

Beatrice Lampedusa was naturally convulsed by the murder of her sister and tried to spend as much time as possible outside Sicily. A cholera epidemic in Palermo provided a good excuse for the family to move to Tuscany for a few months in the summer of 1911. In the autumn the Lampedusas transferred themselves to Rome and did not return to Sicily until the end of the year. Unfortunately, the publicity over the Trigona scandal was about to start up all over again. Paternò del Cugno, who had aimed a bullet through his brain, had failed to kill himself, and after his recovery a year later he was put on trial for Giulia's murder. This event was a terrible ordeal for Beatrice. Not only did she have to appear as a witness at the trial, she had to endure the massive press coverage which included the publication of Giulia's love letters. Worse still, through the evidence of other witnesses, she had to listen to a reconstruction of her sister's last months and to learn of the long campaign of violent threats to which she had been subjected.[46]

At the end of June 1912 Baron Vincenzo Paternò del Cugno was sentenced to life imprisonment with five years at the beginning in solitary confinement. Thirty years later Mussolini's government released him on the grounds of good conduct.

3

The War and Fascism

At the age of fourteen, after the murder of his aunt, Giuseppe went to school for a term in Rome. Following the family's return to Sicily at the end of 1911, he was transferred to the Liceo-Ginnasio 'Garibàldi' in Palermo, where he stayed for nearly three years. The school report for his final year there gave him high marks for those subjects he most enjoyed – history, philosophy and written Italian – and low ones for those in which he was given oral tests: Latin, Greek and spoken Italian.[1]

When he was seventeen, Giuseppe left school and decided to go to university. He intended to study literature, but his father could see no point in this and suggested he should prepare for a diplomatic career like his uncle Pietro. Considering that the only successful career pursued by any member of the family for several generations had been diplomacy, this was not necessarily bad advice. Yet for someone so handicapped by shyness and without any real concern for world affairs, diplomatic life was plainly unsuitable. In addition, Don Giulio wanted his son to study law, a subject equally unsuited to someone of Giuseppe's temperament and interests. Like many southern Italian fathers, however, Don Giulio regarded law as the ideal education for a student, and on this issue his son was forced to capitulate.

There are a number of mysteries about Giuseppe's university career. He seems to have given the impression later on that he went to Turin University and took a degree, but there is no evidence for this. For the year 1914–15 he enrolled at the Law Faculty at Genoa University, yet it is not clear whether in fact he studied there.[2] In any event, we know that he soon left for Rome because a document from the Law Faculty in the capital certifies that he had attended a course of lectures for at least a part of the year.[3] Whatever the reasons for all this, Giuseppe's student life was brief because in May 1915 Italy entered the Great War and the following November he was called up for military service.

There are even more mysteries about Lampedusa's military career, whose length and duration were exaggerated many years later by his widow. An 'Attestation of Good Conduct' of February 1916 declares that he could be admitted into the army as an officer because he was upright and honest and neither a brawler nor addicted to wine and indolence.[4] Giuseppe then joined an artillery regiment stationed at Messina and in May he was promoted to corporal.[5] It is not certain why he joined the artillery but there may have been some family connection: the following year Don Giulio was made a reserve captain of artillery.[6]

Giuseppe's military service was an alarming prospect for his mother. Beatrice bombarded him with letters full of advice and visited him at Messina, when he was ill, and later at Augusta. Her letters, in Italian with French phrases for emphasis, have a rather frenzied tone. They contain a certain amount of gossip about the 'Palermitan *beau monde*' and gratitude for Giuseppe's presents ('I adore them! The violet water *est exquise!*'), but their main concerns were his health and his activities. How was his cold? Had he stayed in bed? What was the journey like? Then there are complaints about the infrequency of his letters. She had received only two recently: why did he not write to her every day?[7]

Beatrice was particularly agitated by a decision to transfer Giuseppe to the infantry which she regarded as the most dangerous branch of the service. It 'has absolutely shattered me', she wrote, urging him to have the decision reversed by a combination of intrigue and determination. If he became friendly with his superiors and told them he planned to become a regular officer, he should be able to choose the branch in which he wished to serve. 'Investigate and find out all possible ways of cheating the law,' she advised, and then make a determined move: '*de l'audace, encore de l'audace*'. Whether this manoeuvre was successful, or whether some other consideration was involved, is not clear; at all events, Giuseppe remained in the artillery.

Beatrice Lampedusa's letters once again reveal the closeness of her relationship with her son, and one has the impression that she was still treating him as a small boy. Many people use embarrassing nicknames and perhaps not too much should be made of her terms of endearment: 'my good and dear Pony' (in the feminine), 'my lovely one' (also in the feminine), 'my sweet little Pony' and so on. But the worries about his health, the endless concern that he might catch a cold in the bad weather, read curiously in letters to a young soldier. And so do some of the sentiments: Giuseppe's barracks at Messina are described as 'the place where all my life is!' Certainly Beatrice was often thinking of earlier times, when Giuseppe was a child and her sisters were still alive. 'The fifth of May! I remember when you were painting pictures in which you tried to give an impression of that fatal day at St Helena.* O blessed and happy times! Where have you gone? Was there really such sunshine?'[8]

Photographs of this period suggest that Giuseppe was not so unsuited to the army as might have been expected: there is a certain self-confidence in his expression, and in his cape and boots he even looks moderately dashing. In May 1917 he was sent to Turin for an officers' training course, and the following September, nearly two years after being called up, he arrived at the front. His first duties were to go out each night and repair the telephone lines brought down by Austrian bombardments. Subsequently he was stationed at an observation post near Asiago in a sector held by Alpine troops of the Edolo battalion. Facing them, to the excitement of the battalion's chaplain, were Bosnian units: the prospect of shooting 'Muslim infidels', Giuseppe later recalled, so aroused the chaplain that he grabbed a rifle and fired madly at them.[9]

Shortly after Giuseppe's arrival at the front, the Italian army was routed at Caporetto, where it suffered 40,000 casualties and 300,000 prisoners, and driven back seventy miles to the line of the Piave. His unit, some way to the west, took no part in the main battle, but in November it was attacked during an Austrian offensive from the Trentino. In his memoirs Giuseppe admitted 'killing a Bosnian with a pistol and who knows how many Christians by shellfire', but this passage may have been an untypical piece of bravado: in recounting the incident many years later to one of his nephews, he gave the impression that he had

*The death of Napoleon, 5 May 1821.

wounded but not killed the soldier. In any case the Bosnians forced the Alpine troops to retreat and in the assault Giuseppe was wounded, knocked unconscious and captured. For several weeks nothing was heard of him and it was suspected that he had been killed: his friend and colleague, the poet Enrico Cardile, even dedicated his poem *Alba Triste* ('Sad Dawn') 'to the dear memory of my corporal, Giuseppe Tomasi, Prince of Lampedusa,* lost near Asiago'.[10] It was not until around Christmas that a telegram arrived in Palermo announcing his imprisonment.

The day after his capture Giuseppe was interrogated by an Austrian officer dressed in a white uniform which seemed to date from the time of the Risorgimento. Subsequently taken outside with other prisoners, he believed he was going to be shot in reprisal for the killing of some Bosnian prisoners by the Edolo battalion. But in fact he received good treatment from the Austrians, a fact he later ascribed to the ducal coronet which they discovered sewn on to his shirt. On his way to a prisoner-of-war camp, he was allowed to do a tour of Vienna on condition he made no attempt to escape. Life in the camp turned out to be reasonably comfortable and he was able to receive news and parcels from his relations in Sicily; they even sent him tennis balls and rackets.[11]

At some stage during his internment, Giuseppe and a friend managed to bribe a guard to procure two Austrian uniforms and train tickets for the Swiss frontier. They then set off and had nearly reached safety when they stumbled into barbed wire connected with an alarm system. A group of guards recaptured them and, believing they were deserters, started to kick them. But as soon as it was realized that they were escaped prisoners, they were once again well treated: reimbursing the Austrians for the train tickets was the sole penalty exacted from them.[12] Giuseppe was then taken back to the camp where he remained for a few months before escaping again. The war was by now virtually over and there were few guards left at the camp. He escaped without difficulty and, a year after his capture, reached the Italian-occupied city of Trieste.

After his return Giuseppe remained in the army for a further

---

*He was not in fact Prince of Lampedusa at this stage. Until his father's death in 1934, he was usually known as the Duke of Palma.

year and was demobilized in February 1920. The post-war years
were for him a period of disillusionment and physical illness. He
spent several months in bed, suffering from nervous exhaustion
and from a combination of nightmares and insomnia that plagued
him for the rest of his life. During his final year in the army he
had resumed his student career to the extent of taking an exam at
Rome University. But neither there nor at Genoa did he settle
down to study. Much to the annoyance of his father and his great-
aunts, who were still hoping he would become a diplomat,
Giuseppe abandoned his law studies without taking a degree. It
seems that even at this early stage he had decided neither to
follow any formal profession nor to make any attempt to earn
himself a living.

His disillusionment extended beyond his own life to Sicily and
Italian politics. It has often been said that Giuseppe di Lampedusa was a convinced anti-fascist who resigned from the army
after Mussolini came to power and refused to accept an official
post under his government. Yet in fact he was never really an
opponent of Mussolini, least of all at the beginning. Indeed, he
was less of an anti-fascist than several of his relations: his
maternal uncle Alessandro was a socialist politician; his paternal
uncle Pietro was foreign minister in the penultimate liberal
government; and his father Don Giulio, like many of his peers,
seems to have viewed the regime with a degree of aristocratic
contempt.*

Throughout his life Lampedusa remained too sceptical and
disillusioned to be a genuine democrat or a liberal, at least as far
as his own country and his own island were concerned. The man
who acquired such admiration for British parliamentarians had
little but disdain for Italian liberals, especially in the south. One
character in *The Leopard* is described as possessing 'the deluded
and rapacious soul of a liberal'. For Lampedusa, liberalism
applied to Sicily was a ridiculous notion, an attempt at veneering
a rough and brutal society that was obviously unready for it. The
sixty years since the Risorgimento had brought little benefit to
the south. Whatever political liberalism may have achieved in
certain areas in the north, it had scarcely been practised in the
southern provinces. Successive governments in Rome, which

*On seeing Mussolini for the first time, one Sicilian prince shook his head and
muttered, 'Too many spats, too many spats!'[13]

needed the support of deputies from the south, found that their
easiest course was simply to make pacts with local landlords
allowing them to retain political power. From Cavour onwards,
liberal politicians in the north had found Sicily impossible to
understand and consequently thought it easier to ignore the place
rather than antagonize different factions with various plans of
reform. For decades there had thus been almost no worthwhile
measures of social or economic reform, few agricultural
improvements and little in the way of public investment.
Communications were still very bad: the Lampedusas took four
hours to travel the twenty-two miles from Partanna to Santa
Margherita in a landau; more remote districts could be reached
only by donkey.

Lampedusa's view of the Italian liberals as corrupt and
ineffectual was shared by other southern intellectuals: for many
years the limitations of the Risorgimento and its failures in the
south had been attacked by writers and political figures such as
Fortunato, Salvemini, Verga and De Roberto. In their eyes
southern liberalism had been merely a euphemism for heavy-
handed political control. In addition, the liberal leaders now
seemed too weak and hesitant to deal with Italy's post-war crisis,
in particular the alleged threat of Bolshevism. In 1919 many
opponents of the liberals applauded the flamboyant D'Annunzio
who invaded the free state of Fiume and demanded its
annexation; Lampedusa, who admired D'Annunzio's writing,
later admitted that he had been among them.[14] Yet they needed
something more stable and serious than the exotic nationalism of
an exhibitionist poet, and most of them found it in Mussolini's
movement. The literary desert of much of the fascist period and
the intellectual incoherence of the regime's doctrines have
perhaps obscured fascism's great attraction to intellectuals in its
first years. Three of Italy's finest musicians, Puccini, Mascagni
and Toscanini, were early supporters of the party;* among
writers, the most famous and enthusiastic adherent was
Pirandello, who joined the fascists just after they had murdered

---

*Toscanini, however, had already become disillusioned by the time of
Mussolini's march on Rome and afterwards refused to conduct the fascist
anthem 'Giovinezza'. Puccini died in 1924 shortly after he had been appointed
a senator by Mussolini. Mascagni remained a zealous fascist and a member of
the Italian Academy.

the socialist deputy Matteotti.[15]

Giuseppe Palma's early admiration for fascism, like that of many junior officers, stemmed from fear of revolution and resentment at the liberals' failures. He recognized that the fascists were not blameless, yet 'with all their excesses and defects' at least they wanted to improve the country while the liberals remained in complacent and corrupt inertia.[16] Besides, he believed that fascism could 'tame Bolshevism', removing the communist threat by imposing much-needed reforms. These views were sometimes expounded in the house of his Piccolo cousins who admired Giuseppe's political intuition. Many years later they were recalled by someone who argued with him there one afternoon in the winter of 1922–3. According to this witness, however, Giuseppe never lost control of himself and, although dogmatic, he did not argue like a 'fervent fascist'. Much of his attitude seemed determined by a 'bitter grudge' against the liberal middle classes.[17]

Some of the greatest figures of Italian liberalism, such as Croce and Giolitti, did not oppose fascism until the end of 1924 or 1925. Giuseppe Palma had lost his enthusiasm for the regime before then, although he did not think that Mussolini was always wrong and later applauded his intervention in Spain.[18] He admitted that the fascists might be necessary in Italy for a certain period, but he was now increasingly disdainful of them. Demagoguery, military parades and all the other paraphernalia of fascism were of course quite alien to his temperament, and he found them boring and rather ridiculous.

Giuseppe had also lost his enthusiasm for living in Sicily. Between the wars the island retreated from the Belle Epoque into a dull provincialism which Mussolini's bureaucracy did little to make more interesting. Furthermore, Giuseppe had personal reasons for disliking his home region. The quarrels between his father and his uncles made the atmosphere of the Lampedusa home disagreeable, and the old palace must have lost much of its charm when a large part of it was let to the municipal gas board. There was still an aristocratic society of sorts, but Giuseppe participated in it with reluctance; years later people remembered him drifting about at dances by himself, vaguely looking for his mother.[19] But if he was disenchanted by Palermo, his feelings for Santa Margherita were even sadder. During a visit in 1921 he was conscious that the place was changing – strolling actors no longer visited and the theatre had been turned into a cinema – but he had no idea that it would soon be lost to him for ever. Three years later, however, his uncle sold the house without warning. Alessandro Tasca had sacrificed his wealth to finance Sicilian socialism and his debts were by now massive.

His illness, his weariness of Sicily and his disinclination to work persuaded Giuseppe to spend many of the post-war years in northern Italy. He had made some intellectual friends during the war and stayed for long periods with them in Genoa, Turin and their home villages. The writer and critic, Bruno Revel, had been a fellow prisoner, and Giuseppe wrote letters and visited him for many years afterwards. Another friend was Guido Lajolo, who emigrated to Brazil in 1930; a quarter of a century later Lampedusa renewed their correspondence to tell him of the novel he was writing. Sometimes he was accompanied on his travels by his mother. During the twenties the two of them stayed in Tuscany and Bologna and made at least one journey to Munich.

At some stage in the early twenties Giuseppe acquired a camera and took quantities of photographs of the places he visited. His surviving albums reveal him as an assiduous tourist but an indifferent photographer: the pictures contain few people, have no artistic pretension and are designed simply to record the architecture of the buildings he looked at.[20] In November 1925 he was in Pistoia, where he photographed the cathedral and various palaces, and then in Florence, where again he visited the most famous sights: the Uffizi, the baptistry, the Ponte Vecchio, the Piazza della Signoria. There is a single picture of Beatrice at San Miniato in December and then several photographs of Rome (the forum, the Spanish Steps, the Trevi fountain), where they spent a few days before returning to Sicily. By 12 December they were staying with Beatrice's sister Teresa, and Giuseppe was taking photographs of the Piccolo estate at Capo d'Orlando.

A photograph taken during this visit shows Giuseppe wearing a bow-tie, a suit and waistcoat, and spats. He has a small clipped moustache and his black hair is brushed straight back without a parting. Like his father and uncles, his eyes are large, round and slightly protruding. Sitting on a sofa with one of his cousins, a cigarette in his left hand, a large book open on his lap, he has the appearance of a well-fed dilettante.

Yet his reading was more serious than that of a dilettante. He did not dabble in different subjects so that he could shine at dinner parties, but concentrated on his major interests. Paying little attention to religion, music, economics or contemporary politics, he devoted his time to literature, history and, to a lesser extent, art and architecture.* By his early twenties his knowledge of literature and history was so impressive that his Piccolo cousins dubbed him *il mostro*, the monster. Nearly all his reading, except for Russian novels, was done in the original language. As a child he had learnt to read Italian, French and German, and later on had acquired English: he had read all of Shakespeare before visiting England in the twenties and must have been one of the first Italians to penetrate Joyce. Giuseppe later compared literature to a forest where it was important to investigate everything, not just the large trees in isolation but the undergrowth and wild flowers as well. They were all part of the great body of literature and contributed to each other's growth.[22] Horace Walpole's *The Castle of Otranto*, for instance, was in itself 'not worth a cigarette end', but it was an important and influential book because it opened the way to novels by Scott and Thackeray, to the supernatural writing of Poe and to certain works of Henry James.[23]

This consuming interest in literature led Giuseppe to the exploration of minor writers from every era. He pursued them through innumerable biographies and acquired an enormous stock of literary anecdotes. With his knowledge of authors and their books, he liked to construct theories and establish unusual connections between different periods and branches of literature. Towards the end of his life he wrote an essay on 'thrillers' or *'romanzi di terrore'* which traced their origins to Shakespeare's lesser tragedies and other Elizabethan drama before sketching their development down to modern times.[24] Elsewhere he argued that history could not be understood properly without a

---

*Giuseppe had catholic tastes in buildings, encompassing Gothic cathedrals and English country houses as well as the Baroque churches of Sicily. About paintings he talked little, though sometimes he liked to compare works of literature to the style of a great artist. One of Shakespeare's sonnets he described later as 'coloured and sumptuous like a Rubens', while *Antony and Cleopatra* 'reflected its epoch with the clarity and colour of a fresco by Tiepolo'.[21] One of his favourite pictures was Reynolds's portrait of Dr Johnson in the National Portrait Gallery.

knowledge of literature, especially minor literature. To find out what shopkeepers and railway workers were thinking in the 1920s, he remarked, there was no point in reading the works of Giovanni Gentile. One had to read the books of second-rate novelists to have an authentic picture of an epoch, and although this might require patience, a strong stomach and a dose of bad taste, it was worth it. 'Ungrammatical, illogical, hysterical, ignorant, fatuous, "snobbish", in short pitiful as they are, they give us the true portrait of Demos, our lord and master. One has to read them.'[25]

Three articles which Giuseppe published in 1926–7 give some indication of his literary tastes as a young man. There are favourable references to Yeats, Joyce, Shaw, Swift and Keats; among the French, to Baudelaire and Anatole France but not Hugo; and among Italians, high marks to Petrarch, D'Annunzio and Leopardi but not Tasso.[26] Many of his judgements did not change (Keats remained his 'archangel';* Leopardi was always his favourite Italian lyric poet), but some did. Over the years Hugo was partially rehabilitated, Lampedusa admitting that after all *Les Misérables* was 'not bad'.[28] He also changed his view of *The Comedy of Errors*: for most of his life he regarded it as a 'comedy of horrors' and did not recognize until 1954 that it had one or two good characters and a few exquisite lines.[29] Lawrence Sterne went through three stages of popularity. *A Sentimental Journey* was one of the first books he had read in English as a child; he liked it, reread it and liked it even more. He then read *Tristram Shandy*, first in Italian and then in English, and thought

---

*Lampedusa enjoyed placing writers in categories. One group contained 'creators of worlds' such as Homer, Shakespeare, Cervantes, Jane Austen, Balzac, Tolstoy and Dickens. Another was reserved for the 'angels':

'To be included among the angels it is necessary to die very young or to cease all artistic activity at an early age. It's necessary, it goes without saying, that their work must be of supreme value and that their presence is short and brilliant, so that they die leaving us grey mortals with the sensation that they are superhuman visitors who watched us for an instant and then returned to the heavens, leaving us gifts of divine quality and also a bitter regret at the fleetingness of the apparition. Among the "angels" I place Raphael and Masaccio, Mozart and Hölderlin, Rimbaud and Maurice de Guérin, Shelley, Marlowe and Keats ... Rupert Brooke and Novalis have just missed promotion to this group, together with Giorgione and Van Gogh. In this list, shining with joy and for us tears, the supreme place goes to John Keats. Of all of them, he alone is absolutely pure ... angel and archangel of the highest degree.'[27]

it a masterpiece. After the First World War he read them both again: 'Complete disappointment! I was already reading Proust and Gide, and Sterne seemed to me to be rosewater.' Thirty years later he read both novels once more and reversed his opinion. Sterne was 'much more subtle and penetrating than the inattentive reader could ever imagine'.[30]

There was a change too in his attitude to what should be explained in a book and how much should be left for the reader to deduce. On rereading Stendhal's autobiography in 1955, he said he 'had not read it since long ago in 1922, when I must have still been obsessed by "explicit beauty" and "subjective interest", for I remember not liking the book. Now I cannot disagree with anyone who judges it to be Stendhal's masterpiece.'[31] This increasing preference for the implicit over the explicit extended to other areas as well and was doubtless a cause of his later distaste for Italian opera.[32]

Another valuable source for Giuseppe's tastes and interests is a surviving volume of his commonplace book.[33] It is undated but the handwriting, the interests and the absence of modern writers suggest that it was compiled in the twenties. A majority of the quotations are from French sources, but there are a good number of Italian writers and the English range from Shakespeare and Pepys to Ruskin and Charlie Chaplin. As people usually use commonplace books to record opinions they agree with, this collection probably gives a good indication of Giuseppe's ideas and prejudices at that time. It contains a derogatory comment about philosophy, which no longer interested him after he left school, and another on the incompetence of democratic government. Bismarck's remark that Italy was made with 'three Ss: Solferino, Sadowa, Sedan' – battles principally between the French, the Prussians and the Austrians – is quoted presumably because it supported Giuseppe's view that the Risorgimento was much less nationalist and heroic than Italian historians liked to pretend. And there are several quotations which record what he liked about the English: their common sense, their stiff upper lip (Charles I on the day of his execution), their taste for paradox (even when exaggerated by Chesterton and Oscar Wilde), and various other qualities he believed they possessed. (Sir Herbert Tree: 'A gentleman is one who does not care a bit whether he is or not.')

Before he visited England in the mid-twenties, Giuseppe bought his English books from the Treves brothers in Milan who published works of British and American authors at five lire each; his earliest purchases included *Gulliver's Travels* and the poems of Edgar Allan Poe.[34] Unlike many of his aristocratic contemporaries, Giuseppe did not have a British nanny or governess, and his English was therefore probably learned from books. When he wrote it, which was seldom, the grammar was usually correct but the choice of phrases suggests that they had been picked up from his reading. Among his papers there is a curious document, partly in Italian and partly in English, which illustrates this. 'From its very beginning,' he started in English,

> English literature shows itself as a solid block, without those crevices, those abeyances of talent which are so painful to behold in German and Italian letters. But, of course, there are more or less brilliant periods; by universal recognition the two brightest phases are the Elizabethan and Victorian ages. Both exhibiting the most varied talents in prose and in verse; though the theatre of the former and the novel of the latter are set down as their most glorious achievements.

On the next page there is an odd dialogue about someone strolling along Piccadilly, followed by two sentences in Italian stating that Keats had greater spirituality or inner feeling than Shelley. There is then an interesting but less well-written passage in English comparing Shakespeare to Dickens.

> The English author who is most like Shakespeare seems to me to be Dickens; he is, in fact, a Shakespeare to whom tragical poetry had been taken away but whose jokes had been amplified and often bettered. Besides he owns Shakespeare's zest for life and unremitting comprehension towards his own characters.

The document ends with a few paragraphs in Italian denying that Milton was an 'English Dante'. Although the characters of the two poets had much in common ('austere, rigid and sometimes hard'), Milton lacked both Dante's concision and his latent sympathy for the damned. 'In any case, how can one compare Dante to Milton when the latter was not in a position, morally or theologically, to imagine Purgatory?'[35]

During his thirtieth year Giuseppe decided to exhibit some of his learning in *Le Opere e i Giorni*, an obscure Genoese journal vaguely connected with D'Annunzio and Pirandello.[36] His three articles are all very different and highly idiosyncratic, full of incidental subjective judgements on writers unrelated to the subject matter of the essays. They also reveal the breadth of his reading, demonstrating a literary knowledge of French, English, German and Italian.

The first article, a commentary on the early works of Paul Morand, praises the author's view of the period immediately after the Great War and admires the irony with which he describes the 'sad caricature' of post-war Europe. It also contains some of Giuseppe's pessimism about the future, including an accurate prediction that the diplomacy of recent years had 'laid firm foundations for future conflicts'. The second article, which he entitled 'W. B. Yeats *e il Risorgimento irlandese*', celebrated the 'spiritual beauty' of Yeats's poetry. Stressing Ireland's Celtic inheritance and the effect of the country's climate and landscape on Yeats and his symbolism, Giuseppe also had time to view the whole sweep of Irish literature and to discuss the caustic satire of writers from Swift to Joyce. With a rather grandiose flourish, the article concluded that 'under the distinguished guidance of W. B. Yeats ... the literature and arts of the new Ireland are assuming a position worthy of the traditions of a people which in all the tragic hours of its history has always found a poet to point out its destiny'.

The third article, a long review of a German biography of Julius Caesar, reveals Giuseppe's fondness for historical heroes. His enthusiasm for Caesar's greatness was even more lavish than his praise for Yeats's poetry, and was presented in even more sonorous prose: 'Caesar, for twenty centuries absent in the flesh, for twenty centuries present in the spirit; without doubt the most alive of all the immortals'. This high-flown, rather ornate style is one of the characteristics of these essays. Another is the quantity of personal opinions, such as his remarks on the importance of reading literature in its original language. And a third is the surprising degree of self-confidence for someone so reserved and inexperienced. The judgement on Victor Hugo is grandiloquently self-assured: Hugo's 'untidy palace', which was 'partly a Gothic cathedral decorated only with monsters and angels, without God and without human effigies', already had, in spite of its recent construction, 'more than one broken pane and more than one piece of peeling plasterwork'.

These articles were not polished pieces of literary criticism but they had a certain originality and made some interesting points. Forty years later Paul Morand read the review of his work and found it excellent.[37] After the publication of the essay on Caesar, a journalist wrote to tell Giuseppe that his admiration for the piece was such that he had been inspired to write a short story on the same subject which had been published in the *Corriere della Sera*.[38] Yet curiously the appearance of his articles did not inspire Giuseppe to continue writing. So far as we know, he wrote nothing else with a view to publication for nearly thirty years.

4

The Wanderer in England

Towards the end of his life Giuseppe di Lampedusa said that he had visited every European country of 'major interest' except Spain and Greece.[1] Much of this travelling on the continent was done in the second half of the 1920s, during which he spent several months of each year abroad. Occasionally he visited Germany and Austria but his usual destinations were Britain and France.

Giuseppe had been visiting Paris since he was a small child, yet his photographic album for May 1926 resembles that of a first-time tourist.[2] There are shots of Notre Dame, the Seine, the Louvre, the Tuileries gardens, the Place Vendôme, the Boulevard St Germain; almost the only thing missing is the Eiffel Tower. Once again the photography is of poor quality, largely caused by his habit of pointing the lens so far downwards that half the photograph was taken up by the tarmac.

In later life Lampedusa used to make jokes about the French, especially about their greed and dirtiness, and claimed that Racine's parsimonious style was 'a sublimated form ... of the national stinginess'.[3] Yet he was also a great admirer of France and its cultural influence on his life was second only to England's. If other people deprecated the French, he talked about their greatness: only in France, he believed, did one find the correct mixture of 'Latin and Germanic elements'.[4] Besides, their writers were unsurpassed in their observation and analysis of human behaviour.[5]

From Paris Giuseppe went to London and stayed the summer of 1926 in England. In August he returned via Folkestone to Boulogne, spending the crossing taking photographs of the Kent

cliffs, and by September he was in Burgundy. The monuments of
Dijon were recorded before travelling to Savoy, where he stayed
briefly at Chambéry and Aix-les-Bains. By the end of the month
he was back in his own country, photographing the north-eastern
town of Bolzano. His five-month absence from Italy was typical
of the pattern of his life during this period.

Giuseppe's long visits to England coincided with the period of
his uncle's embassy in London. Pietro Tomasi, Marquess of
Torretta, looked much like his brother Francesco – rather
dapper, large bulging eyes, a long well-groomed moustache – yet
he had managed to escape from the idle Palermitan world which
the rest of his family still inhabited. Much of his distinguished
diplomatic career had been spent in central Europe, where his
posts had included the Viennese embassy, and Russia, where he
had been head of the Italian delegation during the Revolution; he
had known Lenin and was impressed by him.[6] The year before
Mussolini's 'march' on Rome, Torretta had become foreign
minister in the government of Ivanoe Bonomi. A liberal
conservative by inclination, he was a diplomat rather than a
politician and therefore felt able to continue his career under
Mussolini in spite of his opposition to fascism. In 1922 he went to
London accompanied by his wife Alice, the widow of a Baltic
baron. By then in her sixties, Alice Barbi had behind her a fine
concert career as a mezzosoprano during which time she had been
greatly admired by Brahms. She was not always so highly
regarded as an ambassadress. During a visit to Sicily in 1925 King
George V complained that in Rome he had always been forced to
sit next to her at dinner: 'I get enough of her in England when I
am obliged to put up with her.'[7]

In London Giuseppe often accompanied his uncle to official
functions, and a photograph survives of him in a top hat and
morning coat standing in St James's Park before some formal
occasion. He was also present at official embassy events and *The
Times* recorded his presence with Lord Lucan, the Duke of
Argyll and other British peers at a dinner in July 1926. There
were a great many invitations for that summer as well. He was
invited to a ball at Chandos House by Lady Shaftesbury and to a
concert at Bathurst House. The Swiss minister asked him to an
informal dinner without decorations and the Countess Lützow to
a private cinema show. Sometimes the invitations clashed: on

6 July he was invited by the Polish minister to a concert and by the Spanish ambassadress to a reception for the King and Queen of Spain at which he was expected to wear knee breeches and decorations.[8]

Some of these occasions must have appalled him. One cannot imagine that he enjoyed having tea at the British-Italian League in Grosvenor Street any more than he liked dancing at Mrs Glasgow's in Ennismore Gardens. Nor can he have been enthusiastic about the Lord Mayor's invitation to hear an address by Baron Bernardo Quaranta di San Severino on the 'Reorganization of Public Services and proposed scheme for Greater Rome' – one of several similar schemes of Mussolini's which were not put into practice. Then there were requests from fashionable photographers that he should sit for them and be included in their record of 'distinguished patrons'. It was probably thought that he was more important and his title more illustrious than they were: the invitations were often addressed to the Duke of 'Parma', perhaps in the belief that he was the heir of the former independent duchy rather than an impoverished nobleman whose title came from an obscure town in Sicily. In June the art dealers Frazer & Haws invited him to view 'the Duchess of Urbino', a picture they attributed to Titian, but we do not know if they were impressed by Giuseppe's knowledge of painting or by the fact that the Duke of 'Parma' would have come from an area reasonably close to the duchy of Urbino.[9]

It is unlikely that Giuseppe was sent all these invitations because he was talkative and made a good impression. The lady who met him one afternoon at a concert at the Wigmore Hall, presumably wrote him an invitation the same evening on the strength of his title. Available evidence suggests that he was awkward and shy and refused to speak English. The ambassadress clearly found him difficult to entertain. On his first arrival in London in 1925 he was able to talk about English literature to Alice's daughter Alessandra; yet the following year, after several months in the country, he was still unable to speak to his English contemporaries. In 1926 the ambassadress asked Mrs Walter Runciman to bring her 'high-brow son'* to lunch because she had a 'high-brow' nephew staying at the embassy. Steven

---

*The future historian, Sir Steven Runciman, author of *The Crusades* and many other works of Byzantine and medieval history.

Runciman duly arrived, was unimpressed by Giuseppe and 'left thinking that his [Lampedusa] title was the only interesting thing about him': 'he was pasty-faced and podgy, and very shy – he didn't speak English and his French was not good'. Runciman later suggested that Giuseppe was not prepared to speak English because he was frightened by its irregular pronunciation, while his diffident French was a consequence of shyness rather than ignorance.[10]

Despite this heavy and plainly alarming social life, Giuseppe had time to travel around much of the capital and its surroundings during the summer of 1926. Once again his photograph album is a useful guide to the places he visited, and once again the itineraries tend to be predictable: St Paul's, the Houses of Parliament, Trafalgar Square, Downing Street. He was much taken by the Thames and there is a sequence of all the bridges between the Tower and Westminster. As always, the intention was simply to record the buildings, and the deserted streets indicate that this was done on Sunday mornings. Those photographs which do contain people are typical of the first-time visitor to London: the Lifeguards on horseback, the band of the Coldstream Guards, changing the guard at Buckingham Palace and at Whitehall, a policeman directing the traffic in Oxford Street; the one unusual picture is of a meeting of the Catholic Evidence Guild in Hyde Park. Some excursions are recorded as well, to Primrose Hill and Keats's house at Hampstead, and westwards along the Thames to Hampton Court and Windsor.

Yet the photograph album is deceptive, recording the obvious places he went to and omitting the more interesting things. We know he went to Whitechapel and the City, even if he did not take his camera with him. We know that he saw London not as a tourist in Trafalgar Square but as a reader of Dickens and Dr Johnson. For Giuseppe, Johnson was the quintessential Londoner, 'a countryman in exile' who 'each Sunday went out to the country, had a picnic on the grass and returned to the City with a bunch of wild flowers'.[11] Dickens was the true poet of London who knew the capital in all its moods and in all its corners. If Europe was destroyed by the hydrogen bomb, Giuseppe reflected later, Palermo would disappear for ever, unrecorded by a single decent writer; but London would survive, immortalized by Dickens.[12]

Giuseppe could not take his camera into theatres or libraries, yet he went quite often to the West End and spent a great deal of time in public and private libraries in London. The plays he saw included Sheridan's *School for Scandal*, *Hamlet* and *Much Ado about Nothing*, after a performance of which he left the theatre 'cheered up and with a whirling of exquisite words, like fireworks, before my eyes'.[13] In the libraries he used to read volumes of political journals from the eighteenth and nineteenth centuries. He liked the original *Spectator* and claimed to have read nearly half its back-numbers; he much admired Addison's style, 'lucid, colloquial but elegant', and believed it had set the tone for subsequent British essayists down to Belloc and Huxley.[14] He also liked *The London Magazine* but did not care for either *Blackwood's Magazine* or the *Quarterly Review* which he would not forgive for its ' angelcide' of Keats.[15] Sometimes he refused to listen to advice about works that required 'Carthusian patience' to read through. 'I remember the dismayed look of Mr Clay, a kind old gentleman, when I asked permission to borrow several volumes of Southey from his library. "But my dear duke," he exclaimed, "they are poison!" My studies confirmed the wisdom of the old man. Unreadable from top to toe – unreadable, though read by me.'[16] In later life Giuseppe liked to read Landor's works, 'redolent of leather and good tobacco', because they reminded him of English private libraries 'where the ceilings are a bit too low but one's feet sink softly into large tawny carpets, where the gold leather binding of the books looks down on the green leather armchairs, and where beside the fireplace ... stands the tea table laden with fine bulging silverware'.[17]

Giuseppe was comfortable in London, living at the embassy in Grosvenor Street, his expenses taken care of by his father's allowance. He was also much happier outside Italy. His cousin Lucio Piccolo, who once travelled with him, recalled the change that came over Giuseppe after he had crossed the frontier. He even became quite agile, leaping on to a London bus, his overcoat flapping, like a teenager.[18] (A different change came over Lucio when he saw London: the city so appalled him that on the day of his arrival he took the next train home to Sicily.)[19] One of Giuseppe's favourite occupations was wandering up and down the Charing Cross Road, browsing through second-hand bookstalls. He also enjoyed shopping and was evidently pleased to be given a free copy of the Rubayat of Omar Khayyam after buying more than £5 worth of goods from Selfridges.[20] St James's Street had particular appeal, 'the windows of its minute shops adorned by articles whose quality has been examined with the same scrupulous care with which a poet examines the lyrics which might adorn his collection'. Giuseppe was impressed by its elegance ('even the most self-possessed of men are bemused'), by its exclusiveness ('the prices are in guineas') and above all by its variety: everything needed for 'the noble and combative sport of angling', shops 'overflowing with hooks, rods, bait, lines, barrels and whatever man has ever invented for deceiving and destroying these innocent creatures'; shotguns 'for all sorts of quarry from a thrush to an elephant' with 'every type of cartridge from the lightest for killing a bird without damaging its plumage to the most powerful for shooting dead a charging rhinoceros'. Most remarkable of all were the tobacconists which stocked an inexhaustible supply of pipes, an amazing range of ingenious cigarette lighters, and every kind of tobacco from 'coarse Tuscan' to 'cigarettes of saffron, cinnamon and incense' and 'certain cigars from the Philippines which smell of pineapples'.[21]

But the most important thing for Giuseppe in London was that he could be himself. In the evenings he might have to dress up and assume the role of the Duke of 'Parma', but during the day he could be anonymous. London, he later recalled, was the only city where he could find the satisfaction of 'disappearing, of losing oneself in an ocean, of not being anyone'.[22] Years afterwards he wrote of Giovanni, 'the most loved, the most difficult' of Don Fabrizio's sons, who 'preferred a modest life as a clerk in a coal depot to a pampered (read: "fettered") existence in the ease of Palermo'. Like others of Lampedusa's characters, Giovanni was based partly on one of his relations (in this case his great-uncle Filomeno) and partly on himself. Giuseppe was too timid, too indolent and too tied to his mother to follow Filomeno, and yet Giovanni, like Don Fabrizio in *The Leopard* and La Ciura in the short story 'Lighea', is in some ways the person Lampedusa would have liked to have been.

From London Giuseppe made several journeys to other parts of the country. Like his visits to Hampstead and the City, the destinations often had literary or historical associations; years later a young friend in Palermo teased him for having visited 'every' house in England where a writer had once lived.[23] Naturally he made a pilgrimage to Stratford where he saw Anne Hathaway's cottage and several other places connected with Shakespeare, whom he considered not only 'the greatest poet who ever lived' but also 'the most glorious name in the history of humanity'.[24] He also visited Oxford, Cambridge, the Lake District and Newstead Abbey, where he was struck by Byron's house and its magnificent park. Most impressive of all was the sight of the desolate landscape that surrounded the Brontës' house at Haworth: 'the immense moor, boundless and bare ... always the same colour and totally deserted. The swaying curves of the surrounding hills would invite sleep ... if it was not for the hostile ruler of the place, the wind; an incessant wind that gallops freely as an open sea.'[25]

There were also non-literary goals such as the Gothic cathedrals which Giuseppe regarded as England's 'supreme architectural glory'. [26] Once he was in Liverpool (perhaps on his way to Ireland), where he was compensated for the lack of literary associations by the sight of two men who resembled Henry VIII. Watching the landlord of a pub chase a drunkard from his premises, Giuseppe noticed that 'both men had the physique, the reddish whiskers, the sea-green eyes and the chilly majesty' of 'this most English of kings'. He also went to Scotland and later recalled the

red and purple moors, almost treeless, and the ochre-coloured hills overhanging a frothy greenish sea; the grey squat towns of slate and mist (beautiful) which without transition into suburbs open straight out into the most deserted countryside; this light which is nearly perpetual but never sparkling in summer and which in winter is almost (though not completely) absent; this weird spectral landscape, charged with sorcery, animated (in a manner of speaking) by folk who talk so low they seem almost dumb; among them, though, if one is lucky, one will meet the most beautiful girls of Europe (emerald eyes in faces of milk and roses); this unforgettable, fascinating countryside which I had known already from *Macbeth* and which caused me no surprise when I first saw and experienced it.[27]

On another occasion he went to Wales as the guest of Lord

Powys's daughter Hermione, who was married to a Sicilian nobleman. Many years later Hermione della Grazia recalled Giuseppe as 'a most "shut-in" personality. One "met" him but did not "know" him.' Nevertheless, she persuaded her father to invite him to Powis Castle for a few days. Giuseppe accepted and was taken to a fête in Lymore Park, a large Restoration house near Montgomery that was demolished shortly afterwards. During this event he was plainly ill at ease: 'Poor man, it was not at all his cup of tea.'[28] Yet he was impressed by the place and the countryside. On his return he talked ecstatically to Lucio Piccolo about the castles, the parks and the deer.[29]

There is a frustrating lack of information about Giuseppe's relations with other people during this period. We know of the intense link with his mother, of the mutual incomprehension between him and his father, and of the affection he had for his uncle Pietro. Among contemporaries he had a few male friends such as Revel and Lajolo and he had close ties with his Piccolo cousins. But there is little else, and almost nothing about his relationships with women. One can speculate that he was shy and tentative with girls of his own age, and this may have been the reason for two broken engagements. During the 1920s he was engaged to an Italian girl and to an English girl but their names are a mystery. So is the identity of a Scottish girl 'with enchanting seagreen eyes' with whom he was briefly infatuated.[30]

Although nothing is known of his English friends, or indeed whether he had any friends in Britain, Giuseppe certainly felt at home with the English. He later told his wife that he had an English temperament[31] and he did indeed have some of the qualities he believed the English possessed: their reserve, their self-control, their ironic sense of humour. He was impressed by English manners and admired the woman in a London park who made her son apologize for hitting him in the face with a football.[32] Certain phrases and concepts also impressed him, like 'fair play' and 'the underdog', which led him to make favourable comparisons with the Sicilians.[33] Concern for 'the underdog', he believed, was one of the perennial themes of English literature, recognizable in old English texts and subsequently discernible in many works from *Piers Plowman* to the novels of Dickens.[34] 'Fair play' also had a literary ancestry, which had survived till his own day. During his visits to England Giuseppe enjoyed the literary rivalry between Shaw and Chesterton and was much impressed that the two men, 'faithful to the national traditions' of sportsmanship, should have been friends.[35]

Lampedusa later claimed that he was 'not blind to the many defects of the English character', but the only defect he listed was 'self-satisfaction' and the one example he gave was of a certain smugness about individual liberty* which he admitted was partly justified. That seems to have been his only reservation. Otherwise he delighted in 'Englishness' and English characteristics. He had a particularly high regard for 'understatement' and admired people who did not boast about their achievements. England was 'a most extraordinary country', he once said, because 'there one can spend weeks in daily contact with an elderly gentleman before learning that he is an illustrious admiral or an ex-viceroy of India'. Giuseppe himself had spent some time with Lord Haldane, the former war secretary and Lord Chancellor, without realizing who he was.[37]

But the quality he most liked about the English was their sense of humour. Once again this was a characteristic of their literature which ran all the way from Chaucer to Evelyn Waugh. He thought nonsense verse very funny and argued that 'anyone incapable of laughing at a limerick basically understands nothing about England and its literature'.[38] English eccentricity was also appealing, and he was amused by the dispute between Hilaire Belloc and Sir Charles Oman over military tactics in the Peninsular War. Staying in England at the time, he read the newspaper reports of the two men tramping over Spain with supporters and period weaponry to prove their points. The whole thing was hilarious while it lasted and he regretted that the Spanish government had no sense of humour and asked them to stop.[39] Self-deprecating humour was another variety he liked and among several examples noted in his commonplace book was Lord Palmerston's remark: 'Only three people have ever really understood the Schleswig-Holstein business – the Prince Consort

---

*'Englishmen who talk a lot about the liberty of their writers compared to those on the continent seem to forget that England had had the luck to possess [at the same time] three absolutely top-class poets and that all three had to die in exile, persecuted by a hue and cry of hate from those Englishmen who did not like the political ideas of Byron and Shelley and, worse still, did not approve of the aesthetic ideas of Keats.'[36]

who is dead, a German professor who has gone mad, and I who have forgotten all about it.'

The English, Giuseppe believed, were generally free of humbug and hypocrisy, and thus he approved of Lord Oxford's indignant refusal to become president of the Norwich Bible Society on the grounds that he frequently blasphemed, had long been addicted to the gaming table and had lately taken to the Turf.[40] Of all the Englishmen he admired, the two who incarnated their country for him were Isaak Walton and Dr Johnson. Walton was both 'a scholar and a sportsman', which Giuseppe believed to be a peculiarly English combination. 'The duplication of talents,' he once said, 'is a necessity in England. A student, let's say from Cambridge, who excels in the composition of Greek verses, is morally disqualified if he does not add rowing and boxing exploits to his humanistic feats.' Walton also epitomized the national tendency to understatement. In his biographies of Donne and Herbert, Walton did not mention that the first was 'one of the greatest English lyric poets' or that the second was 'one of the greatest religious poets of the age'; 'for him they were "gentlemen and friends", which was more important'. As a writer Walton was not comparable to Dickens or Browning, said Lampedusa, but if one wanted to understand 'the Englishman' in 'a pure state', one should know him first. 'Hitler and Mussolini,' he later commented, 'had obviously not read Walton.'[41]

Dr Johnson was more English still and his character embraced all the country's national peculiarities so that he was in fact the real John Bull. Lampedusa used to refer to England as 'the country least governed by logic', but any drawbacks this might have had were offset by common sense. 'In any other country Johnson's learning would have forced him to espouse a philosophy', but in England he could do without: 'he was a pure empiricist'. He was also humorous, scrupulous and unconcerned with appearances; he might have dirty fingernails or forget to polish his shoes, but he took a cold bath each morning and changed his shirt every day. Above all he was phlegmatic and, like Walton, a master of understatement. Lampedusa once recounted to friends how Johnson, after being robbed and injured by thieves, had described the affair as a lively exchange of opinions. 'Any of us Sicilians,' he commented, 'would have screamed, "They have killed me!"'[42]

Comparisons between England and Sicily often occurred to Lampedusa, and it may have been the memory of his own upbringing which led him to admire the English public schools. Many continental aristocrats of his generation went to these schools and extolled them afterwards, but they were usually sporting and military types, not men of letters. It is surprising to find Lampedusa praising a system of which he had no direct experience and in which he would not have prospered. Presumably he visited some schools when he was in England (while staying at Staines and visiting Windsor he very likely saw Eton) and talked to people about them, because many years later in Palermo he spoke of the places like a recruiting agent.

> Even more than forming men of culture, they aim to form men of character. Separation from the family and a life with contemporaries eradicates that type of 'mamma's boy' so perniciously frequent the more one travels to the south [of Europe]; compulsory sports in the open air in any weather prevent timidity and physical fear and train one for rapid decisions and teamwork; a singular and complicated system of interdependence between the eldest and the youngest [i.e. fagging] accustoms boys to 'service' without humiliation and to 'command' without believing themselves all-powerful.

There were many other advantages as well; boarding at school, for example, made the boys love their family homes more. Even beating was a good practice, as public-school men recognized when they were adults. It was important in the formation of character though it should not be exercised too often: boys who were never beaten, according to Lampedusa, were despised for being 'meek' whereas those beaten more than five times were apparently considered 'rakes'.[43]

His travels abroad led Giuseppe to look at Italy and Sicily in a different perspective. After his death one of his younger friends suggested that Lampedusa must have suffered considerably from the comparison between Britain and France on the one hand and his own country and island on the other. Not only was Italian inferiority obvious to him from what he could observe; it was made plainer by the indifference or disdain in which Italy seemed to be held abroad.[44] Perhaps Giuseppe exaggerated or

misunderstood foreign attitudes: certainly in Britain there was
still great admiration for the triumphs of the Risorgimento and,
within the British establishment at this stage, plenty of
enthusiasm for Mussolini.

Giuseppe was proud of the Italian role in the history of
European civilization and even, although he was a non-believer,
of parts of the Catholic heritage. When an English clergyman,
who did not realize that he was Italian and a Catholic, asked him
if he was 'High Church or Low Church', Giuseppe replied
haughtily, 'I am of the Highest Church'.[45] Yet this pride in the
past was accompanied by contempt for the achievements of
united Italy. Liberalism in England might be admirable but in
Italy it was a mockery; revolution in France might be a real thing
with real benefits, but in Italy it was an empty charade, 'play-
acting', he wrote later, 'a noisy romantic play with a few spots of
blood on the comic costumes'. It has often been said that
Lampedusa did not 'believe in Progress', but the assertion misses
the point: his opposition was directed mainly against the Italian
liberals and their bogus claims of progressiveness. Real
'Progress', which he recognized had taken place in Britain, was a
different matter. Francesco Orlando, one of the pupils to whom
in the last years of his life he gave lessons in literature, recalled
that he admired it for two reasons:

> It goes without saying that for English social progress ... he
> had the genuine admiration of any civilized European ... But it
> was impossible for Lampedusa not to reflect also that that was
> the only form of progress by which the prosperity, prestige and
> above all vitality of his own social class could have been
> preserved; and therefore he was to deprecate all the more
> bitterly the mortal carelessness of the same class on the lands
> and in the times of the Bourbons, which had such historical
> consequences for himself.[46]

Yet Lampedusa's historical opinions were usually more
detached than this, and it would be a mistake to think that they
were often conditioned by reflections of this kind. There was no
particular 'class solidarity' with the English aristocrats. He
admired them when he thought they were right, but he was
equally capable of appreciating their opponents. He had a 'lively

sympathy' for the Puritans, which not even their attitude to the theatre extinguished, because he regarded them as 'a necessary disinfectant for society': 'without them. rottenness and corruption would invade the world and the polished sceptics and enlightened liberals would all go to the devil'. With all their defects, the Puritans had thus had a beneficial impact on British history and their influence could still be seen, three hundred years later, in the characters of Sir Stafford Cripps and Aneurin Bevan.[47]

Similarly, Lampedusa's attitude to the French Revolution was not governed by any regret for the passing of the Ancien Régime. Instead of being horrified by its excesses, he admired the 'Jacobin insolence' and was impressed by the vigour and courage of the Third Estate. Orlando suggests that he viewed these events through the republican eyes of Stendhal, and certainly there are some unexpected judgements: no one in history, for example, had deserved to have his head cut off more than Louis XVI. Furthermore, there was great admiration for Napoleon and he admitted that he preferred Robespierre to Richelieu, just as he preferred Cromwell to Charles II.[48] Yet the Stendhalien explanation is not really sufficient. Lampedusa often reread the exploits of Julien Sorel and Fabrizio del Dongo, but he read many other things besides. His library contained 1,100 volumes on French history, mostly of the eighteenth and nineteenth centuries. Some of these were memoirs of the period, but many others were works by modern historians: until the final years of his life Lampedusa was collecting the recent publications of Braudel and the *Annales* school.[49]

He was thus able to admire different groups of people abroad – England's Puritans and pragmatic aristocrats or France's determined Third Estate – because they achieved, in their different ways, the transformation of their countries. Yet when he looked at the social classes in Sicily he could find no achievements at all. He pondered over this for the rest of his life and the last thing he wrote – the opening chapter of an unfinished novel – is a diatribe against all Sicilian classes: the aristocracy is condemned for its stupidity and indolence, the middle classes for their avarice, the peasants for their ignorance and violence. In *The Leopard*, written a short time before, Don Fabrizio talks of 'the well-known time lag of a century in our artistic and intellectual life; novelties attract us only when they are dead, incapable of arousing vital currents'. And in an earlier passage Lampedusa had intervened with one of his many statements about the condition of the island: 'In Sicily, partly because of its traditional impermeability to anything new, partly because of the general ignorance of any language whatsoever, partly also ... because of a vexatious Bourbon censorship working through the Customs, no one had ever heard of Dickens, George Eliot, Sand or Flaubert.'

These opinions were not written down until thirty years after Giuseppe's first visit to England, yet the attitudes behind them were the product of those early European journeys and the historical studies that accompanied them. He was fortunate to travel when he was still young and broad-minded enough to absorb new ideas. In fact he was so receptive to the cultures of Britain and France that he became mercilessly critical of Sicily and of what he later called the Sicilians' 'terrifying insularity of mind'. Giuseppe had managed to avoid that insularity but during the rest of his life he became increasingly intolerant of those who had not.

5

A Baltic Marriage

Pietro della Torretta had never been a real supporter of the fascist regime, and in 1927 Mussolini demanded his resignation as ambassador to London. After his uncle's return to Italy, Giuseppe's journeys to England became shorter and less frequent. He appears to have been in London in 1931 and in 1934, but it is not clear whether these were the only visits. Many years later he recalled seeing *Hamlet* in 1931 in modern costume at the St James's Theatre: in spite of the ghost's gasmask, the king in pyjamas and Hamlet appearing variously in khaki, sports clothes and evening dress, the dramatic effect was impressive and Giuseppe found no discrepancy between language and costume.[1] The only trace of another visit three years later is the dedication in a book given him by a friend, the historian Corrado Fatta; *The Love Letters of Henry VIII* are inscribed to '*il mostro, Londra 13/ VIII/34*'.[2]

Giuseppe's continental travels in the late twenties and early thirties were sometimes in the company of his mother. In 1928 he was with her in Bologna, where Beatrice needed medical treatment at a clinic; a letter from Giuseppe to his father describes the excellence of their hotel rooms and then asks him to send 175 lire to pay for 'a pair of yellow shoes (of which, as you know, I have great need)'. A year later he was in Munich, planning to visit Hungary, when he became ill with a phlegmon of the throat. The illness, at first wrongly diagnosed, nearly suffocated him, and he was taken to hospital for an urgent operation in the middle of the night.[3]

From this period Giuseppe's European journeys swung from the north west on to a north-easterly axis, with the Baltic as their usual destination. The precise goal for at least three of these tours was Stomersee Castle near Riga, the home of his uncle Pietro's stepdaughter. Alessandra Wolff, known as Licy, was one of Alice Barbi's two daughters by her first husband, a Latvian baron of German origins who had been a Tsarist official at St Petersburg. Baron Wolff died in 1917 at the outbreak of the Russian revolution, and his widow and daughters returned to Latvia shortly before it became an independent state.

The two sisters were very different characters. Lolette, who took after her Italian mother, was small, mild and charming. Hating the cold and not caring much for Stomersee, she and Alice soon left the Baltic and settled in Italy, where she converted to Catholicism and married Augusto Biancheri. Licy, however, stayed with the Orthodox Church, acquired Latvian nationality and remained at Stomersee. Taking after her father, she stayed loyal to the German traditions of his family and emotionally attached to the old regime in Russia. The Wolffs had been in Latvia for several centuries and she considered it her home, even though she had a rather contemptuous attitude towards the Letts themselves. A handsome and intelligent woman with a formidable personality, Licy was a linguist with a wide knowledge of European literature. Her principal interest was psycho-analysis, which a German lieutenant had explained to her on long walks during the First World War; later she studied for several years in Berlin and afterwards in Vienna where she began to practise. In 1918, at the age of twenty-three, she married an Estonian baron André Pilar, an individual of considerable charm who made little effort, apparently, to conceal his homosexuality. In later life Licy rarely referred to her first marriage, and both the events which led to it and its progress are obscure.* They appear to have lived together for part of the time at Riga, where he

---

*In the summer of 1987 the Italian magazine *L'Espresso* printed an interview Licy was purported to have given shortly before her death five years earlier. Asked about her first marriage, she is alleged to have replied that she married Pilar 'only to escape from the Bosheviks ... We were eating only rough bread and I was becoming a skeleton. The baron, however, was still powerful and in a position to enable me to reach my castle in Latvia.' This explanation is wholly implausible: Pilar was not the sort of person to make marriage a condition of assistance, and Licy was the last person who would have agreed to it. It appears that *L'Espresso* has conflated Licy and a friend of hers, Lila Iljascenko, who apparently did marry someone for similar reasons.[4]

worked and she had patients, but she evidently stayed for long periods away, in central Europe and in London at her stepfather's house.

Licy first met Giuseppe in 1925 when he arrived in London at the moment his uncle and aunt were leaving for a royal reception. She was told to entertain him and years later she recalled how on that occasion they had walked to Whitechapel talking about Shakespeare.[5] It has sometimes been claimed that they did not see each other again for five years, but in fact Giuseppe visited Stomersee in 1927. The castle had been sacked and partially destroyed in the failed revolution of 1905, but Licy's father had rebuilt it in its original style with turrets, pinnacles and battlements. Giuseppe was much impressed by both the house and its surroundings, the expansive lawns, the great trees in the park, the lake and forests, and by the care with which the estate was maintained. In a letter to his aunt, who had not been there for many years, he described various rooms, including Licy's study with the Louis XVI furniture, the books on psychoanalysis and the portrait of Freud.[6]

At this stage Giuseppe probably considered himself as merely a friend of both Licy and her husband. He did not see her again for three years until they met in Rome in 1930. The following year he went again to Stomersee and at Easter 1932 Licy came to Palermo. It seems likely that shortly before this last visit they decided to get married, yet any plans they may have had were made in secret. The main reason for this was doubtless the difficult matter of Licy's divorce and annulment, though her husband does not seem to have caused any problems over this. A further factor may well have been Giuseppe's awareness that his parents did not approve of Licy. A serious-minded and rather imperious woman, already thirty-seven and married to someone else, she cannot have seemed an ideal daughter-in-law to Beatrice.

In April 1932, after Licy's departure from Palermo, Giuseppe wrote a series of love letters in French, the language they were to use throughout their married life both in conversation and in correspondence. Their contents are rather conventional declarations of love written in a style evidently influenced by their joint reading of Proust. After she had gone, he wrote, the days had 'begun to pass by, all the same, one after another, grey, stupid and slow like sheep'; his heart had become like 'an enormous sponge soaked a long time in water which only had to be touched lightly to make a mass of tenderness and memories pour forth'.[7] In one letter he abandons this style to describe in Italian a typical day, which does indeed sound rather boring.

> Palermo 18 May 1932
>
> ... I get up at ten-past nine, as always (the hour I used to ring the bell at Stomersee). Pietro brings me breakfast: coffee and milk, bread and butter, and goes to get my shoes and clothes ready. I eat, reading the newspaper. Wash. At half-past ten I go down to the *Contabilità* [accounts office], a series of rooms you haven't seen at the end of the courtyard.
>
> My father is there trying to pay bills and be paid himself, and it is there that I receive the day's news. Around midday I go out to the post office to receive or not to receive news from Muri [Giuseppe's nickname for Licy], then to the Club where usually I settle down to write, as at this moment, to 'Murilli darling'.* At one o'clock my father arrives, informs himself of the day's news, and at twenty-past one we leave. On the way home we buy a little fruit, in this season cherries and apricots. The usual lunch which you know.
>
> After that we stay in the library chatting: usually my mother complains about servants and workmen. At three I return to my rooms to read or take notes until six. Then I go out with my mother on foot.
>
> We walk along the Via Ingham, past the Politeama, the Via Libertà, and go and have some strawberries and cream (very good). Afterwards, at a quarter-past seven, I leave my mother at her sister's house just opposite the ice-cream parlour, and go to the Club where I shock the timorous souls with my audacious opinions. Yesterday one wretched youth confessed that he had been unable to sleep the night before as a result of the sinister prophecies (very imaginative and detailed) which I had made. At half-past nine (unbelievable!) dinner. In the library till half-past ten, then I go out and meet up with [some friends] and my cousins [the Piccolos] in a cafe or at the club.[8]

During the summer plans for their wedding must have gone

---

*In English in the original.

ahead in secret. Giuseppe hinted at the project in a letter to his friend Bruno Revel,[9] though he kept his parents ignorant of his intentions. In August he left for the north, but a letter which he sent Beatrice from Munich on the 17th gave no intimation of the impending ceremony. It contained descriptions of beautiful views (Bologna and Kufsstein), of the assiduousness of a Munich hotel manager (who asked after *Frau Mutter*) and of the various meals and cups of coffee he had had during the journey.[10] But there was no other news except the times of his trains to Berlin and Riga. On 20 August Giuseppe arrived at the Hotel Petersburg in Riga, and four days later he and Licy were married at a Russian Orthodox church in the city.

On the day of his wedding Giuseppe sent long letters to each of his parents telling them that he had decided to marry and pretending that the ceremony would not take place for a while. To his father he described the feelings that had 'tormented' him to such an extent that he had concluded that a life without Licy had no value for him: 'it is no exaggeration to say that I would have preferred to die rather than to continue to be apart from her, seeing her for a few days every year and undergoing these repeated separations which each time become more intolerable'. He added that the decision had not been a hurried one but 'the fruit of a long period of suffering and meditation', and apologized for not having told him about it beforehand: his introverted character and Licy's complicated situation had prevented him. Now that she was free, however, 'completely free in the eyes of the Church and the State', he could break his silence and admit that she had agreed 'in the future' to become his wife. There then followed some diplomatic passages about Licy's tremendous affection for both of his parents.[11]

There is a more anxious tone in the letter to his mother. Even she, he wrote, who knew everything about him, could not have guessed how 'anguished and painful' his life had become; yet it was only her love that had enabled him to bear such suffering. Now his happiness was immense, disturbed only by the fact that he had been forced to announce it by letter. The only other 'shadow' over his happiness was the postponement of Beatrice's 'projects' – probably travel plans she had made with Giuseppe – which this news would entail. Desperate for his mother's approval, he reminded her of some of Licy's qualities, her

kindness, rectitude and understanding of him, and beseeched a
blessing:

> for your Giuseppe who adores you, write immediately of your
> feelings, complete our happiness, which is so great, let us know
> of your affection. Never, from the earliest days of my
> childhood can I remember having received the very smallest
> refusal from you: one word from you will be enough to give us
> a happiness that would move you if you could see it.[12]

Alarmed by the lack of response, he sent her an even more
desperate letter on 29 August. (The postal services must have
been very good for him to have been able to expect a letter to
reach Palermo from Riga and a reply sent back within five days.)

> I am always hoping, every day, to receive your letter. I beg you
> to let yourself be guided by your heart and by your love for me;
> I beseech you also to have faith in my good sense and capacity
> for reflection. My decision has not been an impulsive step but
> the fruit of years of silent maturation, of a profound
> understanding now of the character and qualities of Licy,
> which you yourselves know as well as me. If it appears
> impulsive it is only because of the particular circumstances,
> because of Licy's reluctance in the past to listen to a word on
> the subject. It is obvious that I could not have said anything to
> anyone before, and it is only now with André's willingness to
> make their dissolution public that I have been able to express
> my feelings plainly to Licy. I beg you: I know how you wish me
> well, I know very well that all your thoughts are for me, but I
> beg you not to let yourself be carried away by a moment of
> irrational anger which could not only spoil my present
> happiness which is immense (and would move you if you could
> see it) but also my future, because Licy, who is good but fully
> conscious of her own irreproachable behaviour, would be
> incurably wounded by any sign of dissent – for which I am
> convinced that I (and up to a point you) would bear the
> consequences in my future married life. A future life, I must
> say, that presents itself, even to an enamoured eye like my
> own, full of promise: Licy is beautiful, an angel of sweetness
> and kindness, who has led a strangely complex life with

incomparable dignity and purity; she is also rich, possessing a net income of 60,000 lire, plus Stomersee and what the land around brings in: her personality and social position make her a sort of queen in this place. She wants to live in Italy except in the hottest part of summer. I don't wish to harp on about the fact that no one understands me or will understand me as she does, because you know it. Therefore I beg of you to reflect before compromising a future so full of good omens with a thoughtless gesture...[13]

Three times during the rest of the letter Giuseppe apologizes to his mother for having 'upset' her like this and begs her not to feel even a fleeting resentment: '...it would torture me to have to be contested between her and you, the people I hold most dear in the world'. There is a brief note of defensiveness, almost of defiance: 'Do not forget that I am past thirty-six,* that I am neither a baby nor a cretin, and that I have chosen according to my heart and my reason – and one can't expect more than that.' But the rest of the six-page letter is a blend of anxiety and apology written by a timid man who knows the contents will upset the reader. The only shadows over his happiness, he wrote, were the fact that Beatrice was not with him, his preoccupation with the delay in her reply, and the thought that he may have upset her and forced her to change her plans. 'I am sure you will forgive me,' he added hopefully, 'and then you will be happy.'[14] But he could not have sounded less sure. The entire letter seems to portend the development he most dreaded: that he would become the battleground over which two powerful characters, his wife and his mother, would wage a long and acerbic struggle.

After such entreaties it would have been churlish of Beatrice to have made a fuss, and two or three suitably agreeable letters soon reached the anxious couple in Riga. Licy reacted positively to her new mother-in-law's goodwill and replied that she was moved by the kindness and affectionate sentiments which animated her letters. She was even tactful enough to write in Italian, admitting that Giuseppe had corrected her two worst mistakes. Only one sentence was in French – *'Tous nos plans sont subordonnés aux vôtres* – followed by the diplomatic assertion that she was waiting to learn of Beatrice's wishes before making any plans.[15]

*In fact he was thirty-five.

Giuseppe's anxiety over his parents' reaction contrasted with Licy's more casual attitude towards the feelings of her mother and stepfather. The news of the engagement – a 'thunderbolt' as Alice described it – reached the Torrettas on 27 August at Latte, Lolette Biancheri's country house by the sea near the French border. They responded with a flurry of congratulatory letters and telegrams to Licy, Giuseppe and the Lampedusas before discovering that the couple were already married. 'We are stupefied,' Alice Torretta noted in her diary. Three weeks later her stupefaction had turned to anger. Neither Licy nor Beatrice had replied to her letters and this had left her so upset and indignant that her husband was forced to send a telegram to the Lampedusas to find out whether Alice's letter had reached them. An affectionate letter from Beatrice duly arrived, but Licy's negligence remained inexplicable. She had not written for a month and had 'failed very badly' by leaving her mother 'in complete ignorance about important details'. How was Alice supposed to tell the news to her friends when she knew nothing about the circumstances of the wedding or the annulment?

In the middle of October Licy sent a telegram from Berlin announcing their imminent arrival in Bolzano. The Torrettas and the Lampedusas then agreed to meet there the following week and a 'very moving' reunion took place at the station. During the following days a number of things were straightened out, including an agreed version of events preceding the marriage which Alice and Beatrice would relate to their friends. It was particularly important to stress the delay in the annulment of Licy's previous marriage and to blame it on the Church. It was also thought necessary to pretend that they had all met up in Berlin rather than Bolzano.

A more serious problem, however, was not solved. When Alice told Giulio that the newly-married couple should have an apartment of their own in Palermo, he replied, to her consternation, that Beatrice did 'not wish to deprive herself of her son'. The following day Licy went to see her mother, 'extremely discontented' at the thought of going to Palermo and living in Beatrice's apartment, which in any case had become smaller and more uncomfortable since part of the Palazzo Lampedusa had been let to the gas board. Giulio's offer to give his son an income of 24,000 lire as well as board and lodging in

Palermo did not mollify her. 'Licy mourns her position in Latvia,' noted Alice, 'where her family, her name and she herself have such great prestige, whereas in Palermo she will be nothing, living in two small rooms where she will not even be able to return the hospitality others will give her. She neither understands nor admits the dignity of the family or the title she now has.'[16]

Although Giuseppe had written 'Proustian' love letters and told his father he would rather die than live without her, his relationship with Licy does not appear to have been a passionate one. Since their first meeting in London, their rapport had been intellectual, founded on common interests and a shared sensitivity to literature. And that is how it probably remained, their best times together, Licy used to recall, being those evenings during which they read aloud to each other passages in various languages from their favourite authors.* 'Flames for a year, ashes for thirty', is Don Fabrizio's view of love in *The Leopard*. But with Giuseppe there may have been no flames at all. There has been some speculation about their sexual relations – or lack of them – but it remains nothing more than unconfirmed, and in some cases scurrilous, speculation. It has been said that Giuseppe was impotent, and one friend recalls rumours that this was the result of his war wound.[17] (If true, this might explain his nervous breakdown after the First World War and the terminations of his two engagements afterwards.) Licy may also have had sexual inhibitions – it is unusual to have one husband who was homosexual and another who may have been impotent – but a journalist's claim that she had a long affair with her Baltic friend, Lila Iljascenko, is not true.[18]

The factor which nearly destroyed their marriage was not so much their physical difficulties as the strength of the bond between Giuseppe and his mother. Like most Sicilian women, Beatrice had always been possessive about her son and her tenacity did not diminish as they got older. Even after his marriage she sent him anxious letters of advice about how to treat earaches and other minor ailments.[19] Giuseppe does not seem to

---

*Giuseppe and Licy both spoke French, English, German and Italian. Licy spoke Russian, which she taught her husband, and Giuseppe later also learnt Spanish.

have had the inclination, and certainly not the willpower, to detach himself from his mother's influence. Although he travelled a great deal, he never considered living anywhere except Palermo in the Palazzo Lampedusa with his parents. Licy's arrival did not loosen his bonds to a mother who dominated him, to a city which bored and annoyed him, and to a family almost submerged by litigation and financial problems.

If Giuseppe, in spite of his cosmopolitanism, remained emotionally tied to Palermo, Licy, despite her travels, was firmly attached to the Baltic. She did not make a good impression in Sicily: she could be peremptory and intolerant, and her direct manners and Teutonic bluntness were found unattractive. Besides, a Freudian psychoanalyst was unlikely to be welcomed by islanders convinced of their incomparable virility. As Giuseppe had feared, she quarrelled almost immediately with Beatrice, and the bitterness between the two women was so great that it soon became clear that there was not enough room for both of them in the Palazzo Lampedusa. If the marriage really had been the passionate affair Giuseppe claimed in his letters, he presumably would have sided with Licy. In the event he struggled vainly to keep the peace and then stuck more or less with his mother. Within a year of their marriage, Licy had settled back in Latvia, returning to Palermo only for brief periods each year. Not until she was forced to leave the Baltic during the Second World War did she agree to live again in Sicily.

Between 1933 and 1939 (and later during the German occupation) Licy lived most of the time at Riga and Stomersee. Giuseppe joined her for the first year and there are photographs of him at the castle dressed in plus fours with his spaniel. He liked Stomersee and spent many hours walking in the woods or rowing timidly on the lake. Shortly after their marriage he also accompanied Licy to Latte to stay with her sister Lolette. His nephews remember him there, reading and giving them sweets; one of them used to call him *'mein süsser Giuseppe'* as a result. Giuseppe was delighted to find in the house an almost complete collection of *Blackwood's Magazine*. Although he disliked its views – it had once attacked his favourite poets and had now 'declined to such rigid conservatism that only retired colonels and civil servants read it' – he found it absorbing and worked his way through the back numbers.[20]

After the first two years of marriage, the couple saw less of each other. Giuseppe's visits to Stomersee became shorter and sometimes he saw Licy only twice a year, at Christmas when she travelled to Rome and Palermo, and in August when he went to Stomersee. In 1937, for example, Licy spent the early months in Riga and moved to Stomersee in the spring. In August Giuseppe joined her but within a month he had gone home and she was sending long descriptions of her psychoanalytical work to him in Palermo.[21] Their marriage became what one commentator has called *un matrimonio epistolare*, based on a lengthy and rather banal correspondence in French.

After her husband's death Licy made much of the intellectual companionship they had enjoyed in their marriage. This may have become stronger during their last years together when they were living in Palermo, but there is not much evidence of it during the thirties. Their letters to each other are strangely uninteresting and even suggest a lack of understanding between them. Giuseppe's 'Proustian' tones have been replaced by mundane reports about their dogs, their friends and the weather. There is little talk of literature, their major common interest, and no demonstrations of great love or even of much affection.

Licy's letters are dominated by her illnesses, descriptions of their symptoms and prescribed diets. In October 1935 she was staying at the Hôtel Bellevue in Riga for a course of injections for serious inflammation of her eyes. Lila Iljascenko visited her every day, with one of Licy's favourite dogs, and wrote frequent bulletins to Giuseppe in Palermo. André Pilar, who was staying nearby, also sent reports of his former wife. Licy was not getting any worse, he wrote to Giuseppe in November, though she had become 'very nervous and irritable', and she now had *'une idée fixe'*, stemming from her experience of the Bolshevik Revolution, about financial matters. Giuseppe himself does not seem to have done much about this long illness beyond sending his wife letters and illustrated magazines.[22] Indeed, Licy saw far more of her first husband during this period than of her second.

In September 1937 Giuseppe wrote to Licy asking her to come soon to Palermo and enclosing quantities of information about train connections and timetables. But she preferred to stay at Stomersee. If Beatrice and Palermo were really more important to Giuseppe than his marriage, Latvia and her patients mattered more to Licy than her husband. During the Second World War, when the Baltic states were invaded twice by the Russians and once by the Germans, Pilar wrote to Giuseppe about the future of her property: '...let us hope that matters sort themselves out and that Licy is happy, because Stomersee is the only thing of real importance in her life'.[23] This is something of an exaggeration because, as her letters show, Licy's psychoanalytical work mattered very much to her too. During the mid-thirties she was particularly occupied by the case of a former housekeeper at Stomersee who suffered from depression and homicidal tendencies. Sometimes, after sessions of analysis that lasted four or five hours, Licy described the situation in a letter to Giuseppe and asked for his opinion. In 1936 her work on this case gained her membership of the Italian Society of Psychoanalysts.[24]

Don Giulio died in June 1934 at the age of sixty-six, and Giuseppe became Prince of Lampedusa. He had never been close to his father and it is unlikely that he was greatly upset by the event. It did, however, mark a new stage in his life because he now decided, for the first time since 1914, to spend most of the year in Palermo. For the next few years he lived with his mother in the family home, attempting to deal with boring administrative problems: among papers found in the ruins of the Palazzo Lampedusa were letters from Giuseppe about rents and receipts, correspondence over an allowance of 200 lire to his uncle Francesco, and details of legal cases being fought between members of the family.[25] Many of these problems stemmed from the saga of his great-grandfather's will which had not yet been concluded. Giuseppe made comprehensive notes about all the heirs, their addresses, deaths, wills and lawyers,[26] but came no nearer to a solution of this tiresome business.

Middle-aged life in the Palazzo Lampedusa was very different from the childhood idyll he later recalled. He still loved the palace but the 'beauty and integrity' he evoked in his memoirs had been lost several years earlier when much of the house had been let; half of the first floor, a part of the second and various store rooms were now occupied by the municipal gas board. The administration of the house and the remaining Lampedusa properties did not of course occupy all his time, and he was able

to spend several hours each day reading. Much emphasis has
rightly been placed on Lampedusa's extraordinary knowledge of
European literature, but his study of history was almost as
extensive. His historical library* consisted mainly of books on
France, Italy, Britain and the First World War. Many of them he
had privately bound in marbled cloth covers with red and white
(sometimes black and white) leather spines. The English
historians he read during this period included the great Whig
writers, Macaulay and G.M. Trevelyan, who may have
influenced his favourable view of English constitutional
development. But he also loved the seventeenth-century diarists,
Pepys and Evelyn, and had great admiration for the biographies
of Carlyle. Among the French he read the books of modern
historians (Bloch, Mathiez and Madelin) as well as the memoir
writers of the Napoleonic era (Marbot, Caulaincourt and the
emperor's disgraced secretary Bourienne). He also advised
people to read a French historian, Halévy, for his long history of
England in the nineteenth century. As for Italians, he studied the
works of contemporary writers such as Chabod and Omodeo,
nineteenth-century politicians including Franchetti, Sonnino and
Cattaneo, as well as Sicilian specialists such as Pitrè and Amari.
The critics who after his death accused Lampedusa of historical
ignorance were quite wrong. His knowledge was remarkable,
although he was more discerning about literature than history
(except on Italian matters). His glorification of heroes, especially
Caesar and Napoleon, was sometimes childish, and there was a
certain naïveté in some of his judgements. His vision of
Elizabethan England, for example, does not sound like the
product of deep consideration: among 'the most attractive, the
most gifted and the most feared people who had ever lived, [the
Elizabethans were] a race of supermen' living happily under laws
that were 'simple, clear and wholly empirical'.[27]

Lampedusa's social life in the 1930s was even more restricted
than in other periods, and his appearance at a fancy-dress ball at
the Palazzo Mazzarino in 1938 was unusual. He spent some time
at the aristocratic club, the Circolo Bellini, but his earlier claim to
Licy – that he went there to 'shock the timorous souls' with his

---

*When he moved to the Via Butera after the Second World War he had two
libraries: one of historical books off the great drawing room and one for
literature on the floor below.

'audacious opinions' – is not entirely convincing. All the evidence suggests that he rarely spoke except to close members of the family and a few intimate friends; one young man who sat beside Lampedusa at a lunch at the Bellini recalls that he could get nothing from him but monosyllables.[28] It is more likely that he observed his contemporaries at the club and listened to their idle conversations with some derision but without taking much part. In the last work he ever wrote – the opening chapter of the novel he planned to call *I gattini ciechi* (*The Blind Kittens*) – he described a ludicrous group of aristocrats lounging about in the club – 'a class with a low consumption of general ideas' – whose absurd and pointless discussions, their 'convulsive gesticulating about nothing', could be seen as 'the tragic jerking of a class which was watching the end of its own land-owning supremacy, that is of its own reason for existence and its own social continuity...'

Lampedusa also sometimes went to a cafe with a group of friends which included the historian Gaetano Falzone. Again he does not seem to have contributed much, though Falzone recalled occasional comments about politics. His attitude towards fascism and Mussolini remained ambivalent: Falzone remembered that it was one of disdainful silence,[29] but his aversion was more aesthetic than real. He liked to ridicule the regime and he was contemptuous of Mussolini's Italian Academy. Yet he considered that fascism was what the Italians needed and deserved, and he also believed that the moderating influence of the monarchy prevented it from being dangerous. In any case, he thought right-wing dictatorships were preferable to left-wing ones and for this reason supported Mussolini's intervention in Spain. He was relieved that the 'Muscovites' had been stopped with the help of the Italian 'volunteers' and believed that this policy may have saved Europe from communism.[30] But he probably took little real interest in the Spanish question and relied upon what he read in the papers: certainly he does not seem to have taken the trouble to find out whether the Italians arrived in Spain before the 'Muscovites' or whether the Republicans really were communists.

6

The Troubles of Don Giuseppe

In June 1940 Mussolini declared war on Britain, which had just evacuated its army from Dunkirk, and France, which was on the point of surrendering to Nazi Germany. Giuseppe di Lampedusa disapproved of the dictator's action, not only because it seemed a cowardly move against his two favourite countries after they had suffered heavy defeats, but also because he was sceptical of Italy's military efficiency.[1] Moreover, he despised Hitler,[2] disliked the Nazis and was horrified when he learnt about the German atrocities.[3] The prince himself played little part in the war. In December 1939 the army command in Palermo ordered him to present himself at the artillery school at Nettuno, but the order was twice returned to the authorities with the word 'unknown' mysteriously stamped on the envelope.[4] Nevertheless, Lampedusa seems to have received the papers eventually and spent some weeks with the artillery near Rome and in Palermo. Subsequently demobilized, he was not called up again until just before Mussolini's declaration when he was sent for three months to the province of Trapani. Discharged in August, he was recalled in January 1942 though within a week periostitis in his right leg ended this period of service.[5] The nationalist feelings which had briefly animated him at the end of the Great War were absent during the second global conflict. For Lampedusa the war was a continual source of personal worry and unhappiness as well as a spectacle which disgusted him. 'When one sees what has happened,' he wrote to Licy in 1943, 'one wants to spit on one's passport of humanity.'[6]

Licy had left Latvia at the end of 1939, shortly after a secret protocol of the Molotov–Ribbentrop Pact had placed her country in the Soviet Union's sphere of influence. 'The departure was awful,' she had written from Riga. 'I smiled [at the servants] and said the whole time that I would always come back, that all this did not concern me, but I saw in their eyes that they did not believe me ... their sobs and cries were heard all over the place.' Licy tried to hide the furniture and pictures: the consoles and large mirror under big bundles of straw, a desk and the Chippendale chairs in the gardener's house underneath his clothes, 'the gouaches and small things' in another cottage. Six packing cases were filled with valuables and sent to a railway station 'at night so that nobody should see them'; it is not clear what their destination was or whether they reached it. Licy eventually arrived in Riga where she found 'real pandemonium' and 'incredible panic and alarm'. The German-speaking Balts had to decide whether to leave, take a German passport and forfeit their property (as the Nazi government, which had effectively abandoned them, was urging), or to wait for the Russians. 'Everyone goes without exception,' reported Licy, 'with two *Handkoffer* as only luggage. In ten days there will not be a person here, not one doctor, not one advocate. The pastors are going, leaving all our old churches to the Letts ... ' Among numerous other worries, including an attempt to send her silver away by ship, there was a problem with her friend Lila Iljascenko, 'who of course neglected to take a passport in time. With dreadful pains and runnings [sic] I now hope to get her one. Thank God she has brothers who have lots of money and will pay.'[7]

When the Soviet Union occupied and annexed Latvia a few months later, Licy was in Sicily, visiting her husband from time to time at his post near Trapani. But the following year she returned to the Baltic, now occupied by German troops, and remained there until the Russian counter-attack in the south at the end of 1942. Staying at Riga, she made frequent journeys to Stomersee to try to preserve control of the castle in conditions which were extremely difficult. Her house and lands and the countryside remained the same, but the world she had known and the people she had grown up with had all gone, destroyed by the Russian occupation.

During these years the Lampedusa marriage reverted to an epistolary relationship, the couple writing regularly from Riga and Palermo to tell each other how impossible conditions were in their respective cities. Giuseppe spent much of his day in the library at the Palazzo Lampedusa, waiting for Licy's letters to arrive and then answering them. It is difficult to believe that she can have been delighted by these replies because her husband had little to say except how bored and depressed he was. On their tenth wedding anniversary he brought himself to declare that there was now nothing solid and unchangeable in his life except his love for her. But this was a rare passage of affection in a correspondence that seldom displayed feeling on either side. Giuseppe's only words of tenderness appeared in English at the beginning of his letters: 'Muri, my dearest and very good one', 'Mury my most sweet and delightful old dear', 'Mury my dearest and very good darling'. Licy's letters did not even have a variety of tender beginnings: she addressed her husband always as *'Mon Ange Chéri'* and signed herself, eccentrically in the masculine, *'Ton Petit'*.[8]

The absence of affectionate phrases is a reflection of Lampedusa's introverted and undemonstrative nature rather than an indication of lack of affection. The persistence and regularity of the correspondence shows that there must have been a genuine attachment between them even if it was not expressed and even if it was sometimes misunderstood. If they had had children, this affection would perhaps have been revealed through descriptions of their offspring; in their absence it showed itself in accounts of the large numbers of dogs which the Lampedusas acquired and treated almost as if they were children. Among the various breeds and mongrels which they collected, the most cherished seems to have been a black spaniel called Crab (named after Launce's dog, one of Giuseppe's favourite characters in *Two Gentlemen of Verona*)[9] to whom they spoke in Italian (each dog was addressed in a different language). Crab was with him in Palermo throughout the war and became his main consolation. Writing to Licy, he described the dog's nervousness at night when the sirens sounded and admitted he had to pick him up and comfort him. He also listed Crab's diet: the same pasta and broccoli which were cooked for Giuseppe and a variety of meat, vegetables and small fish. For his birthday Crab would be given 'an enormous dinner' of pâté, peas and meat followed by bread and honey; afterwards he would spend an hour in the garden with permission to bark at as many cats as he liked.[10]

In Palermo Lampedusa established a sort of daily routine: reading, talking to his mother, looking after the dogs, writing letters to Licy, seeing an occasional friend from the Bellini club. There were the usual administrative chores and further attempts to settle the inheritance of his great-grandfather. These bored and irritated him and in a letter to Licy he complained of '*des entrevues et des réunions partielles et générales avec tous les héritiers* which are a smart remarkable assembly of people, one-third fools, one-third lunatics, and the rest of them rascals'.[11]* In the autumn of 1942 Lampedusa made the puzzling decision to enrol as a student of literature at Palermo University.[12] He was already forty-five and despised academic life, and the idea that he intended to take exams and solemnly gain a degree seems ridiculous. Whatever it was that inspired him to make the move is a mystery, but in any case he appears to have changed his mind soon after matriculation. Perhaps it was the trauma of living in a city under bombardment that persuaded him to abandon his curious project. During the winter of 1941–2 there had been several air-raids on Palermo and in April 1942 the Palazzo Lampedusa lost all its window panes in the dining room and the green drawing room. Over the following year the raids intensified and the damage to the old palace increased until it became almost uninhabitable.

From time to time Lampedusa escaped to Capo d'Orlando, the villa of his Piccolo cousins on the island's northern coast a hundred miles to the east of Palermo. Standing in one of the greenest corners of Sicily, the house was surrounded by citrus groves and gardens of orchids, palms and hydrangeas. For Giuseppe it had always been an enchanted place, an Arcadia to flee to from the problems of Palermo. Among its streams and valleys, where he went for long walks and could find wild strawberries even in early April, he felt transported from the loud cities and arid spaces of modern Sicily to the pastoral world of ancient Greece.[13] Capo d'Orlando's air of unreality was increased by the presence of his eccentric cousins, the relations he was most attached to after his mother. There were three of them, Giovanna who ran the house and garden with her mother (Beatrice's sister Teresa), and her two brothers, Casimiro and Lucio. Their father,

*In French and English in the original.

the baron of Calanovella, had long since departed in pursuit of an actress, and they all lived with their mother and a great many dogs in the extraordinary atmosphere of Capo d'Orlando.

'A fine welcome', Giuseppe reported to Licy after one arrival at the house, 'excellent food and endless ghost stories'.[14] All the Piccolos were interested in spiritualism and were both fascinated and frightened by ghosts. Casimiro, the eldest, was a painter who spent much of his life producing pictures of fairies and goblins in a style influenced by Arthur Rackham and *Alice in Wonderland*. His paintings are delicate and meticulous and took a long time to complete; from an adult life's work of less than a hundred pictures, he gave four to his cousin Giuseppe. Many years earlier Casimiro had studied art in Munich. But his fiancée had died of tuberculosis there and he had returned home with a phobia about becoming contaminated. Terrified of contracting the disease, he had shut himself up at Capo d'Orlando and spent a lot of time washing his hands in alcohol. If someone insisted on shaking hands with him, he was polite enough to return the handshake but took the first opportunity to retire to his bathroom to wash. In the drawing room of the villa his armchair was placed in a sort of quarantine zone well away from the others; in the dining room, where he had to sit next to other people, he had perfected a technique of pulling in his chair with his feet so that he did not have to touch either it or the table with his hands.[15]

Even more eccentric was Casimiro's younger brother Lucio. Thickset and ugly, often dressed in plus fours and shooting stockings, Lucio's appearance masked an astonishing range of talents. He was in a learned if amateur way an astronomer, mathematician, poet and musician. He could read several languages, including Persian and ancient Greek, . and his knowledge of literature was comparable to Lampedusa's. A self-taught pianist who played Wagner by ear, Lucio composed music at a leisurely pace and spent a good deal of time writing an unfinished Magnificat. Like many Sicilians, he did not feel the need to broadcast or publish his talents, but when he finally did publish some poetry he won an important literary prize. Eugenio Montale, the future Nobel winner who had to present Lucio on that occasion, found him 'an accomplished musician, a student of philosophy ... trained Greek scholar, knowledgeable in the entire field of European poetry, old and new ... a savant so

learned and well-informed that truly the idea of having to present
him embarrassed me immeasurably'.[16]

The literary rapport between Lucio and Giuseppe was so
strong and long-lasting that neither of them bothered to look for
other intellectual friends. Visitors to Capo d'Orlando were
amazed by their conversation at meals, the literary games, the
allusions, the rhymes and intellectual jokes, the attempts to catch
each other out. They shared many of the same tastes, such as a
love for Keats, but they enjoyed disagreeing and teasing each
other. Lucio was a great reciter of poetry, prone to declaiming
The Faerie Queene and addicted to lengthy quotations from
Browning. Giuseppe secretly agreed that Browning was the
greatest of the Victorian poets [17] but he disparaged him to Lucio
and said he preferred his wife: men would know nothing of what
women thought about in bed, he once said, were it not for the
sonnets of Sappho, Louise Labé and Elizabeth Barrett
Browning.[18] Between the two of them there was a good-
humoured rivalry exhibited in an intellectual tournament
contested with wit and literary allusion. They wrote verses and
sketches for amusement and then ruthlessly criticized each
other's efforts. It was all an enjoyable game, played out at Capo
d'Orlando and in Palermo restaurants, and for many years it
remained a private one. Only after Lucio published his first
volume of poems in 1954 did Giuseppe feel the need to compete
in print.

One taste Lampedusa did not share with the Piccolos was their
interest in the occult. Casimiro possessed a large library on the
supernatural and both he and Lucio not only believed in the
existence of spirits but could even sense their presence. Both of
them were also convinced by reincarnation and seemed to know
so much about the 'after-life' that Giuseppe suggested they
should compile a Baedeker about it.[19] In the early twenties Lucio
had corresponded with W.B. Yeats not about poetry but about
different sorts of elves, comparing Irish goblins to their Sicilian
equivalents.[20] He was obsessed by 'the twilight zone of the
psyche' and wanted to do for Sicily what Yeats had done for
Ireland in *The Celtic Twilight*: to recover the lost myths ('what are
today called myths but are for me reality') and esoteric traditions,
that interest in the 'penumbra' and the sunset world which the
Sicilians had long lost but still needed. The attempt was not

approved of by his cousin who laughed at him and told him he was 'incorrigible, immersed in base superstitions'.[21] If one had to believe in an after-life, said Giuseppe, the arguments of the Catholic Church were more convincing than Lucio's.[22]

In addition to the conversation and the walks in the countryside, one of the main pleasures of Capo d'Orlando was the food. On Easter Sunday 1942 Giuseppe described to Licy a typical dinner of lasagne, vol-au-vent with lobster, cutlets in breadcrumbs with potatoes, peas and ham, 'an admirable tart from a recipe of Escoffier' (puff pastry, cream and candied cherries) – and 'all in their usual quantities!' The manner in which the Piccolos were able to insulate themselves from the horrors of the Second World War is remarkable. Throughout the summer of 1942, while massive armies confronted each other in Russia and Africa, there was no shortage of food at Capo d'Orlando: on 9 June Giuseppe reported 'tender and tasty beefsteaks two inches thick', exquisite cakes, a slice of tuna fish 'literally as large as a car tyre'. On another day Giovanna announced that they were having a light and mainly cold lunch as it was summer, and afterwards Giuseppe listed for Licy's benefit the contents of this 'light' meal: 'real *fettuccine*' with butter and parmesan cheese, an enormous fish with various sauces, a *pâté de lapin* made 'according to the rules of the old game pâtés: liver purée, black truffles, pistachios and consommé jelly; a very successful product of Giovanna's art'; and finally meringues with real chocolate ice-cream.[23]

Lampedusa's visits to Capo d'Orlando were regular but short and in between he went back to Palermo to look after his house. During 1942 life in the city became increasingly disagreeable. The Palazzo Lampedusa was gloomy and deserted, its windows repeatedly shattered, its furniture and contents stacked in the basement. Apart from the porter, the servants had gone for safety to the country and so had most of his acquaintances. By day he wandered about the Bellini club by himself and at night he lay awake listening to the bombs and the air-raid warnings. By the end of the year he could stand it no longer and decided to take his mother and Crab to live at Capo d'Orlando. For several weeks they stayed with his cousins and their mother in the villa and then rented a small house in a village nearby. During the early part of 1943 Lampedusa's time was occupied by organizing the new house which was unfurnished and without heating or running water. For a while there was no electricity either and he had to buy oil lamps which he thought looked 'very charming'. Beds, chairs, tables, curtains and linen all had to be transported with great difficulty from the Palazzo Lampedusa. He also insisted on bringing a good number of his books which he carried 'with unbelievable effort' in heavy suitcases by train.[24]

Although moving house was tiresome and time-consuming, it was a relief to be out of Palermo; and it was some consolation to be able to walk in a landscape he knew and loved. Even the grey February tones were beautiful, he told Licy, with their mixture of olives and almonds under a grey sky; moreover, it was nearly spring and the countryside was already full of roses and wild narcissi. On his walks Giuseppe was naturally accompanied by Crab who apparently terrified the district's women, children, sheep and other dogs. From photographs Crab seems to have been an ordinary Cocker spaniel, but perhaps this breed was not well known in Capo d'Orlando. Several women, reported his master, asked whether he was a dog or a monkey, to which Giuseppe replied that he was an American ape.[25]

Apart from his anxiety over the Palazzo Lampedusa, which he visited regularly by train, Giuseppe's principal worry was once again the relationship between his mother and his wife. Licy had stayed a considerable time in Latvia in the middle of the war, trying to hold on to her property, but towards the end of 1942 she gave up. She disliked the Nazis but loathed the Bolsheviks far more; she was after all of German origin and the Nazis did not threaten her position at Stomersee as the Russians did. Before the end of that year, however, the German army outside Stalingrad had been surrounded and the Russian offensive in the south had begun. By then the position of the German-speaking remnant in Latvia had become precarious, and Licy decided to leave, aware that she would probably never see Stomersee again.[26*]

Licy left the Baltic for the last time and went to her stepfather's house in Rome. Giuseppe joined her there for Christmas but she refused to return with him to Capo d'Orlando afterwards. From the new house her husband repeatedly implored her to join him

---

*She never did. After the USSR's second annexation of the Baltic countries, the estate was nationalized and the castle turned into an agricultural school.

and Beatrice, and he may have exaggerated the beauties of the countryside to induce her to come. But Licy was not tempted. If she and her mother-in-law could not live together in the great Palazzo Lampedusa, they were unlikely to tolerate each other in a four-room house in the provinces. Giuseppe was of course aware of the dangers but hoped they would be overcome by the good sense of the two ladies. In February 1943 he wrote to Licy:

I have thought of what it will be like ... when we are all downstairs together in the little house. I must say that it is not something which frightens me, because I have so much faith in the good sense of the ladies who will live there. I am sure that they will not wish to stir up a minor civil war during this terrible real war of which we are all the victims; that they will understand the ineluctable nature of the inconveniences we have to put up with; and that the inopportunity and absurdity of any conflicts will backfire on themselves. In a word, I am confident that they will not wish to create for me 'a second front' and that the Italian and Slav subtlety will know how to adjust to conditions which threaten all of us equally.[27]

This exercise in diplomacy, however, did not persuade Licy to leave Rome, and her husband continued his solitary shuttles between Palermo and Capo d'Orlando. Each month the Palazzo Lampedusa endured further damage, but for a time this was nothing more serious than broken window panes and a few holes in the roof. There were no direct hits on the palace in the bombing raids of March 1943, although much of the surrounding district was destroyed. Towards the end of the month an ammunition ship blew up in the port and caused widespread damage in the city; in the Palazzo Lampedusa doors and windows were torn off their hinges and the remaining panes broken. This may have been the occasion Lampedusa referred to in his memoirs when an explosion flung the iron window grilles from the neighbouring Pietraperzia palace into the first-floor rooms of the Palazzo Lampedusa, smashing up the stucco work and the Murano chandeliers.[28]

The structure of the palace remained intact until 5 April, 'the day', Lampedusa later recalled, 'on which bombs brought from beyond the Atlantic searched her out and destroyed her'.

Unaware of the damage, he hurried to Palermo a day or two later and was confronted by 'the terrible spectacle' of its 'repugnant ruins'. [29] He was unable to reach the first floor because the main staircase had been destroyed and the back stairs were blocked by debris 'two storeys high'. The green and yellow drawing room and the gallery were also wrecked, though his father's old apartment and the rooms containing most of the valuable objects survived. Retrieving a large bag containing Licy's slippers and sealskin coat from the porter's lodge, Lampedusa went to the police station and arranged for guards to be posted around the house to deter looters.[30] Then he set out on the road to Bagheria and walked eight miles to the house of Stefano Lanza, Prince of Mirto, on the coast at Santa Flavia. According to Count Sarzana, who was staying there, he arrived covered in dust and unrecognizable, repeating, 'my house has been bombed, it's been completely destroyed'. Then he went to the fire and sat down without saying anything else. For three days he remained at Santa Flavia refusing to talk.[31]

Many years later Lampedusa recalled that the entire palace had been 'literally razed to the ground'[32] and most of its contents destroyed. This, however, was an exaggeration. Although much of the building was ruined, a part of it remained habitable and his mother was able to spend the last year of her life in it. Pictures and furniture were damaged by the bombs and many things were stolen during the pillaging of the palace which took place after either this raid or a subsequent one. But some fine furniture was saved and the Louis XV consoles and mirrors were later installed in Lampedusa's new house in Via Butera. More importantly, as his bookcases withstood the explosions and their contents did not interest the looters, he was able to salvage most of his books. Forty years after the bombing, torn pages of Dickens and Diderot could still be found in the ruins of the palace; among other books he lost was a set of Johnson's *Lives of the Poets* which he had bought at a high price from a second-hand bookshop in Turin.[33] But the bulk of the library had survived and after the war it too was transported, with the original bookcases, to Via Butera.

In the middle of July, at the time of the Allied landings in Sicily, Lampedusa received another blow: a bomb landed on the top of the house he had rented in Capo d'Orlando and flattened it. He and Beatrice were out at the time and returned to find the house destroyed together with all the furniture and belongings he had brought from Palermo. Soon afterwards Licy arrived from Rome and the three of them debated where they should go. With its railway and coastal road, Capo d'Orlando was plainly a potential battlefield, and they decided to leave it for a village in the Nèbrodi hills to the south. This was not necessarily the most sensible decision as there were German troops in the hills and the hazards of the journey included a strafing by Allied aircraft. Even when they reached the village, Ficarra, they were not safe because there was a German battery nearby which drew the fire of the Allied artillery. Yet they must have liked the place because, after the danger had passed and the Germans had left Sicily, they stayed on for a few weeks in Ficarra. During the day Lampedusa went for long walks in the wooded countryside and in the evenings he visited the local club. They were still there in September, when they heard on the wireless that Italy had declared an armistice. Soon afterwards there seems to have been a breakdown in relations between Licy and Beatrice. In any event, Lampedusa and his wife soon departed for Palermo while his mother remained at Ficarra before settling in a hotel in Capo d'Orlando.[34]

The Lampedusas rented a furnished apartment in the Piazza Castelnuovo and remained there for nearly two years. In a life of long and frequent disappointments, this was perhaps the bleakest period of all for Giuseppe. He yearned to rebuild his palace, which might have been possible though difficult and expensive, but eventually he abandoned the project as impractical. The destruction of his home weighed on him oppressively and continuously, and he thought about little else; ten years later, according to a close friend, he still had not recovered from the loss.[35] It is unlikely that Licy was able to do much to raise his spirits because she was almost as depressed by the loss of her home at Stomersee; to her patients she admitted that it was the worst thing that had ever happened to her.[36] Yet although she kept a packed suitcase ready for a quick return to the Baltic, she did not brood on her disaster like Giuseppe because at least she had the distraction of her work. In the post-war years she was the only woman practising as a Freudian psychoanalyst in Italy. Apart from her patients, she also worked hard for the Italian Society of Psychoanalysts in Rome and became its vice-president;

much of 1946 was spent in the capital organizing its conference
and preparing a paper on developments in psychoanalytical
diagnosis and technique.[37] Moreover, Rome itself was a
distraction to her and a much more congenial city than devastated
Palermo. She liked its restaurants, particularly Ranieri's near the
Spanish Steps, and she had colleagues and friends who lived
there. So did her sister's family, the Biancheris, as well as her
mother and stepfather, Pietro della Torretta, who in 1944 had
come out of retirement to be president of the Italian Senate.

Lampedusa also understood the need to immerse himself in
some occupation, though unlike Licy he did not find work he was
well suited to. During their occupation of Sicily the Allies had to
find thousands of people for local government and other
administrative posts vacated by Fascist Party officials.
Regrettably, many of these turned out to be *mafiosi* who had
spent time in the United States or had family connections with the
American underworld, but others were honest men appointed
because of their social position and because they had held no
official post under Mussolini. One of these was Lampedusa who
at the end of 1944 found himself nominated as president of the
Palermo provincial committee of the Italian Red Cross. He
accepted the position and for the next two years most of his time
was taken up with complicated and frustrating administrative
problems. Although his original appointment limited his duties to
the province of Palermo, he was later made regional president of
the association with responsibilities over the whole island.

Lampedusa seems to have been competent and conscientious
in his new job, though often unhappy with his duties. Surviving
letters suggest that his two years there consisted of an
interminable succession of difficulties and disagreements, but it
should be remembered that correspondence on such a subject at
such a time is more likely to concentrate on problems than on
achievements. A letter from General Paolo Berardi in April 1945
thanked Lampedusa for the Red Cross's assistance to the army,
but most of the other letters deal with rivalries between
employees, disputes over salaries, the problems of a hospital or
the poor organization of a warehouse. Lampedusa had to contend
with shortages of sugar and other necessities, to accept and refuse
resignations, and to listen to complaints about the absenteeism
and inefficiency of Red Cross workers. In addition, there were

frequent quarrels between his inspectors who denounced each other in anonymous letters to the Central Committee in Rome. Then there was the problem of money. In July 1945 the inspector-general of the organization urged him to start fund-raising and pointed out that in February the Duke of Misterbianco had organized a ball which raised 100,000 lire. Admitting that it might not be an appropriate moment to plan other balls, the official hoped nevertheless that Lampedusa would arrange some other 'recreation' to raise money.[38]

His principal problem, however, was the fact that his organization was evidently being exploited by its previous officials. In a long letter in May 1946 to the president of the Italian Red Cross, Lampedusa explained why the morale of his organization was 'very far from being satisfactory'.[39] The chief trouble was 'interference' which 'paralysed our main projects' and tried to force him and his colleagues to pursue 'goals incompatible with the seriousness of the Red Cross'. It was caused by 'individuals of the old set'* who continued 'to be domineering, to weave dark intrigues and to present facts in a particular light that suited their interests'. These characters were exceeding their duties in various ways as well as 'setting traps designed to trip us up' and blocking any useful initiatives; although in competition with each other, they could be relied on to unite in preventing the Red Cross from carrying out its duties. As a result, Lampedusa wrote, services were slowing down while costs were rising, and nothing could be done to improve the situation without 'radical remedies'.

Lampedusa suggested going to Rome to explain the problems in greater detail and to reveal various names which he had been careful to avoid mentioning in his letter. But 'urgent business' both in the office and at home (probably the last illness of his mother) prevented him from going until August, and on reaching the capital he found that the president of the Red Cross was not there. By that time new crises had surfaced in hospitals in Catania and San Lorenzo Colli. Such grave incidents had taken place at San Lorenzo, declared Lampedusa in another letter, that his own 'cautious' inspectors could not deal with them: it was necessary to send out an 'Extraordinary Administrative Inspection' from

---

Individui del vecchio ambiente could mean either former Fascist Party officials or unsuitable 'mafia-types' appointed by the Americans.

Rome to find out what was going on.[40] The nature of the incidents and the result of the inspection have not been discovered; nor is it known whether anything was done about the 'individuals of the old set' and their various conspiracies. But it was clearly becoming too much for Lampedusa and after two years in the job he may have become a little less conscientious about his duties. In February 1947 he received an angry letter from the director-general in Rome demanding to know why he had not replied to 'a simple routine request for information on the present state of the Red Cross in Sicily'.[41] Although the official refused to discuss the prince's offer of resignation at that moment, it may have been the final blow to Lampedusa who resigned the following month.

A few weeks earlier the dowager Princess of Lampedusa had died. Until the spring of 1946 Beatrice had been living in a hotel at Capo d'Orlando but had then moved to Palermo and taken up residence in the least damaged part of the Palazzo Lampedusa. She was old and ill and very thin, and she had come home to die in the palace where her son had been born fifty years before. One of her last recorded acts was to vote in favour of the monarchy at the referendum in June 1946; afterwards she complained to the porter's wife that she was no longer a princess and had become a nobody.[42] During her last years Giuseppe had visited her often at Capo d'Orlando but for the first time since his birth they had been living in different houses in Sicily. Beatrice had had a powerful influence over him throughout his life, an influence that seems evenly divided between positive and negative effects. She gave Giuseppe intelligence, sensitivity and much of his education, but she was also domineering and over-protective, traits which did not diminish as he grew older. A shy child in the shadow of a brilliant and extroverted mother, he was almost smothered by her affection and her personality. Their relationship scarcely altered when he became an adult and her treatment of him as a perpetual child had unfortunate consequences.

Life in Palermo after the war offered Lampedusa little more than sadness over his house, problems with his work and anxiety for his mother. A student at the time remembers him sitting over lunch day after day at Renato's restaurant, silent, sad and solitary.[43] But he could still escape occasionally to Capo d'Orlando and drop in on his cousins during his journeys for the

Red Cross to eastern Sicily. One of the few advantages of the job was that Lampedusa, who did not drive, now had a car and a chauffeur at his disposal. For someone with an almost unlimited capacity for nostalgic recall, the visits to Capo d'Orlando were able to assuage some of the pain he felt for the losses of the Palermo palace and his mother's family house at Santa Margherita. In the description of the second house in his childhood memoirs, Lampedusa recalled that

> at my bedhead hung a kind of Louis Seize showcase in white wood, enclosing three ivory statuettes of the Holy Family on a crimson background. This case has been miraculously salvaged and now hangs at the bedhead of the room in which I sleep at my Piccolo cousins' villa at Capo d'Orlando. In that villa, too, I find again not only the 'Holy Family' of my infancy, but a trace, faint certainly but unmistakable, of my childhood; and so I love going there.[44]

As always, though, there was a comic side to Lampedusa's times at Capo d'Orlando. On one visit during his Red Cross years, the Piccolos' mother decided that the family should have an heir to carry on the name and look after the property. None of her children were married or showed any sign of looking for a spouse. In any case it was too late for Giovanna, who was past child-bearing age, while Casimiro's aversion to any form of human contact ruled him out as a potential begetter. Lucio was therefore the only candidate and he accepted the task of producing an heir provided they could find a girl who was beautiful. At this stage Giuseppe made the mistake of mentioning a Red Cross nurse in Syracuse who was both beautiful and unmarried. Lucio became enthusiastic and the two of them set off in Giuseppe's official car to find her. Unfortunately they stopped for lunch in Messina where Lucio ate so much pasta that he was too ill to meet the nurse when later they reached Syracuse. Postponed until the following day, the meeting was not a success because Giuseppe had neglected to do the necessary preparations: he not only failed to warn the girl of Lucio's ugliness and his passionate but off-putting declarations of love; he was also unaware that she wanted to marry a coal merchant of whom her parents disapproved. Nevertheless, she managed to

7

At Home in the Via Butera

After Lampedusa had decided not to attempt the restoration of the Palazzo Lampedusa, he was forced to look for somewhere else to live. While others of his generation, often in similar circumstances, bought modern apartments in the west of Palermo, it was typical of him to move eastwards into an old and dilapidated quarter badly damaged by the bombing. In 1945 he went to live in a house at number 42 Via Butera, which runs east from the old port parallel to the marine drive, and two years later he moved next door and bought number 28. Surrounded by slums and damaged buildings, the seafront ruined by war debris which had been recently dumped there, the house had little to recommend it beyond its architecture. Lampedusa was never particularly fond of it but it had for him the great merit that eighty years earlier it had briefly belonged to his great-grandfather. Coincidentally, the astronomer's will had at last been settled and, with the sale of some of the few remaining plots of land in the provinces, his great-grandson was able to buy back a peripheral piece of the family patrimony.

Number 28 was a small palace with a nineteenth-century front on the Via Butera and an eighteenth-century facade overlooking the marine drive to the north. On the seaward side there was a high, broad terrace with a magnificent view of the bay; by the time the Lampedusas moved there, however, it had been spoilt by the construction of a highway as well as by the great deposits of rubble which had pushed the sea back a hundred yards. A visitor to the Lampedusas in 1950 remembers the couple on their terrace watching with amusement the sight of prostitutes below trying to entice clients into the debris.[1] Inside, the new

Lampedusa home was a curious mixture of grandeur and discomfort. Except in summer, it was a surprisingly cold house because the windows did not fit properly and the wind came in. The weakest point seems to have been the kitchen: Licy was not in any case a good cook, but she cannot have been helped by a dingy kitchen which had neither windows nor, frequently, running water. Little cooking, however, was done there. When her nephew Giuseppe Biancheri came to Palermo with his mother, he was surprised to find that lunch did not exist in the Lampedusa household. Licy, who used to work until four in the morning, was still in bed, while Giuseppe was out of the house, though he sometimes returned in the afternoon with a few pastries.[2] The rare teatime visitor was more fortunate. A pupil of Licy's, Francesco Corrao, remembers a courteous welcome from Lampedusa while the princess was in the kitchen, preparing her own special recipe of Russian savouries.[3]

Coexisting with the discomfort and various hygienic defects, were an impressive staircase in red marble, an enormous salon (used as a store room) and enough space for two libraries. In a large room on the second floor, either side of a mantelpiece rescued from the old palace, were placed the bookcases of Lampedusa's historical collection. It was in fact the only room he decided to restore on that floor, and he did so with doors and windows from ruined buildings nearby. Downstairs the walls of the room where Licy received her patients were covered by his literary books. Lampedusa complained that both libraries were freezing – according to a friend the history room had a 'nordic atmosphere' partly because it was very dark and partly because of the sound of Licy's accent[4] – and bought a noisy and inefficient gas stove which caused them endless trouble and occasionally a minor injury.

They were an unusual couple in post-war Palermo. To the English painter Derek Hill, who visited Sicily in the early fifties, Lampedusa seemed 'a very un-Sicilian man, reticent, retiring and extremely erudite and intellectual'.[5] His appearance, too, was not recognizably Sicilian. One cousin, who said he had 'the typical colouring of someone who has never lived in the open air', remarked that Nature had given him a generous portion of 'spiritual assets' but had been 'correspondingly parsimonious with her physical gifts'.[6] This was a little unfair. Lampedusa may not have been handsome but he had an impressive appearance which reminded people variously of a retired general, a Hungarian and T.S. Eliot.[7] He was a heavy man of medium height, with large eyes and slow movements. He rarely drank anything except water, which he said had always been his favourite drink, but he ate well and smoked incessantly, 'never noticing the ash which rained on his jacket'.[8] Conscious that he was too heavy, he used to note his weight in his diary; during 1955, while he was writing *The Leopard*, it hovered around 102 and 104 kilograms.[9] There is no record, however, that he attempted to go on a diet.

Strict diets in the Via Butera seen to have been reserved for the dogs. The Lampedusas were members of the 'National League for the Defence of the Dog' and the health of their own pets was one of their major preoccupations. Most of Licy's diary for 1952 is taken up by the long illness of a dog called Pop, detailed analysis of his digestive problems combined with daily records of his temperature, diet and medicines.[10] When Derek Hill met her in 1950, she was nearly always carrying a small dog under each arm; 'We call this one Sissy,' she told him confusingly, 'because she's really a pansy.'[11]

Licy had also become stouter over the years and her top-heaviness reminded Hill of 'one of those figures which if you pushed it over would bounce back'.[12] According to Lampedusa's cousin, Francesco Caravita di Sirignano, she 'was a woman of extraordinary intelligence but lacking in femininity and very authoritarian with gentle Giuseppe'.[13] The art historian, Bernard Berenson, received a similar impression after he had lunch with the Lampedusas in 1953, a few days before his eighty-eighth birthday: 'she deep-voiced, arrogant, but well-bred', he recorded in his diary; 'he charming, cultivated, gentle'.[14]

Lampedusa's shyness did not diminish as he grew older. He felt at ease only at home, at Capo d'Orlando or with young people interested in history and literature. In other circumstances acquaintances remembered little about him except his large pallid appearance and the fact that he seldom spoke. It was the same whenever he met people in public, whether at the Bellini club, a cocktail party, the Caflisch cafe or the film society: an ironic smile, a few monosyllables and nothing more. When he was introduced to people, he shook hands without looking at them. Even when he was being driven home once from Capo d'Orlando, he was too timid to complain that his young cousin, Vences Lanza, was driving so fast that he felt 'seasick'. He only admitted the fact the following day because he had dreamt about the journey and his 'seasickness' throughout the night.[15]

Lampedusa's taciturnity and shyness were not, however, part of a timid character afraid even of expressing uncontroversial opinions. They were the result of an inability to communicate with other people, a problem which he had had since childhood and which no doubt had impelled him into the world of books. The impression he gave Berenson and Caravita – 'bashful, modest, timid, incredibly courteous',[16] a man dominated by his wife – is partly misleading. They did not know Lampedusa well and they saw only the shy and gentle exterior which the self-conscious prince employed to conceal strong feelings and opinions. Licy was a formidable woman of whom her husband was a little afraid, but his character was also a powerful one and the relationship between them was more equal than outsiders guessed. His eyes may have dropped when shaking hands, but at other moments they would dominate a group of people he knew well or felt at ease with. He had a strong presence which drew others' attention, not because of his size but because of his imposing head and large dark eyes.[17] And once the diffidence had been conquered, he revealed sides to his character which few people suspected: pride, original thought, powerful opinions and a bitter, ironic sense of humour. After the publication of *The Leopard*, Palermitan society was astonished as well as shocked that such a shy and apparently timid man could have written such sarcastic things about Sicily.

Lampedusa and his wife kept very different hours. While Licy used to get up after midday and work for much of the night, he was an early riser. Before the war he had spent much of the day in the Palazzo Lampedusa, but the new house, in spite of the family connection, had little hold over him and he liked to spend most of his day outside it.* Rising at about seven, he would be walking down the Corso Vittorio Emanuele towards the centre of the city by eight. Turning west at the Via Roma or a little further on at

---

*In his childhood memoirs, written in 1955, Lampedusa criticized the house 'that I now have, that I do not like at all, that I bought to please my wife and that I am happy to put in her name, because really it *is not* my house'. The passage was crossed out by himself in the manuscript.[18]

the Quattro Canti, he then walked westwards until he reached one of his favourite cafes, the Pasticceria del Massimo in Via Ruggero Settimo. There he had a long breakfast and read one of the books he had brought with him. He ate cakes and pastry with particular pleasure, recalled Francesco Orlando, if he had before him a volume of sixteenth-century French poetry.[19] Once he sat in the Pasticceria for four hours and read a whole Balzac novel at a sitting. Afterwards he wrote to Licy, who was in Rome: *'Quel talent, nom d'un chien! Et non seulement talent de romancier mais aussi de grand historien.'*[20] Before leaving the Massimo, he bought some more cakes, which he put in his bag, and then wandered off to Flaccovio's or one of the other bookshops. Buying books, which he often had privately bound, was his only real extravagance. He felt guilty, however, about buying so many and used to pretend to Licy that he had found them in a sale.[21]

Lampedusa in the crowded streets in mid-morning, recalled Orlando, was a sight difficult to forget: a large bulky figure, very distinct and shabby, his eyes alert and his leather bag always overloaded with books and confectionery which had to last him for the rest of the day.[22] Flaccovio had a similar memory of Lampedusa entering his shop not in the least embarrassed by his bag containing courgettes and several volumes of Proust.[23] According to the bookseller, he went there almost every morning for ten years, often spending a couple of hours leafing through books. After Flaccovio's he used to go to another cafe, the Caflisch, where a group of intellectuals of his own age met regularly to exchange ideas. These included a number of people, such as the historians Virgilio Titone and Gaetano Falzone, who shared the prince's intellectual interests as well as some of his historical views. Yet Lampedusa never fitted well into this group and probably did not have a high opinion of its members. Presumably he went to the Caflisch to escape from the isolation and depression into which he often sank, but even with these people he remained a solitary figure. To the other intellectuals he was an enigma, sitting for hours with them yet seldom taking part in the conversation.* Sometimes he read a book or a newspaper

---

*Lampedusa's presence at the cafe evidently puzzled them. One of those present, a pupil of the French historian Braudel and a student of the Neapolitan Bourbons, believed that the prince's marriage was such a 'catastrophe' that he was forced to flee each morning to the cafe.[24]

while the others talked, and sometimes he listened without any desire to join in. He seemed to want to be anonymous even there and rarely spoke unless asked a direct question. Then he would give a brief answer, might mention a few facts, even occasionally offer a diffident hypothesis. But he soon returned to that strange solitude which puzzled his companions and prevented them from being close friends.[25]

After Lampedusa's death, Gaetano Falzone tried to recall the few things he had said, recognizing how important his thoughts were and comparing them to pearls thrown into the depths of the sea which had to be fished out because of their importance for Sicilians. But they could seldom be found in his conversation, except with that minuscule group of aristocratic intellectuals whom he saw in Palermo, the Duchess of Arenella, Lucio Piccolo, Corrado Fatta, Baron Sgàdari di lo Monaco and his young student friends, Francesco Orlando, Gioacchino Lanza and Francesco Agnello. In the Caflisch, as elsewhere, he exhibited timidity of expression rather than timidity of thought. His gentleness and courtesy masked a person Falzone described as 'sceptical, disenchanted and bitter'.[26] In the early fifties, when the film *Moulin Rouge* was being shown in Palermo, a professor at the Caflisch asked Lampedusa whether Toulouse Lautrec was a real or imaginary character.

> Lampedusa did not bat an eyelid, assumed his expression of an enormous thoughtful cat with his great head bent down and his eyes staring over his spectacles, and promised to do some research on the matter in his library; the following morning he reported that he had been unable to find any indication that a painter of that name had ever existed.

When explaining this behaviour afterwards, he said 'it is always necessary to leave other people in their ignorance'.[27]

Yet this was not a maxim he applied to people to whom he was close. With them, especially if they were younger than he, he could be caustic and sarcastic. He was sceptical of human motives but he concealed this from all except those who knew him well. His scepticism was partly a product of his great learning, his enormous knowledge of the follies of history and especially of the absurdities of Sicilian history, but it also stemmed from a misunderstanding of human nature and a certain indifference towards other people. No doubt much of his scepticism was justified, but the extremes to which he went, in particular the belief that any generous action must have a hidden motive, seem excessive.[28] At times they even seemed excessive to him and he recognized that hard-heartedness was one of the misfortunes of his life. To Gioacchino Lanza, the young cousin whom he later adopted, he often used to say, 'Be careful. *Cave obdurationem cordis*' ('Beware of the hardness of the heart').[29]

Lampedusa's misanthropic tendencies were probably reinforced by loneliness and a sense of failure which cut him off still further from his fellow men. Alienated from society, unable and often unwilling to communicate with any but a handful of intimates, he remained aloof and disdainful of other people without attempting to get to know them. An unattractive side to his character, which he may not have been aware of, was his tendency to treat friends according to their class and family background.* Gioacchino Lanza, for example, was a member of one of Sicily's greatest families and therefore treated as an equal although he was thirty-seven years younger than Lampedusa. Francesco Agnello and 'Bebbuzzo' Lo Monaco, who was a friend and contemporary of the prince, belonged to the minor nobility and therefore had to put up with a certain amount of condescension. As for Francesco Orlando, who came from a middle-class professional family, he was addressed by his surname and treated in an overbearing way despite the fact that his great-uncle had been prime minister of Italy.

Lampedusa's scepticism extended to matters of politics and religion. He thought all political systems bad, but communism in his view was worse than the rest. For fascism he had had a fastidious aversion, mocking its pretensions while believing the Italians deserved nothing better. He had admired the development of the British constitution and approved of certain aspects of French radicalism. But he had thought little of the Italian parliamentary system before Mussolini and he thought little of it afterwards. He voted for the christian democrats or the monarchists after the war but he was scathing about the

---

*The evidence for this comes from two people who saw Lampedusa frequently and considered themselves to be victims of this attitude. Their criticism may have been unduly harsh but clearly had some validity.

immaturity of Italy's new democrats.[30] Political compromise was, he recognized, the only rational way to govern a country; but it was a shabby business[31] and made shabbier by the Italians. Several years after the abolition of the monarchy, a cousin urged him to stand as a Monarchist Party candidate for the Senate, but Lampedusa smiled and said he preferred to keep out of politics.[32] In *The Leopard* he was critical of both the Savoyard monarchy and the Neapolitan kings who preceded it, yet he remained, probably for nostalgic reasons, a monarchist. To Gaetano Falzone he once said, 'I am a monarchist. I have never joined and never will join the Monarchist Party, and I am certain that the monarchy will never return to Italy. I remain, however, a monarchist.'[33]

If Lampedusa cared little about politics, religion interested him even less. After his death Licy declared that he was a believer though not a practising Christian,[34] but this is borne out neither by his writing nor the evidence of his friends. Falzone declared that he was 'certainly secular' while, according to Orlando, Lampedusa once said in a tone more serious than usual, 'It all ends down here [on earth].'[35] Discussing the last chapter of his novel, he claimed never to have practised religion nor known a priest in his life, though this was certainly an exaggeration.[36]* Yet he was an agnostic rather than an atheist, sceptical enough not to believe but not sure enough to reject religion altogether. In some ways he was an old-fashioned anti-clerical who, according to one acquaintance, might have accepted the Church in a Protestant country but was too aware of Catholicism's shortcomings in Italy to be able to support the Roman Church.

Lampedusa was depressed that his own country lacked the intellectual Catholic traditions of France and England. Italy's Catholic writers existed in an atmosphere of 'tepid soup whose temperature favoured the germination of microbes but not of good writers'. There were anti-clericals in Italy but no anti-Catholics (with the exception of Giovanni Gentile who was, however, predominantly a fascist), and therefore the Catholic writers had no challenge to face. Combined with the Italian 'formalistic temperament which makes us shrink from polemics

---

*His diary records that he had met the archpriest of Palma di Montechiaro on two occasions the previous year (1955) and had attended Mass on Christmas Eve.

about ideas', this induced a sense of sterility in the work of writers like Foggazzaro, Salvadori and Fausto Maria Martini whose books reeked of 'the odour of the sacristy'. In France, by contrast, there had been a terrific 'dialogue between Faith and Free Thought since the sixteenth century: Pascal replied to Montaigne; Maistre countered Voltaire, and Veuillot would not have existed without Renan'. More recently, there had been a 'magnificent flowering of French Catholic writers', culminating with his own contemporaries, Bernanos, Claudel and Mauriac.[37]

Lampedusa admired Catholics in adversity, on the defensive against rival faiths or hostile governments. He had much sympathy for the Jansenist reformers, for the convent of Port Royal and for Pascal, and in a typical throwaway remark to Orlando he once said that 'whoever wants to call himself a man and not an animal on two legs must have read Pascal's *Pensées*'.[38] He also admired the doggedness of English Catholics. Centuries of persecution had rid them of their lukewarm followers and forced the remainder to abandon the worst and most dogmatic aspects of Catholicism. 'The way of being a Catholic in England is completely different, perhaps even opposite, from being one in Italy.' Graham Greene, for instance, was always considering Catholic doctrines instead of merely accepting them. 'His warmest admirers,' Lampedusa once remarked,

> are often surprised how much he is attracted, without repugnance, by everything that is repulsive and putrid. But his is simply *the* Christian attitude. If Christ had refused to touch the lepers or talk to the Samaritan woman, the first would have remained ill and the second sinful. The Christian *must* be attracted by fetid carcases, like hyenas, like Baudelaire, like the angel of the Resurrection.

In some of his novels, such as *The Heart of the Matter*, Greene evoked the original spirit of Christianity in its compassion and charity, and in *The Power and the Glory* he had produced 'one of the most powerful figures in English literature: this priest, immersed in mortal sin, who is also the salvation of other sinners'. Lampedusa regarded Greene not only as the greatest modern English writer after Eliot but also as one of the most

remarkable Catholic thinkers. 'It is very unlikely,' he once said,
'that Greene will ever become Pope. But if he does, we will all
become Catholics with him.'[39]

After several years of regular but silent visits to the Caflisch,
Lampedusa abandoned the cafe at some time in 1954; in the
diaries of his last years, where visits to cafes and restaurants are
meticulously recorded, the Caflisch is scarcely mentioned. Its
place was taken by the Mazzara, another cafe in an ugly modern
building off the Via Ruggero Settimo. Lampedusa did not go
there for company but to read and later to work on his novel. But
he was seldom left alone. Gioacchino Lanza, Francesco Agnello
and other friends went to the Mazzara to question him about
literature, and in their company he was able to talk in a relaxed
way he had found impossible at the Caflisch. He was also visited
by his agent, a man called Aridon, who administered his
remaining property and organized his taxes. In his fifties
Lampedusa's grasp of financial matters was as weak as ever.
Worried by shortage of money, he showed his perennial lack of
interest in improving the situation: a friend's suggestion that he
should speculate on the stock exchange produced incredulity.[40]
The Lampedusas lived a frugal existence, based on the meagre
rents of a few scattered properties, but probably they did not
want a more extravagant lifestyle. Apart from running the house,
their main expenses were books, cinema tickets and meals in
modest restaurants. They rarely travelled, except to Rome, they
did not drive a car, and they belonged to a generation that had
managed without modern conveniences; neither Stomersee nor
Santa Margherita had had running water.
   Having walked to his various cafes and bookshops during the
morning, Lampedusa used to take a bus back in the early
afternoon. He often had lunch at the Pizzeria Bellini, in a square
behind the town hall, beside the small Norman churches of San
Cataldo and La Martorana. One of the friends he ate with was
Licy's first husband, André Pilar, who had lost his Baltic property
during the war and afterwards worked in Italy for a Swiss
pharmaceutical company. During a lecture visit to Sicily in 1950
Derek Hill lunched several times with Pilar and Lampedusa in a
self-service restaurant before going on a tour of the city. Years

later he recalled that they had taken him each afternoon to see ancient remains, the Mazzarino and Salaparuta palaces or the villas at Bagheria.[41] Pilar also remained a friend of Licy to whom he had been helpful during her various illnesses in Latvia in the thirties. A friend remembers the two of them in Palermo twenty years later, often reminiscing about life in St Petersburg and speculating on the complicated subject of the Romanov heir.[42]

Another lunchtime companion was his cousin Lucio Piccolo. Lampedusa's diaries often record the 'unexpected arrival of Lucio' – sometimes with a brief mention of his extraordinary clothes – followed by 'Extra-Bar', the restaurant they often went out to eat in. Orlando later recalled a couple of long lunches in which the two cousins quoted poetry at length to each other in different languages.[43] In congenial and familiar company Lampedusa lost his shyness and became a witty and entertaining talker. He no longer muttered occasional monosyllables but spoke with elegance and lucidity in a clear, rather high-pitched voice. His conversation was simple, free from jargon and technical terms, yet at the same time subtle and allusive. When at ease he had the breadth of knowledge and command of words to make conversations brilliant and memorable.[44] Yet this skill was known only to a small circle; most of his acquaintances believed him incapable of completing a sentence.

Lampedusa rarely saw his wife before the evening. Licy got up after midday, spent all afternoon on her cases and returned to her study late at night. She was engrossed in her work, relentlessly probing the phobias and obsessions of her patients, listing their fears and weaknesses in small black notebooks. She relaxed for a few hours in the evening, talking to her husband or reading. One of her pastimes was to draw quick portraits; some of these have survived, including two of Churchill and Hitler and a couple of unflattering sketches of Giuseppe.[45] Some evenings were spent reading aloud, in five languages, passages from their favourite authors.'We had completely the same tastes,' recalled Licy, though they argued about the merits of the great Russians, her favourite being Dostoyevsky whereas her husband preferred Tolstoy. They read from their favourite poets, who included Goethe, Keats and Shelley, and they discovered Trollope together; both of them loved Shakespeare but for some reason preferred not to read him aloud.[46] Sometimes they had minor disagreements over literature or historical events, Giuseppe teasing Licy good-naturedly and she replying brusquely and dogmatically. A friend remembers her extolling 'in deep Teutonic tones' the Russian victories against Napoleon while Lampedusa contradicted her with mocking but affectionate irony.[47]

After her husband's death, Licy seems to have contributed to the impression that most of their evenings were spent in this way. According to his diaries, however, they spent a good deal of time outside the house. In January 1955 they spent twelve evenings at the Cine-Club or another cinema and the following month went back on nine occasions. Then there were dinners at the Pizzeria Bellini and various social occasions in other houses. Lampedusa had a horror of cocktail parties but sometimes felt obliged to attend them; such receptions at places like the Villa Niscemi or the Palazzo Gangi are recorded in his diaries, often followed by a comment such as 'basically boring'. Less formal dinners used to take place at the house of Pietro Sgàdari di Lo Monaco, known as 'Bebbuzzo', music critic of *Il Giornale di Sicilia* and a man whose cultural interests made him nearly the equal of Lucio and Giuseppe. The Lampedusas did not themselves entertain, though on Sunday evenings they were 'at home' – in the historical library in winter and on the terrace for the rest of the year – to a restricted group of friends.

Other evenings were spent listening to music, either going to concerts and operas or hearing gramophone records in someone else's house. Lampedusa's attitude towards music was ambivalent. According to Gioacchino Lanza, it was 'a waste of time' trying to educate him musically; he cared little about music and made nineteenth-century opera a frequent target for his sarcasm.[48] Yet if this was the case, it was eccentric of him to see *Parsifal* and *La Traviata* at the Teatro Massimo in the same week; and if, when Gioacchino called *La Traviata* a queen of operas, he replied that she was thus a 'queen of the zulus',[49] it was odd that he should have been prepared to listen to her on a gramophone afterwards.[50] Stendhal's love for opera, wrote Lampedusa in his notes on French literature, was 'a defect of taste extenuated by the fact that the operas he preferred were those of Cimarosa, Mozart and the young Rossini...'[51] Mozart, certainly, was exempt from his sarcasm. *Così fan tutte* was 'very beautiful', he noted after listening to it on Gioacchino's gramophone, and he also liked Mozart's religious music. When in his memoirs he came to write about his mother's boudoir in the Palazzo Lampedusa, he described the design of the ceiling as 'gentle and corporeal as a piece of music by Mozart'.[52]

Italian opera of the nineteenth century had none of the features Lampedusa increasingly admired in literature. The works of Stendhal, for example, were subtle and implicit, whereas opera was sentimental, painfully explicit and left nothing to the imagination or intelligence of the listener.[53] In the story 'Lighea' he gave the protagonist lines that could have been his own: 'Important words can't be yelled; the scream of love or hate is only heard in melodrama or among the most uncivilized, which comes to the same thing.'[54] Writers invariably produced their worst work when they became melodramatic. Dickens, for instance, who was one of Lampedusa's favourite authors, had 'sunk to his lowest depths' with *Dombey and Son*, Paul's delirium and death being 'worthy of Donizetti'.[55] On the other hand it might have been a good thing, Lampedusa once jested, if Wordsworth's life had ended in melodrama and he had been guillotined in Paris in place of the French poet André Chenier: the impossibility of pronouncing the Englishman's name would surely have preserved him from being chosen as the hero of an Italian opera.[56]

Lampedusa exaggerated his dislike of operatic music in order to tease his musicologist friends, Gioacchino, Bebbuzzo Lo Monaco and Francesco Agnello. His distaste was in any case intellectual and theoretical rather than activated by aversion to the music itself. He objected to Boito's manhandling of Shakespeare, lifting passages of *King Henry IV* as well as *The Merry Wives of Windsor* into the libretto of Verdi's *Fàlstaff*.[57] (This seemed to him a double betrayal because Shakespeare had already been treacherous to 'the real' Sir John Falstaff [of *King Henry IV* and *King Henry V*] by creating a naïve and ridiculous character of the same name for 'the merry wives'.)[58] He also lamented the fact that 'for Italians the opera *Otello* had killed the tragedy *Othello*'. Boito's libretto was certainly superior to any of the others used by Verdi, but was still 'fundamentally wrong' and 'deformed the whole play'. He had 'mutilated' individual scenes, particularly those dealing with Iago's envy and Brabantio's warning to Othello,* and his 'apocalyptic vision of Iago's character' had unjustifiably transformed the man into Satan.[59]

Yet there was also a more serious argument underlying Lampedusa's criticism of opera. He felt passionately that melodrama had destroyed the Italians' sensibility to art and made them impervious to the subtlety of fine writing. Jane Austen, for instance, was not appreciated in Italy because she was *'l'anti-melodramma'*: Italians consequently complained that nothing happened in her novels.[60] The problem so engrossed Lampedusa that one day he decided he had to write down his objections to melodrama in order to stop himself lying awake at night:

> The infection began immediately after the Napoleonic wars and spread with giant steps. For more than a hundred years, tens of thousands, hundreds of thousands of Italians went to the opera, in the great cities for eight months a year, in the lesser cities for four months a year and in the small towns for two or three weeks each year. And they saw tyrants killed, lovers committing suicide, generous clowns, multiparous nuns and every sort of nonsense dished out in front of them in a continual whirling of cardboard boots, plaster-cast chickens, leading ladies with blackened faces and devils springing from the ground making awful grimaces. All this synthesized, without psychological passages, without developments, all bare, crude, brutal and irrefutable.
>
> This unfathomable stupidity was not considered as common enjoyment, as an excusable distraction for illiterate layabouts; it was passed off as Art, as real Art, and horrors! sometimes it really was Art. The cancer had absorbed all the artistic energies of the nation: Music was Opera, Drama was Opera, Painting was Opera. And other musical forms like the symphony and chamber music languished and died: during the nineteenth century Italy lacked all of them. The drama which with its slow build-ups could not resist the waves of *'Do di*

---

*Brabantio's warning is not mutilated in the opera but omitted together with the rest of the Venetian scenes. Lampedusa felt that the lines – 'Look to her Moor, have a quick eye to see/She has deceiv'd her father, may do thee' – were indispensable in explaining Othello's subsequent rage. He plainly had little sympathy with Boito's problem of having to reduce 3,500 lines in the play to less than 800 lines for the opera.

petto',* died also. Painters neglected their noble canvases to throw themselves headlong into designing the prisons of *Don Carlos* or the sacred groves of *Norma*.

When Opera mania diminished after 1910, Italian intellectual life was like a field in which locusts had spent a hundred years in a row. Italians had become accustomed to citing as gospel truth the lines of Francesco Mario Piave or Cammarano;** to thinking that Enrico Caruso or Adelina Patti† were the flowers of the race; and to believing that War was like the chorus of *Norma*. The influence of all this on the national character is before our eyes.

Art had to be easy and the music singable. Drama consisted of sword-trusts flavoured with musical trills. What was not simple, violent, within the grasp equally of a professor and a dustman, was beyond the pale.

But there was worse than this. Saturated and swollen-headed by so much noisy foolishness, the Italians sincerely believed that they knew everything. Did they not go almost every evening that God gave them to listen to Shakespeare, Schiller, Victor Hugo and Goethe? Signor Gattoni from Milan or Cavaliere Pantisi from Palermo were convinced that universal literature had been revealed to them because they knew the above-mentioned poets having heard them through the notes of Verdi and Gounod ... And so now we are the nation least interested in literature that exists, fed up (or so it seems) with Opera, but unready to listen to anything else.[61]

There was little variation in the Lampedusas' life in Palermo in the early fifties. Licy went to Rome to work and Giuseppe often accompanied her, usually staying at his uncle Pietro's house in the Via Brenta though on some occasions he went to the Albergo Quirinale. They often had meals with Licy's sister Lolette at her house in the Piazza d'Indipendenza. His Biancheri nephews remember Lampedusa as affable and ironic, more talkative than he could be in Palermo society though less relaxed than he was

---

*A phrase signifying a tenor's highest notes.
**Two of Verdi's librettists.
†Respectively the most famous tenor and the most celebrated soprano around the turn of the century.

with Gioacchino or the Piccolos; his favourite conversation with them was history, and Boris Biancheri recalls an interminable discussion about General Monck in a *carrozza* in Palermo. They also saw him at their country house at Latte near the French border, where the Biancheri family spent two months in the summer. The Lampedusas visited Latte together at least once after the war, at the same time, to Torretta's annoyance, as André Pilar. His uncle felt that Giuseppe should have resented the presence of Licy's first husband under the same roof and was irritated by his nonchalance. On the final day of the holiday there was a regular ceremony consisting of the two sisters and Lila Iljascenko singing Russian songs on an out-of-tune piano.[62]

Apart from visits to Rome and the Italian Riviera, and occasional journeys elsewhere, Lampedusa's only regular diversion from Palermo was Capo d'Orlando which he visited nearly every month for about four days at a time. Licy did not go with him. According to a fellow guest, she had offended the Piccolos on one visit by forgetting to look at their dog cemetery which they took very seriously. But it hardly needed an incident of such insignificance to reveal the differences between Licy and the Piccolo family. They were complete opposites: a serious-minded, peremptory Teutonic lady could not have been expected to appreciate the frivolous brilliance of Lucio. Nor did she appreciate his poetry: in her diary she complained that Lucio tried all the time to talk about his poems.[63]

So Lampedusa went to Capo d'Orlando without her, usually driven by Gioacchino Lanza along the coastal road to his cousins' villa. They tried to go more often in summer than in winter because the house was so cold; when Lucio acknowledged this defect, he installed central heating which made it too hot.[64] The atmosphere at Capo d'Orlando was madder than ever. Lucio was a scooter fanatic and had bought several models, and Casimiro had become obsessed with photography: he was particularly proud of two expensive cameras he had bought from Bologna which produced very small negatives and rather blurred prints. In addition, visitors were now assigned 'roles' which they were expected to play throughout their stay: Francesco Agnello, who was given the part of a bishop and was meant to behave as 'a hypocrite and false mediator', found it so unbearable that he stopped going there.[65] There was also the perennial hazard of their dogs which were untrained. When a car arrived, a young cousin of Lampedusa's later recalled, it was besieged by a pack of dogs barking furiously and ready to bite. It was not possible to get out of the car until someone had come out of the house and called them off.[66]

Yet with all its eccentricities, Capo d'Orlando remained Giuseppe's favourite place. He was at his happiest there, wandering in the garden, eating Giovanna's excellent food, mocking his cousins for their latest enthusiasms. There were few inhibitions and rare irritants, and he and the three Piccolos could talk about their favourite subjects – literature, dogs, reincarnation and memories of their childhood.

8

The Consolation of Literature

'I am a person,' noted Lampedusa in 1954, 'who is very much alone. Of my sixteen hours of daily wakefulness, at least ten are spent in solitude. I do not claim to be reading for all that time though; sometimes I amuse myself by constructing literary theories...'[1] In fact he was not really thinking up theories but simply cogitating on writers, placing them in categories and making comparisons between them. It was, in the literal sense of the word, his pastime. As Francesco Orlando recalled after his death, 'Literature was the great occupation and consolation of this nobleman from whom various patrimonial misfortunes had removed all worldliness and practical usefulness, and who was reduced to living isolated, without any luxury other than his considerable expenditure on books...'[2]

Literature was essential to Lampedusa's life. It gave him most of his ideas and much of his happiness, and it also attenuated the heavy depressions to which he was increasingly prone. According to Licy, 'he never left the house without a copy of Shakespeare in his bag, with which he would console himself when he saw something disagreeable'.[3] 'There were several editions of Shakespeare's works: some of them were portable, and these he took with him on his walks to the club; others were large volumes to read during sleepless nights ....'[4] *The Pickwick Papers*, which may have been his favourite book of all, was also crucial: 'He had a copy on the bedside table at night, he took it with him when he travelled, he kept rereading it.'[5] Literature aroused emotions in Lampedusa in a way that human relations could not. He was capable of laughing aloud at Shakespeare's characters and confessed that he had once wept at the beauty of Milton's *Lycidas* 6.

After decades of solid reading, Lampedusa's enthusiasm for literature never weakened. In his mid-fifties he might regret that he had read almost everything and even envy younger friends when he discovered they had not yet read works which would give them hours of delight.[7] But he still went to great lengths to discover new books for himself, even if it meant learning new languages. In his final years he was taught Spanish by Gioacchino Lanza, whose mother came from Spain, and the two of them read Calderón and Góngora together. He also liked to improve his Russian and astonished a Sicilian student in the 1950s with his knowledge of Russian culture. Giuseppe Paolo Samonà recalls Lampedusa's considerable interest in its poetry as well as his knowledge of Russian pronunciation.[8] Yet this great learning was displayed without the least ostentation or pretentiousness. To Orlando, his understanding of literature was so much a part of him as to seem natural and innate.[9]

Lampedusa was knowledgeable about literary currents but he despised critics. The only four who escaped his scorn were Hazlitt, Lamb, Sainte-Beuve and De Sanctis.[10] Literature did not require complicated theoretical criticism; it could be appreciated by anyone capable of reading with intelligence and sensitivity. Those who wanted to write about literature should follow Swinburne who employed 'no theorizing and no pedantic contrivances'.[11] Lampedusa himself read a book, thought about it, studied the author, made comparisons with other writers and other periods, and then reflected. Why did fiction and theatre never flourish in any literature at the same time? Why had literary critics 'remained blind to the tragic quality of Defoe's work'?[12] He also liked to consider the problems of writing novels. How should writers, who must not use timetables, deal with the question of time? How should they describe characters, through their words or through their actions? And where should the narrator stand, inside or outside the narrative, or in a combination of both which could be dangerous and ridiculous unless controlled by a genius like Proust?[13]

For several years after the Second World War, Lampedusa had led a largely solitary, often silent existence, seeing few people regularly. His life changed at the beginning of the fifties when Gioacchino Lanza and Francesco Agnello began to visit him to talk about literature and history. Lampedusa found them easy to

talk to and in their company, and that of their friends, he was able
to relax and talk expansively about his favourite subjects. Soon
Licy suggested that he might turn these conversations into
informal courses of literature for their new friends. Giuseppe was
delighted with the idea. It gave him, Licy later recalled, 'a pretext
for rereading authors almost unknown to Italian teaching and
allowed young people to share those interests which had given
him so many pleasurable hours'.[14] He had enjoyed literature all
his life and he wanted to convey that enjoyment to others by
showing them how to understand and appreciate books. He also
seems to have been suited to the role of sagacious teacher with
young disciples; some years later he described a similar
relationship between an elderly Hellenist and a young journalist
in his beautiful story 'Lighea'.

The two principal pupils for Lampedusa's course in English
literature were Francesco Orlando and Gioacchino Lanza,
though some of their friends were also present at the lessons on
Joyce and T. S. Eliot. Gioacchino was a grandson of the Count of
Mazzarino and a cousin of Lampedusa; charming and intelligent,
he had a mocking sense of humour which greatly appealed to the
older man. With Francesco Orlando the prince had a less
personal relationship; Francesco was a law student at Palermo
University, intelligent but reserved and without Gioacchino's
natural charm. He had been introduced to Lampedusa by
Bebbuzzo Lo Monaco who had advised him to go to the Via
Butera for some literary advice. Subsequently Giuseppe invited
Francesco to lunch at a restaurant with Lucio Piccolo, where
the two cousins amazed him by their knowledge of foreign
writers. A little later, towards the end of 1953, Lampedusa
suggested he might teach Francesco to read English by
means of some grammatical lessons followed by a course in
literature.

Lampedusa's informal chats with Lanza, Orlando, Agnello and
their friends used to take place in the mornings at the Mazzara
cafe. But the lessons on literature, for which he wrote pages of
notes, were given in the Via Butera on the first floor next to the
room where Licy received her patients; in the summer of 1954,
when more people attended, they were sometimes held on the
terrace. Lampedusa used to prepare his talks in the afternoons
before the lessons, which began, three times a week, at six

o'clock. Two of Orlando's clearest memories of these visits to the Via Butera were of Giubino, the trembling elderly man-servant who was stationed in the ante-room, and of the 'noisy and eye-watering gas stove' whose bass rumbling accompanied their discussions.[15]

A few pages of Lampedusa's language lessons have survived in the basement of the Via Butera. Notes on the use of the definite article are accompanied by advice on plural nouns: 'brother', he told Orlando, becomes 'brothers' except in the sense of *confratelli* when they become 'brethren'. Then there are warnings against 'easy' words, many of which came from Latin but had different meanings from similar Italian words. 'Affluent', he pointed out does not mean *affluente*, 'savage' is not the same as *selvaggio*, and 'concrete' should not be translated by *concreto* but by *cemento armato*.

Orlando was evidently expected to learn English very quickly because the grammar lessons were soon finished and the literary course begun. This was a massive task for Lampedusa, perhaps the most laborious piece of work he had ever done in his life. Between the end of 1953 and September of the following year, he wrote over a thousand pages on British writers from Bede to Graham Greene. Even allowing for the fact that he had spent most of his life reading and absorbing books, they reveal an astonishing knowledge of British literature. Not only had he read and remembered all the novels of Scott; he knew the plays of the lesser Elizabethan playwrights and the poems of the most minor Restoration poets.

Although he discussed writers singly, in chronological order, Lampedusa always tried to place them in the context of their period and to explain the historical background. His pupils did not care much for these historical digressions – according to one of them, they were reading Gramsci and saw the past in Marxist simplifications – but Lampedusa persevered. How could one understand why English writing between Milton and Wordsworth was essentially political literature if one did not understand the political background? He was also fond of drawing attention to particular themes which he traced down the centuries. The appeal of the sea, which had fascinated poets as different as Raleigh, Coleridge and Kipling, could be traced back to Old English poems such as 'The Wanderer'. Compassion for the 'underdog', which Lampedusa thought was a 'sporting' rather than a Christian attitude, could be found in the same period, and so could an interest in ruins. In 'The Ruin', a short poem which may be a lament for the sack of Bath, could be found the seed of that romantic interest which later populated so many English parks with follies. Additional themes were visible in Chaucer such as humour, perhaps the most important quality of English literature and one shared by most of its contributors with the obvious exception of Milton. Interest in the fantastic or magical, referred to by Lampedusa as 'eeriness', also pervaded the different periods: Shakespeare, Marlowe, Keats, Coleridge and James were among the many writers fascinated by this 'fourth dimension'.[16]

The course was divided into five sections. Most of the first was taken up by Shakespeare, a glance at each of the sonnets being followed by an examination of all of the plays. Some of Lampedusa's favourite sonnets were discussed and their beauty extolled; others were dismissed with single adjectives – 'horrendous', 'worthless' – or awarded a solitary noun – 'a summit', 'a miracle'. 'The most profound and painful of all' was number 129 describing the poet's

> final separation from sensuality. When the lustful present themselves at the Last Judgement they will hear the Angel pronounce these definitive lines on the uselessness and innate filthiness of the flesh. The technique is surprising. We are dealing no longer with church bells but hammer blows: the middle rhymes, the alliterations and the booming of the final rhyme create a paroxysmal atmosphere, and the sonnet staggers off to hell, which is in fact its last word.

Lampedusa considered that about eighty of Shakespeare's sonnets had little or no aesthetic value. Thirty of the others, however, had beautiful lines, and 'the remaining forty were among the finest things in world literature'.[17]

Shakespeare's early plays did not greatly impress him. '*Henry VI* was perhaps the first, certainly the longest and probably the worst of his works.' *Titus Andronicus* was also very bad, written to please its Elizabethan audience and 'unreadable' for everyone else. *The Comedy of Errors* and *Richard III* were second-rate works though the first was not so awful as he used to think and the hunchback king in the second play 'with his sinister grandeur, his perverted gaiety and his mocking smile towards his victims', was very much alive. *The Taming of the Shrew* was 'a little jewel' but *Two Gentlemen of Verona* was not a good play, its most interesting characters being the buffoon Launce and his dog Crab. *Love's Labour's Lost* was also worth little, and the drama in *King John* was 'awkward and a little boring' (besides, Arthur's death was 'too obvious'). Nearly all the later plays, however, had great merit and some of them were masterpieces. Only *All's Well that Ends Well* was 'inferior', 'boring', and 'crammed with repellent characters'; for Lampedusa it was something to be read as a Lenten penance.[18]

'Just as there are seven wonders of the world (and seven mortal sins), so are there (in my opinion) seven supreme peaks reached by Shakespeare: *Henry IV*, *Hamlet*, *Measure for Measure*, *Othello*, *King Lear*, *Macbeth* and *Antony and Cleopatra*.' *Henry IV* parts I and II was the masterpiece of the historical plays, without 'either a mediocre scene or a false character'. Its chief glory was Falstaff, of whom Lampedusa said that he would sacrifice ten years of his life for the privilege of meeting him for an hour. *Henry V* was a fine sequel and it was regrettable that the incomparable night scene had 'been barbarously mutilated in the film by either Olivier or our translators'.[19] The first time one reads *Hamlet* in English, he told Orlando, is an important date in one's life.[20] He had also seen the play several times, at Santa Margherita as a child, in London in 1931, three times in Italian productions, and in Olivier's 'admirable interpretation' at the cinema. *Macbeth* was 'technically the most perfect' of the plays and, unlike *Othello*, had not been destroyed by the operatic version. *King Lear* was luckier still, its 'Michelangelesque' protagonist 'escaping Boito by a hair's breadth'.[21]

Shakespeare's great plays gave Lampedusa an opportunity to form a new private category, that of literary lovers. If his 'wife' was *Hamlet*, his 'public mistresses' were Cordelia, Desdemona, Lady Macbeth and Falstaff, and his secret, underground and favourite 'lover' was *Measure for Measure*.

If I was told that all the works of Shakespeare had to perish except one that I could select, I would first try to kill the monster who had made the suggestion; if I failed, I would then try to kill myself; and if I could not manage even this, well then, eventually, I would choose *Measure for Measure*.

The pessimism and 'absolute moral nihilism' of this play, even more profound than in *King Lear*, appealed to Lampedusa whose own view of the world was not dissimilar. So did the atmosphere of Vienna, a 'ghostly city consisting of brothels, prisons and attics where abandoned women weep', a place where 'even the stones had been corrupted by Evil'; it was strange, he reflected, that the Vienna of Shakespeare's imagination should have so closely resembled the desolate post-war city described 350 years later in Graham Greene's *The Third Man*.[22]

The second part of the course was delivered in January and February 1954. It covered the Puritans, the Restoration and most of the eighteenth century, ending with the forgeries of Macpherson and Chatterton. A good portion of the lessons was devoted to British history, Lampedusa discoursing at length on his admiration for the Puritans, his disapproval of Charles II's character and his less partisan views on William III, the Hanoverians and the growth of the British empire. The first literary figure he dealt with was Milton whom he admired both as a man and a poet in spite of various lapses such as the 'mediocre and awkward' Italian sonnets. He was particularly moved by Milton in old age: 'under the transparent mask of Samson, Milton, like him a champion of God, like him blind, like him a slave of the impious, breathes out his pain and his pride'. Of the numerous other writers discussed in this part, Lampedusa praised especially Marvell, Walton, Dryden, Pepys, Defoe, Swift, Richardson, Fielding, Sterne, Gray and of course Johnson. *Tom Jones* was singled out as a great novel that should last for ever, and Gibbon's *Decline and Fall of the Roman Empire* was described as 'one of the greatest monuments of English prose'. Swift, whose humour and pessimistic outlook were admired and in some ways shared by Lampedusa, was the author of 'one of the masterly books of humanity': *Gulliver's Travels* was 'a prodigious research into the depths of human misery, an explosion of sorrowful misanthropy'.[23]

In March Lampedusa moved on to the Romantics, concentrating particularly on Byron because he was the era's representative, 'Romanticism dressed up as a man'. He wrote over forty pages of notes on Byron's life and drew attention to the private lives of other poets as well. Shelley, Coleridge and Byron, all of whom he adored, together formed a 'triad of the worst husbands of the world'. Wordsworth was Lampedusa's least favourite among the major poets of the period. One did not have to read all his poems because they were uneven, some of them lacking in inspiration and technical mastery: there were fine poems such as 'The Prelude' and 'Tintern Abbey', but others, like 'The Recluse', were unbearable. The works of Blake, Shelley and Keats, however, should be read in their entirety. Some of Shelley's poems, such as 'Adonais' and 'Prometheus Unbound', were sublime; reading the second poem just before the lesson, he found it even more admirable than he had on his previous reading, eight or nine years before. As for Keats, one could say little about his poems except that they were 'miracles', and in 'Kubla Khan' Coleridge had produced one of the greatest poems in literature. Turning to prose, he discussed Jane Austen who, with Emily Brontë, was her country's greatest female writer, William Beckford ('an excellent example of that race of eccentrics which is one of England's glories'), and novelists such as Ann Radcliffe, author of *Mysteries of Udolpho*, and Matthew Lewis, author of *The Monk*. Many people who have tackled the Waverley novels with less perseverance would share Lampedusa's opinion of Scott's beginnings:

The start of every novel is truly unbearable. Scott describes hair by hair, line by line, the face of each character; after that there is no ribbon of a dress or buckle of a boot left uncounted; and after that the castle is described with the scruple of an architect and the surrounding countryside with the pedantry of an official from the land register. And all of this is done without any talent or well-chosen adjective which evokes the scene. A hundred pages or so go by and one is astonished how such a bore could even, in any age, have enjoyed such a great reputation.

But after page 100 ... one realizes that the faces and places have remained imprinted on one's memory... And the drama is described in masterly fashion: the psychology of the characters is solid, the action alive and rapid – just as much movement as in Dumas but incomparably more 'fleshy'. Athos etc ... are abstractions, geometrical figures. Guy Mannering and the Antiquary ... are full-blooded characters.[24]

By the spring of 1954 Lampedusa was dissatisfied with his lessons. At the bottom of a page in the second part he had written, 'this has been reeled off too quickly; *il faudrait nuancer*'. But the third part, in his opinion, was far worse. From the beginning, he said when he was halfway through, it had been 'planned badly and developed worse. If I was not too lazy I would tear it up and begin again... My hands are itching to burn these pages as soon as you have read them.' By the end of it, he was even more depressed by his efforts. His recent lessons, he said quoting Dr Johnson's verdict on a piece of mutton, were 'as bad as bad can be. Ill-killed, ill-quartered, ill-cooked, ill-seasoned and ill-served.' They were 'the worst pages that had ever been written by a human pen', particularly those on Byron's life which were an 'endless abomination'. He consoled himself with his pupils, however, by saying that 'the fire had returned them all to nothingness'.[25] On several occasions Lampedusa pretended to have destroyed the lessons, but fortunately there is very little missing and the thousand-page manuscript is the most important document on his life that exists.

Despite his doubts on the value of the exercise, Lampedusa persevered and in the early summer wrote the fourth part on the Victorians. He had just reread *Wuthering Heights* and found it one of the greatest of all masterpieces: Emily Brontë had 'descended down, deep down into the human spirit and had naturally arrived in hell'. She and Dickens were the supreme writers of the age, although the prince was also very fond of Hardy, Thackeray (except for *The Virginians* which was 'unreadable'), George Eliot and Disraeli. Dickens's work was sometimes marred by an 'exasperating sentimentalism' but he was still a 'demi-God'. After *The Pickwick Papers*, Lampedusa's favourite Dickens novel was *David Copperfield* and he loved Micawber whom he considered 'Falstaff's only brother in all literature'. He discussed various minor novelists – Captain Marryat, William Ainsworth, Martin Tupper and the 'unreadable' Theodore Hook – and the poets Arnold, Swinburne, Browning and Tennyson ('Pangloss turned poet'), whom he

Giuseppe di Lampedusa, aged two.

Giulio Tomasi, Prince of Lampedusa.
Giuseppe's great-grandfather.

The ruins of Santa Margherita di Belice, country house of the Filangeri di Cutò and inspiration for Donnafugata. *Above*, the facade.

Left, the family's private balcony in the chapel.

Beatrice Mastrogiovanni Tasca e Filangeri di Cutò, Duchess of Palma, later Princess of Lampedusa. Giuseppe's mother. (Photo courtesy of Gioacchino Lanza Tomasi)

Giuseppe, aged about twelve, with his French governess and an unidentified man.

Giuseppe posing in military uniform in a photographer's studio, probably in 1917. (Photo courtesy of Gioacchino Lanza Tomasi)

Capo d'Orlando, the home of the Piccolo family, overlooking the sea on Sicily's northern coast.

Giuseppe at Capo d'Orlando in December 1926, a few days before his thirtieth birthday. On the left is his cousin Lucio Piccolo. (Photo courtesy of Scafidi Foto)

Stomersee, Latvia, the family home of Giuseppe's wife, Alessandra Wolff. (Photo courtesy of Giuseppe Biancheri)

Giuseppe and Alessandra with two of their dogs at Stomersee. (Photo courtesy of Scafidi Foto)

The dilapidated Villa Lampedusa today. Although Giuseppe never lived there, he used it as a model for the Villa Salina in *The Leopard*.

The cathedral at Palma di Montechiaro, the town that was once the feudal base of the Lampedusas.

The Lampedusas in Palermo in the 1930s. (Photo courtesy of Giuseppe Biancheri)

Via Butera, Palermo. Giuseppe di Lampedusa's home for the last decade of his life.

Left, the terrace and the eighteenth-century front overlooking the marine drive. The former Hotel Trinacria (where Don Fabrizio died in *The Leopard*) is in the background.

Right, the nineteenth-century facade in Via Butera.

Lampedusa's library of historical books in Via Butera.

Crab, the favourite spaniel of the Lampedusas. (Photo courtesy of Gioacchino Lanza Tomasi)

Left to right, Gioacchino Lanza, Lucio Piccolo and Giuseppe di Lampedusa. (Photo courtesy of Gioacchino Lanza Tomasi)

Lampedusa and Gioacchino Lanza in the ruined castle of Montechiaro, 1955.
(Photo courtesy of Giuseppe Biancheri)

One of the last photographs of Giuseppe di Lampedusa. (Photo courtesy of Scafidi Foto)

The tomb of Giuseppe and Alessandra di Lampedusa in the Capuchin cemetery in Palermo.

thought inferior to their Romantic predecessors. Ruskin and Cardinal Newman were both fine writers, and the only major literary figure he did not like at all was Meredith, whom he found florid and verbose. To end the course on the Victorians, he tried to explain 'nonsense' verse to his young listeners, though without illusions of their capacity to see its point: 'clouds of smoke from the stakes of the Counter-Reformation' still hung too heavily over Palermo for them to be able to appreciate Edward Lear and Lewis Carroll. '"Nonsense" verse can have no success in this place. As Anatole France says, *"nous sommes sérieux comme les ânes"*.'[26]

Before embarking on the fifth and final part, Lampedusa again wondered whether he was wasting his time. For eight months he had been covering hundreds of pages in blue biro and he was now fed up. Besides, it was August and very warm, and he started writing in the early afternoon, which was the hottest time of the day. Then there was the problem of finding the right books. It was difficult to give lessons on contemporary writers when there were no biographies available. In many cases he could not even get hold of their novels.

> Not only do the works of modern English writers not reach Palermo; you cannot even hear their echo. Flaccovio condescendingly displays as 'novelties' in his window *The Cocktail Party* and *The Family Reunion* which are twenty years old.* One knows Graham Greene exists through his fame but not in any tangible way through his books. To find a copy of a recent book one has to go at least as far as Rome, or else endure the torment of 'ordering' (which two times out of three is unsuccessful).[27]

These reasons against finishing the course were written down, presumably for the benefit of his pupils. There was another reason, however, which he did not mention and which he may not have been wholly aware of himself. In July, when he was completing the previous part, he had accompanied Lucio Piccolo to a literary conference at San Pellegrino Terme where his cousin was awarded a prize.** This unique contact with the literary

---

The Cocktail Party was in fact four years old, *The Family Reunion* fifteen.
**See below pp. 126–8.

world, combined with Lucio's success, undoubtedly encouraged
Lampedusa to try his own hand at a novel. So, probably, did his
recent rereading of so many English books. In any case, the idea
of writing a novel, which he had often thought about in the past,
began to absorb him so that he became less single-minded and a
little less enthusiastic about the course of literature.

Nevertheless, he did write the fifth part, though he began with
a characteristic preamble. 'Will it be of any use for anything? But
what is really useful? The things that are most obviously
indispensable, a kilo of bread say, only serve to allow a rascal to
go on being a rascal for another twenty-four hours.'[28] The
novelists of the twentieth century he most admired were Conrad,
Joyce, Virginia Woolf, Evelyn Waugh and Graham Greene. He
liked E. M. Forster's first two novels and *A Passage to India*, but
thought there was 'a long period of inferior production' in
between. He did not care much for H. G. Wells or the early
works of Rosamond Lehmann, though he admired one of her
recent novels and talked to Berenson about her when they met in
1953. In one of the lessons he dwelt at length on Gerard Manley
Hopkins, whom he thought 'the greatest English lyric poet since
Keats', and he spent much time on Chesterton whom he admired
as a poet, polemicist and writer of detective stories. His poems
were 'among the most enjoyable that exist' (Lampedusa's
favourites were 'Wine and Water', 'Lepanto' and 'The Ballad of
the White Horse'), though some of his stories were mediocre.
The greatest contemporary poet, however, was Eliot, whose
principal masterpieces were the 'Four Quartets' and 'Ash
Wednesday'. To demonstrate Eliot's mastery, Lampedusa
translated passages of 'The Waste Land': the greater length of the
translation revealed the poet's ability to compress his meaning.[29]

In lighter mood Lampedusa devoted an entire lesson to
thrillers and detective novels even though he admitted that only
one per cent of them was any good. The oldest ones were
generally the best because more recent detective novels were
written according to formulas. They had become even worse
since the war largely as a result of the domination of American
writers who had mixed pornography with their mysteries.
Detective novels could only be successful if they took place in
'Anglo-Saxon countries, that is in countries where *habeas corpus*
is not a vain formula'. In Italy, where murder was followed by

'the arrest of wife, children, parents, brothers and sisters, uncles and aunts, cousins and all the acquaintances of the victim ... the detective who investigates cigarette ash and specks of coffee appears, as he is, ridiculous'. In Lampedusa's view the only 'artistically valid' detective novels were those of Conan Doyle and Chesterton in England, and Simenon in France. In the tales of Dorothy L. Sayers and others, one might find traces of art but when he tried

> to recall the aesthetic emotion obtained from the hundreds of detective novels [he had] read, there remained only the vision of a middle-aged gentleman, dry, sarcastic, addicted to morphine and supremely intelligent – Sherlock Holmes; and that of a poor little priest, his umbrella under his arm in the wind of an autumn sunset, who, on the deserted heath of Hampstead, is about to meditate on the problems of original sin and on the just punishment for the robbery of two silver teaspoons – Father Brown.[30]

Lampedusa's lessons were full of advice, humorous as well as serious, about what ought to be read and why. Conrad, for example, should be used 'as an antidote to the unbearable stagnation of Palermitan life'; fortunately there were 'good Italian translations available to save one the trouble of looking up endless nautical terms in a dictionary'. Lampedusa had just reread Arnold Bennett's Clayhanger series and recommended one of the novels for a long train journey. They were 'witty and enjoyable' and 'would pass the time well'; furthermore, the reader would not feel 'encumbered on arrival because he ·could leave the book in the luggage rack without remorse'. Burns could also be useful, though one got little satisfaction from reading him: he was 'the typical *faux bonhomme* type of writer who makes an affectation of extreme simplicity'. Nevertheless, if anyone wished to charm a girl in Scotland or even in England, he should quote lines of Burns at her: this, apparently, would 'inebriate her to such an extent that she would lose all notion of purity'.[31] Presumably this remark was based on some kind of personal observation, but we do not know if he had once quoted Burns in these circumstances or whether he had watched someone else trying it.

Francesco Orlando later described Lampedusa as an excellent teacher, particularly with difficult texts like Eliot's 'Four Quartets' or the poems of Rimbaud and Mallarmé which they studied afterwards. In spite of his reservations about the value of his lessons, the prince approached the task with enthusiasm. 'He was undoubtedly happy to have broken his intellectual isolation,' recalled Orlando, 'to be able to talk so much about literature, to get to know young people and transmit something to them.' He was also 'generous and kind beyond all description', showing great patience in the teaching, lending countless books and also giving many away as presents. If he bought a modern edition of the French classics, he used to give Orlando a duplicate copy from his library.[32]

When the course ended in January 1955, Lampedusa decided to start straight away on another one in French literature. It was shorter than the English and its only regular student was Orlando, though Gioacchino Lanza was sometimes present as well. This time Lampedusa did not attempt to reveal the entire panorama of a nation's literature from the formation of its language, but concentrated on certain periods. The sixteenth century was dealt with in great detail, and so was a part of the seventeenth, but the eighteenth century was omitted altogether as Lampedusa said it would bore him to write about it.[33] From the nineteenth century he gave lessons on only a few writers, concentrating particularly on Stendhal to whom he devoted almost as much time as he had given to Shakespeare the year before.

Lampedusa's knowledge of sixteenth-century French writers was as profound as his understanding of their Elizabethan contemporaries. He had read all seventy-two short stories of the Queen of Navarre and had studied the most obscure imitators of Rabelais. As before, he liked to fill in the background, not only of the writers themselves but also of the historical events of the time; it was important, for example, to realize that in this period Paris was not France's literary capital and that it was less influential, in artistic fields, than Lyon, Bordeaux and Montpellier. He was also once again full of illuminating points and original comparisons. Calvin, for whom he had some of the sympathy he had already shown for the English Puritans, was taught as a contrast to Rabelais. He was an extremely rare type in

France: searching through the centuries of French history, Lampedusa could find only one similar figure, the revolutionary leader Saint-Just. Other unusual comparisons were made between poets from the sixteenth and nineteenth centuries. In Clément Marot there was 'the same oscillation between sensuality and piety that three centuries later' could be found in Verlaine; likewise, in some respects, Maurice Scève was 'a very distant anticipation of Mallarmé'.[34]

Some of Lampedusa's favourite poets belonged to the group from the Loire called the Pléiade, whose works he enthusiastically collected. He had just been rereading Ronsard and was struck by the contrast between his epic works, which were almost uniformly bad, and about twenty lyric poems, written in haste and given no importance by the poet, which were incredibly beautiful. The long odes and other poems that were supposed to give him immortality, had understandably ruined his reputation which the rediscovery of the lyrics had only partially restored. Poor Ronsard, said Lampedusa, must be sitting in the Elysian fields feeling like someone who, having just bought a fabulous Cadillac, finds that his friends admire it only for the internal cigarette lighter. In his *Amours*, however, Ronsard showed great psychological knowledge and thus began 'the glorious procession of those analysts of passions and human behaviour which from him to Proust has been the most wonderful factor in French literature, of the literature of this observant people, deductive and lucid in their sensuality'.[35]

France's greatest prose writer of this period was, in Lampedusa's eyes, Montaigne. Like Shakespeare, he represented 'the spirit of the Renaissance in its supreme state of distillation'. The work of the two men may have been very different but their ideas were almost identical. Both of them were unreligious themselves but understanding of the religious feelings of others; both combined universal compassion with 'a light tincture of contempt'; both had the same serene scepticism and showed 'the same persistence in dismantling the mechanism of the human psyche'. Above all, they were both sharp observers of 'the human ant-nest' who did not try to make it fit into a cosmic pattern: 'they were both totally averse to ready-made systems'.[36] It was a great point in Montaigne's favour that dictators, including Napoleon, should hate him:

Mussolini, in that encyclopaedia of ignorance and conceit
called the *Prolusione all'anno accademico dell' Università per
stranieri di Perugia*, called him an 'empty rhetorician', thereby
demonstrating that he had never read a line of the *Essais*,
because no one was less of a rhetorician than Montaigne. As
for Hitler, he called him in his 'table-talk' *'ein ungezähmter
jüdischer Rebell'*. If *'jüdischer'* is half-true, 'untamed' and
'rebel' are of a mendacity quite worthy of Hitler. The only
surprising thing about these errors is the fact that Mussolini
and Hitler should have heard of the name (and only the name)
of Montaigne.[37]

Once again the lessons were accompanied by useful and
idiosyncratic advice about what to read and in which edition to
read it. Montaigne was straightforward: his essays 'should be
read, reread and re-reread fifty times, from the first to the last
word'; no other writer could give such sustained pleasure on each
page. Ronsard was more difficult. The reader had to be in 'a sort
of state of grace to extract the honey' from the elegies. If he was
in a good mood and had plenty of time, he would appreciate
them; if, on the other hand, he was impatient or irritable, he
might find them too long and not amusing. Another curious piece
of information concerned the copy of Caesar's *Commentaries*
annotated by Montaigne which the Duke of Aumale had found at
a bookstall by the Seine. Should Orlando ever go to the library at
Chantilly, he would find it sandwiched between a copy of
Aristophanes annotated by Rabelais and one of Aeschylus
annotated by Racine.[38]

Some of Lampedusa's most inspired teaching dealt with
Stendhal, though many of his points came from 'Prévost's
magnificent book'. Stendhal was one of those figures Lampedusa
adored even when he was writing a *'mezzo fiasco'* like *De
l'Amour*. His faults had redeeming qualities; even when he
plagiarized, he produced original works. The life of Haydn, for
example, took its information from Carpini's *Vita di Haydn*, but
the two books were completely different. Stendhal added
personal memories of other things, inserted moral maxims that
were always cynical and sometimes profound, and made some
original points about Haydn's music which, like French melons,
he considered 'always passable'. Lampedusa also liked his books

on Italy and considered *Promenades dans Rome* to be the only 'travel guide' which was a literary masterpiece.[39]

Like André Gide, Lampedusa spent much time trying to decide whether *Le Rouge et le Noir* or *La Chartreuse de Parme* was the greatest novel in any language. A year before he had awarded the prize to the first book, but since then he had changed his mind: 'from a lyrical, artistic and human point of view, *La Chartreuse* won'. There was a wonderful 'mellowness' (one of Lampedusa's favourite English words) about the second half of the novel. Stendhal was writing about fears and intrigues, sinister characters and terrible prisons, and yet one read about them with great serenity; he had wanted to portray Hell, but he had created 'the most adorable Dantesque purgatory'. 'Written by an old man for old people, one has to be over forty before one can understand it. Then one sees that this book, bare even of artistic illusions, almost bare of adjectives, nostalgic, ironic, self-possessed and gentle, is the summit of all world fiction.'[40]

Stendhal's style was a miracle of conciseness. He did not have set-piece conversations or 'the ten-page interior monologues' of modern novels; he did not describe buildings in minute detail like Balzac or employ 'universes of adjectives' like Hugo. He could summarize Fabrizio's conquest of Clelia in five words* or Julien Sorel's night of love in a semi-colon.** Yet this sparse, compressed style was able to convey human feelings with unparalleled sensitivity to those capable of reading between the lines. Stendhal's work, said Lampedusa, was 'written in two columns, composed in equal measure of sensations expressed and transmitted and a second series of sensations expressed only through a marked silence intended to attract the attention of the attentive reader'. Thus he did indeed write 'for "the happy few" gifted with intuition and not for those needing explanations'. There was little point in teaching Stendhal to the boorish or inattentive: 'It is useless to explain,' Lampedusa declared, 'the pathos of [Julien's last hours] to those who do not have the sensibility to perceive it for themselves.'[41]

Stendhal was a good example of another of Lampedusa's

Aucune résistance ne fut opposée.
**La vertu de Julien fut égale à son bonheur; il faut que je descende par l'échelle dit-il à Mathilde, quand il vit l'aube du jour paraître.*

categories, the *magri* or 'lean' writers, those who wrote through allusion and implication and thus made the reader labour to understand them. Nearly all the *magri* (Racine, Calvin, Laclos, Madame de la Fayette etc) and indeed the *supermagri* (La Rochefoucauld and Mallarmé) were French. But there were also some French in the opposing group of *grassi* or 'plump' writers, who explained all their nuances and left nothing for the reader to deduce; they included Dante, Rabelais, Montaigne, Shakespeare, Balzac, Thomas Mann and Proust. Lampedusa did not prefer the *magri* to the *grassi* (Shakespeare, a leading *grasso*, was his favourite writer of all) but he had great admiration for the dry, concise style of writers like Stendhal and felt that that was how novels should be written.[42] Perhaps this reflected his taste for puritanism, which he admired from afar, and which he may have been more conscious of than his taste for the baroque, which is what he had been born into and had lived with all his life. His puritanism, however, was primarily an intellectual attitude which did not much affect the way he led his life; the baroque was always a more important influence on his character. At all events, the explicit style and occasionally baroque prose of *The Leopard* place Lampedusa firmly among the *grassi*.

Lampedusa did not give any further courses in literature, though he later read Goethe with Orlando, studied Spanish writers with Gioacchino Lanza, and gave lessons in Sicilian history to Gioacchino's fiancée Mirella Radice.[43] He did little more than allude to Balzac and Proust, both of whom he had reread with admiration five years earlier.[44]* Nor did he give any lessons on Italian writers, an omission which has led people to speculate that he either despised them or was ignorant of his own country's literature. The second speculation is entirely erroneous and the first needs to be qualified. Certainly he was critical of Italian literature and thought it had become ever more provincial

---

*In a letter to Licy in 1950 Lampedusa had written: 'I have also read a very curious book about Proust by Fallois which gives the 'key' to all the characters in *La Recherche*. Albertine is simply Proust's chauffeur! An Italian called Agostinelli. Gilberte is also a monsieur. I admit that it rather disgusted me. But immediately I reread some pages [of Proust] and the strange charm of the style and analysis reconciled me.'[45] Five years later, however, he still seemed disgusted, describing Proust in the Sicilian dialect as 'a right little pederast'. He recognized the Frenchman's genius but told Orlando that he must have been an odious person.[46]

between the death of Tasso at the end of the sixteenth century and the First World War.[47] But he appreciated some modern writers, such as the poet Montale, and he admired some of the works of Manzoni, Verga, D'Annunzio, Ungaretti and Moravia. The one major figure of Italian literature he disparaged was Ariosto, whom he considered a bad writer whose work consisted of 'verbal games'.[48] The difference between Ariosto and Leopardi 'in the hierarchy of poets was the same as that between a cabin boy and an admiral in the hierarchy of sailors'.[49] It has been suggested that Lampedusa underestimated Leopardi,[50] but this was not the case. He admired his descriptions of nature and thought them superior to Wordsworth's; furthermore, Leopardi's *Canti* were of a remarkably fine standard and their consistency was even higher than that of Shakespeare's sonnets. Lampedusa referred to him and Keats as 'two "most supreme" poets' who shared 'the cult of the beautiful'. They were also two of the greatest exponents of '*anti-melodramma*': 'Let us rejoice,' said the prince, 'that one of these two was an Italian, belonging to the country which more than any other has reason to beg forgiveness for this incurable injury to Art.'[51]

Lampedusa's principal grievance was not so much that Italians were bad writers but that Italy was not a literary country. He used to complain that Italians neither read books nor liked poets.[52] If, with great reluctance, one of them did decide to spend a thousand lire on a book, he did so with contradictory feelings. To give himself the satisfaction of feeling that he had 'made a great sacrifice for cultural reasons', the book should be as 'boring as a university lecture'. At the same time 'the terrible regret at having spent a thousand lire in this way when it could have been used more delightfully in casinos, cake shops or buying neckties' made him want the book to be 'a substitute for lost pleasures and consequently it should be enjoyable, exciting and thoughtless – that is, in absolute contrast to the academic ideal which the other half of his mind yearned for'. As a result, the Italian reader basically did not like books and provided no incentive for other people to write them.[53]

If the readers were largely responsible for the lamentable state of Italian literary life, the writers themselves were not blameless. To begin with, said Lampedusa, they had no sense of humour, or at least they conveyed none in their writing. Whereas the most serious English writers could write humorously, you could scarcely find in Italy a book that was both well-written and funny.[54] In addition, Italian writers tended to be either adventurous and superficial or else narrow and provincial. Journalists, for example, would go to Chile for ten days and then return and write daily articles for two months about a country they could not have learnt much about. This sort of thing had probably encouraged the belief that adventurous novels were for children and the only proper settings for literature were places like Aci-Trezza* or the Via Veneto in Rome. Subjects like childhood, the Malayan islands, Tibet or the scruples of naval captains on long voyages – subjects which could be made interesting by fine writers such as Kipling, Stevenson, Malraux and Conrad – were taboo for Italian literature.[55]

Yet the narrow fields of Italy's writers really only reflected the *campanilismo* or provincialism of the country as a whole. 'A lady whom we all know,' Lampedusa recounted to his pupils,

> was returning to Palermo with me by car after an absence of *two* days. On reaching Porta Felice she made the sign of the Cross and thanked the Lord for allowing her to see her native city once more ('*O tu, Palermo, terra adorata*').** How is it possible that this lady could ever be interested in Conrad, who for twenty years wandered around the Pacific, or Kipling, who spent half his time between London and India?[56]

The real trouble, then, was the fact that Italy was not a country that encouraged writers. The Rossettis, Lampedusa believed, had needed the 'atmosphere and education of England' in which to flourish. Had they stayed in Italy they would have produced nothing worthwhile; the cultural condition of the country in that 'barren period that goes from *I Promessi Sposi* to *I Malavoglia*,'† could not have stimulated their creative talents.[57]

---

*The village in eastern Sicily where Verga's *I Malavoglia* takes place.
**A line sung by Giovanni da Procida in Verdi's opera *I Vespri Siciliani*.
†i.e. between 1840-2, when the Tuscan edition of Manzoni's novel was published, and 1881.

9

The Reluctant Writer

In the spring of 1954 the poet Eugenio Montale received a yellow envelope, insufficiently stamped, containing a few barely legible poems printed in Capo d'Orlando. Accompanying them was a letter from Lucio Piccolo explaining his intention to evoke 'a unique Sicilian world – more precisely that of Palermo – which now finds itself on the verge of disappearing without having had the good fortune to be preserved in any art form'. His poems, he went on, described 'that world of baroque churches, of old convents, of souls suited to these places, who spent their lives here without leaving a trace'.[1]

Montale was not encouraged by the letter, which had in fact been written by Lampedusa and was perhaps more a description of his future novel than a summary of Lucio's poetry.[2] But he started reading the poems, partly to see whether they were worth the money he had been forced to spend on the extra stamps. After reading the first five lyrics 'without straining to understand them', Montale suddenly became fascinated by the little book and later described its author as a 'sedentary piper who can draw unheard-of melodies even from a broken reed'.[3] The *Canti Barocchi*, or Baroque songs, are indeed hauntingly beautiful, delicate but densely scented, their luxuriant verbiage cultivated over decades in the almost tropical atmosphere of Capo d'Orlando.

Shortly after reading them, Montale was invited to take part in a literary conference at San Pellegrino Terme, a small town in Lombardy, where a group of distinguished literary figures would each introduce a younger, unknown writer. On being asked whom he would present, Montale replied impulsively, without knowing anything about him, that his protégé would be Lucio Piccolo. He was subsequently astonished to meet Lucio and discover that he was a Sicilian baron of almost the same age as himself. Furthermore, the unknown poet was so learned and knowledgeable that the prospect of presenting him to the conference was embarrassing.[4]

Lucio, who had had no contact with the literary world, was apprehensive about going to San Pellegrino and asked Bebbuzzo Lo Monaco to accompany him. But Bebbuzzo was in a lazy mood and Lucio had to approach his cousin the *mostro* for moral support. Lampedusa agreed to go and in the middle of July 1954 the two of them, accompanied by a servant, took the train to Milan. The novelist Giorgio Bassani later recalled this 'bizarre trio' at the conference, the two cousins going around together followed by 'the bronzed and sturdy servant' who never took his eyes off them. The literati were astonished by the elderly Sicilian gentlemen but impressed by their manners and bearing. Lucio seemed a most untypical writer, timid, kind and aristocratic, dressed in dark unfashionable Sicilian clothes and without any kind of histrionics.[5] According to Montale, Lucio 'came and went without saying a word',[6] though Bassani remembered him introducing his cousin, 'tall, stout and silent, a pale face – that greyish pallor of dark-skinned southerners'. Although it was mid-summer, Lampedusa wore a hat and an overcoat 'buttoned up with precision'; when he walked, he leant heavily on a gnarled walking-stick. During the conference, Bassani recalled, he was 'always silent, with the same bitter twist to his lips'; even during introductions he said nothing but merely gave a slight bow.[7] Yet there is evidence that he did talk, at any rate to Montale and the critic Emilio Cecchi, and that he even managed to have an esoteric conversation with them. On his return to Palermo he wrote a note about the obscure English writer Martin Tupper: 'I am now mathematically certain of being the only person in Italy to have read him. Cecchi and Montale do not know about him, let it be said to their credit...'[8] It is unlikely that Lampedusa could have acquired this information without speaking to them.

Some years after his cousin's death, Lucio Piccolo was asked why Lampedusa had not begun writing until so near the end of his life. 'Oh!' exclaimed Lucio, 'we Sicilians are so afraid of being badly judged on the mainland that we prefer to keep silent.'[9] Too many fine and prolific writers have come from Sicily since unification for this explanation to be applicable to the island as a whole. Yet it does contain an element of truth in the cases of both Lampedusa and Piccolo. Giuseppe had been thinking of writing a novel for many years but had never felt sufficiently impelled to begin. Licy, who had encouraged him to write, later explained that he would have begun earlier had it not been for the war, the loss of the family palace and the problems of buying a new house.[10] But these are excuses rather than reasons for inactivity; if shortage of time had been the real problem, he could have started at the end of his brief career in the Red Cross almost eight years earlier. The truth is that he needed something to overcome his doubts and inertia, and he found it at San Pellegrino.

Like many Sicilians, Lampedusa had shown little desire to compete in the outside world and even as a child he had not been competitive. But the conference in northern Italy, with its parade of literati and its success for Lucio, did at last arouse some feeling of competitiveness. As Gioacchino Lanza later noted, the combination of the *Canti Barocchi*, a couple of days at San Pellegrino, and the literary lessons in Palermo, provided the crucial incentive.[11] Lampedusa was not particularly impressed by the eminent figures he had observed: 'Montale and Cecchi,' he told Orlando, 'had the unmistakable air of people who know their own importance, the air of marshals of France.'[12] He believed, rightly as it turned out, that he could write prose as well as any of the literati. And if Lucio, whom he had been teasing and trying to deflate for decades, could win a prize, surely he could do so as well. The following year he wrote to his old friend Guido Lajolo in Brazil: 'Being mathematically certain that I was no more foolish [than Lucio], I sat down at my desk and wrote a novel.'[13]

The reasons for his need to write go far deeper, of course. Lampedusa was the ultimate descendant of an ancient noble line whose economic and physical extinction culminated in himself. The consciousness of his family's decadence often depressed him, and he felt the need to record something of the process which had caused it. Like Don Fabrizio in *The Leopard*, he was the last member of the family to have 'vital memories', the last one capable, in the words he wrote for Lucio, of evoking that 'unique Sicilian world' before it disappeared. No one was better placed than Lampedusa to depict that vanishing society. He had been part of it and yet had managed to remain detached and critical. Besides, unlike the other major Sicilian writers of his and the two previous generations, he had stayed on the island and did not look at it with the sentimental eyes of an exile in the north.

Lampedusa's nostalgia for the houses he had lost was another important factor in his decision to write. The sale of the country house at Santa Margherita and the destruction of the family palace in Palermo had an effect on him that is difficult to exaggerate.* Their evocation on paper,** populated by their inhabitants of fifty years before, alleviated that misery and released him from some of the restrictions which had prevented him-from writing. For most of his life he had felt constrained by family decline, the loss of his homes and the overpowering influence of his mother and wife. Writing provided an escape from the years of disappointment and an opportunity to redeem what he recognized had been a largely wasted life. At the end of 1954 he knew he should begin. If the San Pellegrino visit had given him confidence, the state of his health convinced him he could not delay further. Unaware of the illness that would eventually kill him, he nevertheless realized that he was not well; he was having increasing difficulty in breathing and in January 1955 was told he had emphysema. Although only in his late fifties, Lampedusa already resembled a man of seventy.

He started writing with diffidence. *'Je fais ça pour m'amuser,'* he told Licy, and when Pietro della Torretta asked him what he was doing, scribbling away, he replied, 'Enjoying myself.'[15] Yet this nonchalance was a pretence. Once he had taken the decision to start, he committed himself to his writing. During the last thirty months of his life, he worked almost every day on his novel and stories, writing painstakingly in blue biro at a table at the Mazzara cafe or in his library at home.

---

*The fact that Santa Margherita had not been destroyed but belonged to someone else only increased his regrets. Lampedusa made the mistake of revisiting it during his brief military service at Poggioreale in the Second World War. According to Gioacchino Lanza, it pained him that the house should still exist, in alien and uncaring hands.[14]

**Both are described at length in Lampedusa's childhood memoirs. Santa Margherita also appears, rather enlarged, as Donnafugata in *The Leopard*. Some of the rooms in the Palazzo Lampedusa are also portrayed in the novel but the building itself is not. The fictional Villa Salina is based on the Villa Lampedusa outside Palermo at San Lorenzo.

It was a slow process to begin with. Lampedusa had written very little in Italian, apart from business letters and his hurried notes on literature, since the three published articles in the 1920s. In some ways he was more comfortable in French, in which he had written hundreds of letters to Licy over the previous two decades. Knowing half-a-dozen languages but inexperienced in their use, his Italian sometimes gives the impression of being a translation. Yet his unfamiliarity with writing made him particularly thoughtful about the choice of words and he avoided clichés and easy conventions. The phrases and imagery are highly original and there is an intensity about his language which sometimes recalls Conrad. His English translator found *The Leopard* 'so full of subtle word-play and irony both delicate and grandiose' that he considered it 'some of the most allusive prose written since Manzoni'.[16]

More than twenty years earlier, Lampedusa had first thought of writing a book. According to his wife, it was intended to be 'an historical novel set in Sicily at the time of Garibaldi's landing at Marsala, and based on the character of his great-grandfather, the astronomer Giulio di Lampedusa'.[17] It is possible that some notes may have been made or pages written before the Second World War, but none of these has been found among his papers.[18] In any event, the plan remained unaltered for many years. 'It will be twenty-four hours in the life of my great-grandfather on the day of Garibaldi's landing,' he told Gioacchino Lanza after he had begun.[19] But he soon found the time limit too constricting. 'I don't know how to do a *Ulysses*,' he confessed to Gioacchino, and decided to divide the novel into three separate years: 1860 (Garibaldi's invasion), 1885 (the death of Prince Giulio), and 1910, when the fiftieth anniversary of Italian unification would reveal both the failures of the Risorgimento and the decadence of the protagonist's family.

For the long opening chapter Lampedusa retained the twenty-four-hour scheme of 1860. He spent about four months on it, writing and rewriting, altering names and changing characters: Don Fabrizio's nephew Tancredi, for instance, originated as his second son Manfredi. The later chapters were written much more quickly and were afterwards expanded and altered. But the first was corrected and polished before the others were begun and remained almost unchanged in later drafts. It contained several descriptive passages of which the author was particularly proud:[20] the discovery of the corpse of the young Bourbon soldier; the description of Palermo at night, the monasteries and convents 'despots of the scene', giving 'the city its grimness and its character, its sedateness and also the sense of death which not even the vibrant Sicilian light could ever manage to disperse'; and the passages on the garden, its scents 'cloying, fleshy and slightly putrid, like the aromatic liquids distilled from the relics of certain saints', and its roses corrupted, 'first stimulated and then enfeebled by the strong if languid pull of Sicilian earth, burnt by apocalyptic Julys ... changed into objects like flesh-coloured cabbages, obscene and distilling a dense, almost indecent scent...'*

In June 1955 Lampedusa decided to interrupt his novel in order to write his autobiography: only the first part, the memories of childhood, were written and later published as 'The Places of My Early Childhood'. It has usually been assumed that he planned only to describe the houses he had known as a child but a passage in the first draft of the introduction reveals his true intention: 'I would like to divide these memoirs into three parts. The first, "childhood", would end with my going to school; the second, "youth", to 1925; the third, "maturity", to now, the date I consider I have begun "old age".'

His widow afterwards declared that the childhood fragment was written before *The Leopard* had been begun, but her memory for dates declined in old age. She may have been more justified in claiming that she had encouraged her husband to write it in order to mitigate the desolation suffered from the loss of his homes and to 'neutralize his nostalgia'.[21] But the memories were recorded to assist the writing of future chapters as well as to aid Lampedusa's problems with his regrets; the descriptions of Santa Margherita certainly helped him to imagine the great palace at Donnafugata. Another contributory factor to the childhood memoirs was Stendhal's autobiography, *Vie de Henry Brulard*, which Lampedusa was then rereading. It is discussed and praised at the beginning of 'The Places of My Early Childhood' and in some places imitated: 'I will try,' he wrote in a passage later crossed out, 'to adhere as closely as possible to the method of Henry Brulard, even as far as drawing little maps of the principal

---

*The ideas and themes of *The Leopard* are discussed in chapters 12 and 13.

scenes.' The manuscript does indeed contain a few drawings
similar to those found in Stendhal's book; among others there
was a sketch of a wooded hill near Santa Margherita and a
diagram of his mother's dressing room (Giuseppe's position
playing on the floor marked with a x) when his father told them
about the assassination of King Umberto.[22]

After quickly writing his childhood memoirs, Lampedusa
decided to return to his novel rather than continue with his
autobiography. The plan was now to write three more chapters:
another in 1860 (but set in Donnafugata rather than Palermo) and
the other two in 1885 and 1910. But the writing was done less
systematically than before. The assembling of *The Leopard* was a
laborious business, complicated by the insertions of numerous
extra passages and the addition of more chapters. The projected
chapter on Donnafugata eventually became three, while the
chapter on the prince's death, originally intended to come third,
ended up as number seven. The novel was finally published with
eight chapters; it was first sent to a publisher with only four and
was accepted by another with only six.

In the second half of 1955 Francesco Orlando found that a
change had come over Lampedusa. He was 'more reserved, less
patient, prouder, less inclined to take the lessons [on literature]
seriously'. He had become sharp-tongued and critical, sometimes
brusquely dismissing Orlando's views with a curt, 'it's clear you
haven't the first idea...'[23] Orlando, deeply sensitive and
uncomfortably aware of the class differences between them, was
bewildered and hurt. He did not understand why his teacher had
turned against him. One of their friends confirms that Lampedusa
treated Orlando badly, though another maintains that the pupil
overreacted: Orlando was preparing for an academic career and
resented Lampedusa's sense of humour and his jokes about
professors. Whatever the reason, the prince was becoming
increasingly irritable and his diary reveals that much of his
irritation was caused by what Orlando said or did: diary entries
for December 1955 include remarks such as 'inopportune laugh
from Orlando' and 'Orlando with ... much superfluous
conversation'.[24]

Later, on reflection, Orlando attributed the change to
Lampedusa's discovery of his vocation as a writer. The older
man's 'sixty years of training' were over and he had 'nothing more

to discuss or to teach or to learn';[25] he merely wanted to write. The absorption with his novel may well have made him more peevish, impatient and distracted during the lessons, but the deteriorating relationship between master and pupil was caused by the differences in character. Lampedusa did not, for example, become irritable with Gioacchino Lanza during this period; on the contrary, their relationship became closer and eventually he adopted him. Francesco Orlando also noticed his growing affection for Gioacchino and believed that it was a symptom of Lampedusa's aristocratic 'reversion'. During the second half of 1955, he wrote later, the prince discarded the personality of the literary intellectual and reverted to his original aristocratic self. 'The Leopard' had become self-projection; like Don Fabrizio, he wanted to be amused by someone with aristocratic charm and an irreverent sense of humour.[26]

During his first year as a writer, Lampedusa's habits changed little. He did not go into retreat, shutting himself away and refusing to see people. Most of his friends indeed, including Francesco Orlando, were not aware that he was writing a book; he did not discuss it with them or even mention it in his diary. He still visited the cinema or cine-club two or three evenings a week and summed up the films briefly in his diary afterwards: 'bellissimo', 'mediocre', 'poetico', and (for 20,000 Leagues under the Sea) 'spettacolare'. He still ate often in restaurants, usually at Renato, the Extra-Bar or the Pizzeria Bellini, and sometimes he subjected himself to 'basically boring' cocktail parties. Occasionally he used to be taken to listen to gramophone records in a friend's house; with Antonio Pasqualino, who attended a few of the literature lessons, he enjoyed listening to records of Romeo and Juliet and A Midsummer Night's Dream. But some evenings he ended up doing things he knew he would hate, like listening to 'horrendous songs' broadcast from San Remo or going to the 'Miss Italy' beauty competition at Mondello.[27]

The diaries hint at some interesting conversations – 'Licy expresses her new theory on religion' – but generally they record as briefly as possible only where he had been and what he had been doing. Lampedusa was scrupulous about noting the weather, his weight and the purchase of articles such as shoes, paraffin or a waterproof beret. Illnesses were sometimes mentioned, whether his, Licy's or a dog's: among other things, he had nose bleeds and backaches whereas Licy suffered from sore throats and was once 'poisoned by a pizza'. There is a single reference to the fact that he might have had emphysema, but it is not mentioned again. In general the diaries give the impression of a man finding it hard to cope with the minor irritations of life. They record endless payments of bills, 'a useless discussion' about property, 'a useless and painful visit to the Banco di Sicilia'. He seems to have been prone to losing and breaking things, or leaving his glasses behind. Once he bought a Remington electric razor which he dropped and broke after using for the first time. Little incidents, like a conversation with an 'unpleasant builder', could leave him distraught. Even the most insignificant arrangements seemed to go wrong. Returning without his keys from Capo d'Orlando one night, he found his Florentine servant sleeping so deeply that he had to spend the night in the Hotel Jolly. One day, when he went to the cleaner's to retrieve his raincoat, he was told it was not ready, and on his return the following afternoon he got soaked in a thunderstorm.[28]

The diaries also record the arrival of books and foreign newspapers; in January 1955 he received the *Observer* and *The Times Literary Supplement* from his friend Corrado Fatta. In the same month he was reading *War and Peace*, followed by some French books he was teaching Francesco Orlando. At about this time, or perhaps a little earlier, he was also reading accounts of Garibaldi's Sicilian campaign by some of the participants. In the evenings at the Via Butera he was still holding his 'seminars', though they appear to have been organized less systematically than before. The English course came to an end in January with assorted lessons on Greene, Saki, Henry James and T.S. Eliot, and within a week he had started on Rabelais and Calvin. The French course continued for much of the year (Racine and Molière in August, Gide in September) but was then superseded by a mixture of English and German literature. In October Francesco Orlando received tuition in Joyce and Heine, and the following month he went on to Goethe with *Werther* and back to Shakespeare with *Richard II*. After Christmas Lampedusa suspended his lessons on Goethe to discuss Napoleon's tactics in the Italian campaigns of 1796 and 1800. At the same time he was giving other lessons to Gioacchino Lanza and Mirella Radice. In

November he read *A Winter's Tale* with both of them, sometimes at the Mazzara cafe, and in December he read Lope de Vega in Spanish with Gioacchino and gave a course on medieval Sicilian history to Mirella. By the end of 1955, when he had nearly completed the first draft of *The Leopard*, he was giving lessons nearly every day.[29]

A few people make regular appearances throughout the diaries of the last years: Gioacchino, Mirella, Francesco, Antonio Pasqualino and Francesco Agnello were the young people he saw most of; among his contemporaries the only friends he met regularly were the Piccolos, the historian Corrado Fatta, Bebbuzzo Lo Monaco, Licy's first husband André, and her old friend from the Baltic, Lila Iljascenko. He used to see them at the Mazzara, where his younger friends knew they could find him almost every day, and sometimes at restaurants; occasionally he visited a friend's house and on Sunday evenings he and Licy were 'at home' in the Via Butera. Lampedusa did not make any new friends during this period though occasionally he met interesting people such as Freya Stark and Bernard Berenson. He saw Miss Stark several times during her visit to Palermo in 1955. It was a '*crowded* week' she later recalled, 'like a Grand Tour of the old sort with churches by day and receptions in the evening. There is still a Spanish tradition of grandeur in the palaces ... dinners and lunches, princes and duchesses.'[30] Lampedusa may have found her rather fierce because in his diary he referred to Miss Stark and her companion as 'the Lions'.[31]

From time to time the diaries record the 'unexpected arrival of Lucio', once wearing 'a small pink tie', followed by lunch in a restaurant. Lampedusa also saw his cousin in Capo d'Orlando where Gioacchino drove him to spend a few days each month. In his diary he noted walks in the orange groves, during which he got mud on his shoes, 'interminable lunches' and recitals of Lucio's new lyrics. Gioacchino recalled later that much of the time was spent reminiscing with the Piccolos about their grandmother's house at Santa Margherita.[32] The chief peril of these visits remained the Piccolo dogs. On one arrival a creature called Gippi bit Gioacchino and Francesco Agnello three times and on the following day it again savaged Francesco; not until the third day of the stay was Gippi chained up. On a subsequent visit Lucio presented Lampedusa with a copy of *Canti Barocchi* containing the inscription: 'To the *Mostro*, in recognition of his kindness, talent and erudition, in dutiful, affectionate homage and as a signal of protest against vain, pretentious and impertinent youth, the humble author dedicates these simple pages.'[33]

The most important journeys Lampedusa made in 1955 were to Palma di Montechiaro. Curiously, he had never been there although it had been the family's territorial base and for many years his title had been Duke of Palma.* In the breakup of the Tomasi estates he had received neither the ducal palace nor other property in the town (though he had been awarded the ruined and worthless castle of Montechiaro nearby), but it is still strange that someone with his historical curiosity had not gone to see the houses of his ancestors. Even in 1955 he required some persuasion before agreeing to go. Nevertheless, on 3 September he and Gioacchino took a train from Palermo to Agrigento where they were met by Francesco Agnello. Francesco then drove them to his country estate at Siculiana and the following day they visited Palma. Before reaching the town they stopped at the castle of Montechiaro and took photographs, and then went on to the cathedral, built by Lampedusa's ancestor the 'saint-duke' at the end of the seventeenth century. The prince was in fact still the 'patron' of the cathedral and his unexpected arrival was warmly welcomed. He met the archpriest, drank iced lemon juice in the sacristy, and looked at the Tomasi portraits on the walls.[34]

On leaving the cathedral the party visited the Benedictine convent, a former palace of the Tomasi which the saint-duke had turned into a religious house. Lampedusa was 'patron' here also, a position which gave him the privilege of visiting the enclosed convent accompanied by 'two gentlemen of his suite'. After a 'joyful and courteous welcome', the 'gracious abbess' offered him the house's special almond cakes (oddly recorded in the diary as 'birthday cake') and a sprig of jasmine. Then she took the prince on a tour of the convent, ringing a silver bell to warn the nuns to hide themselves from the gentlemen. Lampedusa was shown the cell of the Venerable Maria Crocifissa (Isabella) and various objects including her instruments of flagellation and a letter sent her by the devil. Afterwards he summed up the visit with a single word: *commosso* ('moved').[35]

---

*It is less curious that he had never visited the island of Lampedusa, where the Tomasi had had no house and which brought them, until its sale, no benefit.

The party spent the following day inspecting the ruins and museum of Agrigento, and the next day Gioacchino and the prince returned to Palermo. But the visit to Palma had left a strong impression on Lampedusa and a few weeks later he decided to return to Siculiana with an expanded party including Licy and Mirella. This visit was attended by a number of typically Lampedusian mishaps. They had problems with lice, and Licy was attacked by fleas in the castle at Montechiaro; on one day the motor-car had a puncture near Agrigento and then another the next day at Palma. But the visit was again a moving experience. Licy was very taken by the ruined castle and suggested restoring a part of it so they could stay there. Lampedusa was particularly touched by his return to the cathedral, where the archpriest made a public act of homage, and again by his visit to the convent. That evening they decided to stay an extra day and had to telegraph Licy's patients to cancel their appointments. After the journey to Palma, Lampedusa confessed in his diary that he felt 'orphaned and melancholic'. The following day probably added to his nostalgia because the party made a lengthy detour on the way back to Palermo, driving through Sciacca, Castelvetrano, Santa Ninfa and Gibellina, all places he had known during his childhood holidays at Santa Margherita. Nevertheless, the trip provided great inspiration for Lampedusa. In the Donnafugata chapter he worked on that autumn, he used much of the material he had gathered at Palma, including descriptions of the cathedral and his patronal visit to the Benedictine convent.[36]

The rest of the year was depressing. A week after their return from Siculiana, Francesco Agnello was kidnapped by bandits demanding a ransom. He remained in captivity for seven weeks while negotiations went on for his release, and eventually appeared in Palermo, in a highly nervous state, around the middle of December. Lampedusa did not have an easy relationship with Francesco, who disapproved of his treatment of Orlando, disliked the charades at Capo d'Orlando and felt that the older man had sided against him over a private dispute with Gioacchino. But he was undoubtedly fond of him and his diary records great concern about the kidnapping. After Francesco's release, he wrote and rewrote an article on the incident for the magazine *Oggi*.

Christmas that year was a melancholy affair. Several of his acquaintances died, he noted in his diary, though they were not close friends. On Christmas Eve Licy sang Russian carols 'badly', which may have driven him out to hear Mass for the first time that year; but although Santa Maria della Catena was a beautiful church, the music there was 'horrendous'. Christmas was even worse. It rained all day, lunch was cold and Bebbuzzo did not visit them; 'one of the worst Christmases of my life', he noted in English in his diary. On Boxing Day he went to a boring cocktail party at the Gangi palace, where there were few people and a 'mildly tasteless atmosphere', and the next day it was back to the usual routine, teaching Mirella about Conrad of Swabia and Orlando about Napoleon.[37]

New Year opened with various ailments. He had severe backaches, which were alleviated in February by a change of mattress, and a sore knee bruised in a fall. The behaviour of his gas system was an additional irritation. He used an 'Agipgas' *bombola* for his stove and a 'Liquigas' cylinder for the kitchen, both of which invariably ran out at inopportune moments. One evening in February, in the middle of translating Goethe to Orlando, the Agipgas ran out when it was too late to buy a new one. Lampedusa's diary for the next day is largely taken up by the arrival of the new *bombola* followed by the discovery that the Liquigas was also exhausted. The following week he and his wife were nearly asphixiated by the Agipgas: although Licy was panting breathlessly and he had collapsed and hurt his leg, they just managed to force open the window. Two days later, this 'dangerous *bombola*' (as he called it) ran out and he was able to order a new one. But the gas stove, noisy and evil-smelling at the best of times, was now malfunctioning with any *bombola*. In early March Licy fainted from the fumes of this 'pernicious stove' and several other people felt ill.[38]

Lampedusa continued his teaching: Austerlitz and Wagram and then back to Goethe for Orlando; Spanish texts for Gioacchino, Guelphs, Ghibellines and Joan of Arc for Mirella, and *Cymbeline* for them both together. On some evenings he went out to listen to music, Bach records on a friend's gramophone or a delightful concert of religious music by Mozart. In February he went to the Teatro Massimo to see *Die Meistersinger*, but this was no more successful than his previous visit to a Wagnerian opera the year before. Whereas *Parsifal* had been 'too long and, on the whole badly directed', *Die Meistersinger* was 'poorly performed' and the directing 'feeble'. Yet in spite of all the references to lessons, cinemas and music, Lampedusa's 1956 diary reveals that he was concentrating on his novel and determined to finish it soon. At the end of February there is evidence that it was hard going – 'I am struggling with Salina'; 'I am labouring with the prince' – but in early March he triumphed. On the 8th, he noted, his *'Histoire sans nom'* was finished.[39]

When Francesco Orlando arrived for his lesson that same day, Lampedusa 'with an impenetrable smile' handed him an exercise book and asked him to start reading it. Francesco, who had no idea that the novel was being written, read the first chapter aloud and then repeated it to a group of people in Bebbuzzo Lo Monaco's house. Having kept the project a secret for some time, Lampedusa was now anxious for people to know about it. On 17 March, instead of reading Goethe to Francesco and Góngora to Gioacchino, they read his novel. One evening he even read the first chapter to Lila Iljascenko who, he noted in his diary, did not understand a word of it.[40]

After Lampedusa had read him the third or fourth chapter, Francesco offered to type out the manuscript. The prince gratefully agreed but thought it would be easier for him to dictate it. That summer he used to take his pupil out to lunch and afterwards, when the employees had gone home for a meal and a siesta, they went to the legal office of Francesco's father and used a typewriter. Later Francesco recalled the great heat of those early afternoons in high summer, Lampedusa sitting in an armchair in grey or tobacco-coloured shirts, smoking and perspiring as he dictated.[41] The chronology of the dictation is confusing because Lampedusa added a lot to the earlier chapters and wrote the last couple before the two preceding ones. A typescript of four chapters was impetuously despatched to a publisher at the end of May, but almost immediately Lampedusa realized he wished to add to it. He went back to the Donnafugata section and added so much material that it became three chapters. He then returned to the heat of the lawyer's office and dictated them to Francesco. Not until 23 August, he recorded in his diary, was the task finished.

By now a considerable number of people had read or listened to a reading of *The Leopard*. Apart from Licy, Lucio, Gioacchino and Francesco, these included the historians Corrado Fatta and Virgilio Titone, Francesco Agnello, Enrico Merlo and Gioacchino's brother Giuseppe. Everyone seemed impressed but no one was sure whether it could be published. Francesco Orlando found it beautiful and humorous but thought it unsuitable for publication in the 'neo-realist' climate prevailing in Italian literature at that time.[42] Unsure about how it might be judged by the literati, Lampedusa's other friends were reticent about advice. Only Licy was absolutely convinced of its quality.[43]

Lampedusa himself was reasonably sure of the book's worth, though lack of enthusiasm from publishers later instilled some doubts. He had reservations about certain passages and seems to have been disappointed that the writing had turned out to be explicit rather that subtle and *magro* like Stendhal's. But in letters to his old friend Guido Lajolo, who had been living in Brazil for a quarter of a century, he seemed confident and even complacent about the book's merits. This correspondence contains several inaccuracies, including the claim that a publisher had accepted his novel for publication, but it probably does state his own opinion of his writing. The book, he told Lajolo, was 'ironic, bitter and not lacking in malice'. It was necessary 'to read it with great attention because every word is weighted and every episode has a hidden sense'. There were many personal recollections and the descriptions of some of the places were 'absolutely authentic'. All things considered, it was 'not too badly written' and some phrases, he announced, had already become 'proverbial' among the few people who had read it.[44]

10

Vocation and Commitment

In May 1956 Lampedusa's novel was sent to the Milanese publishers Mondadori. The '*Histoire sans nom*' at last had a name, *Il Gattopardo*,* but it still lacked half its chapters; only the first two and the last couple were sent at this stage. They were accompanied by a letter from Lucio Piccolo, who knew an editor at the publishing house, in which he described them curiously as 'a cycle of short stories'. 'On reading them,' he added, 'it seemed to me that they might have a certain interest as they present not without vividness an aspect of the Sicilian past, which though not distant has something legendary about it, seen from inside an aristocracy faced by problems it did not suspect...'[2]

During the summer Lampedusa added two Donnafugata chapters, containing some of the most important passages in the book, and in October Lucio sent these to the editor, Federico Federici, asking him to insert them as chapters three and four in

---

*A *gattopardo* is not in fact a leopard in Italian. It can mean either an ocelot, a cat found in central and southern America, or a serval, another member of the cat family, which lives in Africa south of the Sahara. It is unlikely, though, that the author had either of these creatures in mind when he was thinking of an animal to represent the prince. His family's coat of arms contained a leopard, which people at Torretta used to refer to as a '*gattupardu*' in the local dialect, and the title presumably derives from this circumstance.[1] Lampedusa certainly envisaged Don Fabrizio as a proud and massive leopard rather than one of the more meagre cats, but probably thought *Il Leopardo* was an inferior title to *Il Gattopardo*.

The choice caused much perplexity among the book's translators. The English and Germans played safe with *The Leopard* and *Der Leopard*, but the Dutch and French went for entirely different animals: the French chose *Le Guépard* (a cheetah) while the Dutch selected *De Tijger Kat*, a margay or tiger cat, which looks like an ocelot but has a longer tail.

the original typescript. In his previous reply Federici had warned
Lucio that there would be a long delay before the publishers
could make a decision and now he apologized for the 'extreme
slowness' with which they functioned. Not until 10 December,
when Federici was on holiday, did Mondadori reply, announcing
'with intense regret' that they had turned down *Il Gattopardo*.
'The book has interested us a lot, and has had more than one
reading. Nevertheless, the opinions of our advisers, though
favourable, were not without reservations, and for that reason,
bearing in mind our current burdensome commitments, we have
come to the decision that it is not possible for us to publish the
book...'[3]

Lucio brought the letter of rejection to Lampedusa at Bebbuzzo's house in Palermo. Gioacchino noticed that the prince was
disappointed although, typically, he did not show it.[4]* Licy noted
bitterly in her diary, *'Refus de ce cochon de Mondadori'*.[6]

Lucio was puzzled by the rejection and in January 1957 he
wrote to Basilio Reale, a young Sicilian friend living in Milan,
requesting more information. Mondadori, he said, had alluded to
the work's merit and to 'some reservations of its readers' which
had left him with 'extreme curiosity' to know more. Reale replied
that negative judgements of three readers had been submitted to
Elio Vittorini, the Sicilian novelist working as a consultant for
Mondadori, who had subsequently noted down that the text,
though worthy, lacked unity and completeness. Nevertheless,
Vittorini had advised the publishers to suggest that the author
should revise the novel before sending it back ·to them.
Mondadori accepted the advice about not publishing the book as
it stood but not the recommendation that they should consider a
revised version.[7]

This episode has led to accusations that Lucio falsified· the
contents of Mondadori's letter and that he was secretly pleased
about *Il Gattopardo*'s rejection. The first, by a writer who had not
seen the rejection letter, is untrue.[8] The second, made by Reale
himself, seems to be an exaggeration. It may be true that Lucio

---

*It was probably because Lampedusa had been so sure of Mondadori's
acceptance that he had written to Lajolo the previous summer to say that the
publishers had already sent him a contract. After the rejection he told Lajolo
that Mondadori were making 'a heap of difficulties' and he was therefore
sending the typescript to other publishers.[5]

was 'maliciously curious' about the reasons for Mondadori's rejection, but it is unlikely that he had hoped the book would be turned down. Perhaps there was an ambivalence in Lucio's attitude which may have been close to love-hate (though Lampedusa was probably unaware of it).[9] Certainly Lucio later became jealous of Lampedusa's posthumous reputation (the writer Leonardo Sciascia sympathized with Lucio's feeling that Lampedusa ought to be known as Piccolo's cousin instead of Lucio always being referred to as Lampedusa's cousin).[10] But although they were rivals and had scoffed at each other for forty years, Lucio cannot have wanted his cousin to fail completely.

A few days after receiving Mondadori's rejection, Lampedusa adopted Gioacchino Lanza as his son. For many years he had been thinking of adoption as a means of preserving the family name and titles.* His first choice had probably been Giuseppe, the son of his uncle Francesco and the only first cousin on his father's side. But Giuseppe had died young in 1945 and Lampedusa next considered a more distant cousin, Alvaro Caravita, whose father had inherited much of the Lampedusa wealth in the 1920s.** At some time, probably around 1950, Francesco Caravita took his wife and son to Palermo to meet the Lampedusas. The visit was not a success. To his mother's dismay, the boy was offered chocolate by Licy which had become bleached with age. 'You think I should allow my son to be adopted by people who give sweets like that?' she hissed afterwards to her husband. 'Because of my usual cowardly love of peace,' Caravita recorded later, 'I let the matter drop.'[12]

Although there might have been a certain historical aptness in the adoption of Alvaro Caravita, it would have been done merely for dynastic reasons. Gioacchino's adoption, on the other hand, was a more sentimental matter for Lampedusa because he

---

*Noble titles had officially been abolished after the establishment of the Republic in 1946, but many people continued – and continue today – to use them. In fact titles seem to have proliferated since their abolition: according to Luigi Barzini, writing in the late sixties, there were then about ten times as many titles in use as there had been during the monarchy.[11]

**Francesco Caravita di Sirignano was the heir of Stella Caravita e Tomasi, daughter-in-law of the astronomer, who had received the inheritance of four of Prince Giulio's children (Concetta, Carolina, Caterina and her own husband Francesco Paolo) and a half share in a fifth (Filomeno).

already thought of him as the son that he had not been able to have. Writing to a friend, he even pointed out that Gioacchino was 'exactly the same age as our first child would have been, had there been one'. Furthermore, he added, Gioacchino was very like himself, with both his merits and his defects: 'He is sarcastic and indolent, has a vivid curiosity for intellectual matters, is full of spirit, has much superficial malice and a good deal of fundamental kindness. Besides, more than with me, one can see a mile off that he is a "gentleman". In short my wife and I are mad about him.'[13]

This affection for Gioacchino was extended to his fiancée Mirella who, coming from a difficult and unstable family background, really did need adoptive parents.* For the Lampedusas the young couple managed to combine the attributes of friends, pupils and children. 'The good that these two young ones have done for us,' the prince told a friend, 'is inestimable. We are getting a bit old and wizened, and the constant presence of these two fine twenty-year-olds has rejuvenated us.'[15] During his last years he saw them nearly every day, at the Mazzara or the Via Butera or for a meal in a restaurant. His diary records these meetings followed by affectionate comments in English: 'Mazzara – Giò [as he used to call him] and Mirella, "Both charming",' and that evening, 'Giò, Mirella and Licy to the pizzeria, "Delightful people".' Sometimes Gioacchino's name is followed by the words 'more charming than ever', occasionally abbreviated to 'm c t e'. When Giò went away or failed to turn up, Lampedusa was despondent. 'Sorrowful glimpse', he wrote in English in his diary one evening after putting him on the train to Venice. On one occasion, when Giò did not arrive punctually at the Via Butera, the older man was so upset that he went out and took a bus all the way to the end of the line; when he finally returned home, he found that Gioacchino had been waiting there for hours.[16]

After he had decided to adopt Giò, Lampedusa hoped to

---

*The Lampedusas' treatment of Mirella Radice was a more loving and caring version of Professor Higgins's programme for Eliza Doolittle in *Pygmalion*: 'By now her manners are perfect,' wrote Lampedusa in January 1957. 'As for culture, she has three weekly lessons of French, two of English and two of history, given by my wife. As she is intelligent she is making progress and, by the time she marries, she will be ready.'[14]

persuade the Piccolos to adopt Mirella, a scheme which would
have served the interests of Capo d'Orlando much better than
Lucio's quest to beget an heir. He was confident of success, he
wrote to Guido Lajolo, because the Piccolos had been
'conquered by the aristocratic charm of Gioacchino and by the
extraordinary beauty of' Mirella. But the project came to
nothing, perhaps because of Lucio's ambivalent feelings for his
cousin, perhaps because his sister Giovanna was not entirely
'conquered' by the couple's attractions. She was 'an old spinster',
Lampedusa told Lajolo, 'more rigid than ever in her moral
principles. She keeps to the old rule that engaged couples must
not sleep under the same roof; so when we are there poor Giò has
to get in his car at midnight and drive off to sleep in the nearest
hotel which is thirteen kilometres away!'[17]

The diaries of both Lampedusas record that on 15 January
1956, at Renato's restaurant, Licy suggested that her husband
should adopt Gioacchino. Giuseppe was enthusiastic about the
idea and so was Giò. A potential obstacle was the boy's family
because Gioacchino's parents and brothers were living happily in
the Mazzarino palace and found the plan bizarre. But in the end
they did not object. In May Licy noted that Conchita (his mother)
was happy about it while Lampedusa recorded 'Fabrizio
Mazzarino's unexpected enthusiasm'.[18] In August the adoption
documents were organized and by the end of the year the
arrangements were finished. Shortly before the adoption
Lampedusa put in an unusual appearance at the Bellini club – 'a
lunch of unspeakable boredom' – to assist Gioacchino's election
as a member. Three days before Christmas the ceremony took
place, a simple affair in a lawyer's office followed by champagne
at the Via Butera. Licy gave Giò a gold watch and Lampedusa
handed him a box of visiting cards bearing the title 'Duke of
Palma'. In the evening the Lanza family gave a large cocktail
party in the Mazzarino palace at which Mirella appeared.
Gioacchino's parents had originally opposed the marriage but
now she was presented as his fiancée, 'her brilliance', reported
Lampedusa, 'overwhelming all the other girls who stood around,
jealous but subdued'.[19]

The Christmas of 1956 was celebrated, as usual, by Licy's
rendering of Russian carols. A panettone was delivered to their
house as a Christmas cake and its arrival gave Lampedusa an

idea. 'I want to write something about this,' he told his wife; 'a short story about a panettone.'[20] He may have been disappointed by Mondadori's rejection, but it did not prevent him from writing. He had at last discovered his vocation and was determined to write as much as he could. The story about the panettone, *'La Gioia e la Legge'* ('Joy and the Law') was written in a few days over Christmas. It was unlike anything else he ever wrote, a sad and compassionate tale about a poor clerk and his family in Palermo. There seem to be traces of auto-biography in the bus-ride ('through streets where rustic baroque fronts hid a wretched hinterland which emerged at each street corner in the yellow light of eighty-year-old shops'), in the protagonist's clumsiness on the bus, and in the district he inhabits ('a decrepit street to which the bombardments of fifteen years previously had given the finishing touches'). But the other vicissitudes of the little clerk were entirely outside his own experience.

Girolamo is on his way home from the office with a huge panettone, weighing seven kilos, which he has been given as a reward for hard work. Neither the complaints on the bus nor the realization that the reward was 'an act of rather condescending pity from his fellow-employees' disturbs his happiness. He can only think of the delight of presenting his family with 'seven kilos of luxury food' when provisions in the household usually came in hectograms and half-litres. But when he gives her the cake, his wife Maria insists on sending it, despite Girolamo's objections, to a lawyer to whom they are under a minor obligation. The clerk then has to buy a smaller panettone for the children and after Christmas a third cake, 'which, disguised by slicing, he took to his colleagues who were teasing him because they hadn't been offered a morsel of the sumptuous trophy'. Meanwhile, Girolamo has received no acknowledgement of their gift and goes anxiously to the agency to make sure it has been delivered. 'Just after Twelfth Night a visiting card arrived "with sincerest thanks and best wishes". Honour was saved.'

It is a short and unambitious story about the hardships of lower-middle-class society in Sicily which are made harsher by the absurd code of honour with which people are forced to live. There is no reference to the Mafia or hint of violence but more pacific aspects of Sicilian corruption (patronage and exploitation) are handled with skill. So is the description of Girolamo's humiliation on the bus and his attempt to deal with it: when the clerk hears a three-syllabled word (*cornuto*) 'alluding to his presumed marital disgrace, his sense of honour compelled him to turn his head [towards the back of the bus] and make his exhausted eyes assume what he imagined to be a threatening expression'. Maria is also a well-drawn character: 'only the soul of a saint survived within her, inflexible and bereft of tenderness; deep-seated virtue expressing itself in rebukes and restrictions'.[21]

After '*La Gioia e la Legge*' Lampedusa wrote a second story that could hardly have been more different. Instead of focusing on a single banal incident of provincial life, 'Lighea' (translated into English as 'The Professor and the Siren') is a fable about death and immortality which spans the classical Mediterranean and the world of the twentieth century. The earlier tale, told with some of the simplicity of Verga, is reminiscent of the *verismo* ('realism') movement that had dominated southern literature two generations earlier. Nothing could be further from Verga than 'Lighea', its themes inspired by pagan mythology, its language allusive, complicated and lyrical. The writing is as beautiful as in *The Leopard*, particularly the descriptions of landscape and the Sicilian sea, and Lampedusa was justly proud of it. He was even persuaded by Gioacchino to read 'Lighea' aloud into a microphone; the tape, which records Lampedusa reading with great expression in a clear, rather high-pitched voice, still exists.[22]

The story deals with the relationship of two Sicilians, Paolo Corbera and Rosario La Ciura, living in Turin during the fascist period, and ends with La Ciura's revelations about his encounter with a siren fifty years earlier. Corbera is a young journalist who, after being deserted by his mistresses, spends his free time in a cafe in the Via Po, 'a kind of Hades peopled by bloodless shades of lieutenant colonels, magistrates and professors'. There he meets a cross, elderly gentleman who occupies the next-door table, constantly smoking and spitting during his reading of foreign magazines. On discovering that this is Rosario La Ciura, 'the must illustrious Hellenist' of his time and famed for his 'almost carnal sense of classical antiquity', Corbera tries to get to know him. The old professor, however, almost rebuffs him. Arrogant, rude, dismissive of his colleagues, contemptuous of Sicily ('a lovely land, though inhabited by donkeys'), he seems at first 'just an ordinary academic priest-baiter with a dash of Nietzschean fascism added'. But Corbera perseveres and eventually La Ciura warms to him. He remains dogmatic and patronizing but accepts that the young journalist, 'as happens with a few Sicilians of the better kind', has 'succeeded in achieving a synthesis between' his senses and his reason. He therefore decides to tell him the story of the siren.

Fifty years before, La Ciura had been lent a hut near Augusta where he could study for the competition to gain the chair in Greek literature at Pavia University. After some days of 'sun, solitude, nights spent beneath rotating stars, silence, sparse feeding [and the] study of remote subjects', he is surprised in his rowing boat by a girl emerging from the sea with a smile that 'expressed nothing but itself, that is an almost animal joy, an almost divine delight in existence'. She climbs aboard, the scales of blue and mother-of-pearl on her lower half revealing her as a siren.* La Ciura has already told Corbera that the story of Odysseus is untrue. It was 'all nonsense', 'petty-bourgeois poets' tales', that the sirens had flung themselves on the rocks after allowing their prey to elude them: 'no one ever escapes the sirens, and even if someone did they would never have died for so little'. Later he says: 'The song of the sirens does not exist, Corbera: the music from which there is no escaping is that of their voices.'

The siren declares herself to be Lighea, daughter of Calliope. 'Don't believe in the tales invented about us,' she pleads: 'we kill no one, we only love.' For three weeks she visits him and during that time La Ciura 'loved as much as a hundred ... Don Juans put together in their whole lives'. Yet it was a true and immortal love, 'quite the opposite of dreary animal lust' and immune to 'the rage of *commendatori* and the trivialities of Leporello'. Like *la Belle Dame sans Merci* of Keats's poem, she keeps him enthralled and, like the knight in his dream, he learns of all the lovers she has had during her 'millennial adolescence'. Lighea abandons him when her companions call her for the storm festival but, unlike Keats's

---

*The ancient Homeric sirens were in fact bird-women, similar to Egyptian harpies. Lampedusa's siren, however, had to be a mermaid and thus he accepted the creature's metamorphosis which, according to Norman Douglas, took place at about the time of Saint Augustine. In Italian the word *sirena* can be translated by either siren or mermaid, and Lampedusa himself translated Shakespeare's Mermaid Tavern as the *Taverna della Sirena*.[23]

lady, she leaves him hope. La Ciura's contentment in the modern world has been destroyed – 'she had shown me the way ... towards an asceticism derived not from renunciation but from an incapacity to accept other inferior pleasures' – but she has offered him the escape of death together with immortality. Fifty years later, he eventually accepts that offer, throwing himself from a ship steaming towards Naples. In his will he has left his books to Catania University; a recent codicil bequeaths a Greek vase with siren figures and a photograph of the Koré on the Acropolis to Corbera. But none of them survived. There is no money for shelves in the university and the books rot away in the cellars; meanwhile the vase has been smashed and the photograph burnt in the looting of Corbera's Palermo home during the Second World War.

The decay and destruction in the final paragraph are a deliberate contrast to the life-giving force of Lighea. 'I am everything,' she declares, 'because I am simply the current of life, with its detail eliminated; I am immortal because in me every death meets, from that of the fish [she has just eaten] to that of Zeus, and conjoined in me they turn again into a life that is no longer individual and determined but Pan's and so free.' Lampedusa's attitude towards death and immortality, one of the principal subjects of the story, will be discussed, together with Don Fabrizio's, in chapter twelve. Another major theme is the corruption of the classical Mediterranean world by subsequent history. Lighea may have been 'ignorant of all culture, unaware of all wisdom, contemptuous of any moral inhibitions, [but] she belonged, even so, to the fountainhead of all culture, of all wisdom, of all ethics, and could express this primigenial superiority of hers in terms of rugged beauty'. She was part of an ancient, innocent and, above all, vital world, the archaic Sicily of the first Greek colonists, the fertile, wooded and primeval island of the pagan deities. Lucio Piccolo would have endorsed this view of mythological Sicily as 'real' Sicily, 'nature's Sicily', its vocation 'that of serving as pasturage for the herds of the sun'. All this had been swept away, though, in the accumulating centuries of man's progress. *The Leopard* describes the decay of a noble family and the destruction of a certain society; 'Lighea' has a grander theme, the ruin of the Mediterranean and the classical world over more than two thousand years.

Both express a part of Lampedusa's view of history.

The author put much of himself into 'Lighea'. Like Paolo Corbera, he had been in Augusta as a recruit and in Turin as a young man; although not a professional journalist, he had written those three essays on literature for a Genoese review. Like Corbera, too, he was an aristocrat whose house had been destroyed by 'Liberators' in the Second World War. He also gave the character the same family name as Don Fabrizio in *The Leopard* and the same family situation as his own: 'I confessed myself to be indeed a Corbera di Salina, in fact the only surviving specimen of that family; all the splendours, all the sins, all the unexacted rents, all the unpaid bills, all the Leopard's ways in fact, were concentrated in me alone.' Rosario La Ciura shares many of the tastes and characteristics of his creator. If the dogmatism and irritability are more pronounced, they come from the same sources: a distaste for academics, a hatred of melodrama, a dislike of H.G. Wells (mainly for having written such a bad story about a siren), a contempt for the 'donkeys' who inhabit Sicily ('I imagine nothing good ever happens there, as it hasn't for three thousand years'). La Ciura even shares some of Lampedusa's enthusiasms. 'He examined my few books. "Good, good, maybe you're less ignorant than you seem. This man here," he added, taking up my Shakespeare, "this man here did understand something. 'A sea change into something rich, and strange.' 'What potions have I drunk of siren tears?'"'[24]*

The third short work Lampedusa wrote in the weeks after Christmas 1956 contains no autobiographical character. It is the first chapter of a novel he intended to call *I gattini ciechi* ('the blind kittens') and was probably written in March 1957. The first few pages describe the rise of the Ibba family, within the space of two generations, from illiterate share-croppers to large (but still uncivilized) landowners. They have gobbled up the estates of foolish nobles as well as ecclesiastical lands sold after the Risorgimento for a tenth of their value. The whole operation had been 'an epic of cunning and perfidy, of ruthlessness and defiance of law, of luck too and of daring'. Extortionate loans have been one of the principal weapons and violence the other. There had been some difficulty over a corpse which the Bourbons had inconveniently   investigated,   but   incriminating   papers

*Quotations from the first act of *The Tempest* and the 119th sonnet.

disappeared during Garibaldi's campaign and Gaspare Ibba was able to return home to enjoy his ill-gotten properties. These were subsequently extended with the same single-minded avarice by his son. For all his wealth though, Don Batassano Ibba remains ignorant, mean, brutal (he kicks his horse when it throws him) and vulgar (although he has a fine English saddle, he uses twisted ropes instead of stirrups). For Lampedusa there is nothing to be said in the Ibbas' favour: as E.M. Forster describes them in the preface of the English edition, 'they stumble blindly into a world which they cannot understand but are capable of damaging'.[25]

The scene changes to the aristocratic club in Palermo where a group of fatuous nobles is discussing the Ibba phenomenon with dogmatic ignorance. Their conversation is prefaced with some observations from the author on the upper classes of those days (1901), their 'frothy and infantile imaginations' and their 'low consumption of general ideas'. But their silly talk with its absurd exaggerations is 'anything but comic': it is a pitiful spectacle, 'the tragic jerking of a class' a few minutes from oblivion. Among this group is Fabrizio Salina, the grandson of Don Fabrizio who appears briefly in *The Leopard* as the 'odious' Fabrizietto. On his deathbed Don Fabrizio had reflected that the Salina heirlooms – the tapestries, the almond groves, even the fountain of Amphitrite – 'might suffer a grotesque metamorphosis [when Fabrizietto succeeds him] from the age-old muted things they had been into pots of quickly-swallowed *foie gras*, or can-can girls transient as their own rouge'. In *I gattini ciechi*, placed eighteen years after the old prince's death, Lampedusa seems to confirm this prediction with references to Fabrizietto's most treasured dishes at Prunier's and the Pré-Catelan. Whether or not these were the favourite Parisian restaurants of Lampedusa's own father, it seems clear that Fabrizietto is partly based on Don Giulio just as Paolo resembles Lampedusa's grandfather and the astronomer is taken from his great-grandfather. In short, *I gattini ciechi* suggests little piety on Lampedusa's part for his father, his father's family or the society in which he was brought up.

The central figures in the novel, however, were intended to be the Ibbas: Lampedusa planned to describe their future rise to the ranks of the minor nobility and their decline shortly afterwards, when land reforms following the Second World War reduced their so greedily accumulated estates. The theme, based on the family history of a friend (who did not find it funny),[26] is a meagre one compared to those which animated *The Leopard* or 'Lighea'. Although it is difficult to judge the quality of a novel from the first chapter, it seems unlikely that *I gattini ciechi* would have been in the same class as its predecessor. One of the problems was that it had no character Lampedusa could identify with, a protagonist of the intelligence or sensibility of La Ciura or Don Fabrizio. The first chapter, wholly devoid of any human sympathy whatever, is written in an irritable and almost cantankerous style: it reads like the overture to a novel in which the Ibbas and the nobles would merely compete as targets for Lampedusa's unceasing sarcasm.

The early months of 1957 were the most productive of Lampedusa's life. He wrote not only the two stories and the opening of *I gattini ciechi*, but also two further chapters of *The Leopard* and a new draft of the whole novel. Further attempts were made to find a publisher and an anonymous copy of the typescript was sent to Benedetto Croce's daughter, Elena, who worked as a literary agent. She does not seem to have read it at this stage, however, and did not bother to reply. Another copy was read by Flaccovio, the Palermitan bookseller and publisher, who could not accept it himself because he did not publish fiction. In March, though, he sent the typescript to Vittorini, who was a director of Einaudi as well as an adviser for Mondadori, suggesting that the novel might be published in Einaudi's series '*I Gettoni*'. The accompanying letter from Flaccovio was sensible and understanding of the book's merits, but directed to a wholly inappropriate person. It is astonishing that Flaccovio, who worked in the literary world, should have considered Vittorini as a suitable recipient for a novel like *The Leopard*. Presumably he felt that the Einaudi director, as a Sicilian, would welcome a novel about Sicily, but anyone with the slightest knowledge of Vittorini's own writing should have anticipated his reaction. A man who saw himself as a moulder of post-war Italian literature, a prophet of neo-realism and experiment, was bound to find *The Leopard* reactionary and regressive. If Lampedusa and Flaccovio were searching for a literary figure to promote the book, it is curious they did not think of Eugenio Montale, who had met the prince at San Pellegrino and who had been responsible for Lucio's success. Montale, who later became one of *The Leopard*'s foremost defenders, would certainly have recommended its publication.

Meanwhile, Lampedusa had been adding to his novel. The two new chapters, 'Father Pirrone Pays a Visit' (1861) and 'A Ball' (1862), eventually became chapters five and six. A further chapter, describing Don Fabrizio's passion for Angelica, was planned to go between 'A Ball' and 'Death of a Prince' (now dated 1883 instead of 1885), but Lampedusa abandoned it after a few pages.[27] He also had doubts, shared by Licy, about the chapter on Father Pirrone because it seemed an 'explicit' apology for aristocracy justified not by Don Fabrizio's behaviour but by the words of the priest.[28]

At the beginning of April 1957 Lampedusa read the two new chapters to Francesco Orlando and asked him to type them out. But Orlando, who had typed the rest of the novel, had various student commitments at that time and asked for a postponement.[29] In the meantime the prince had been writing a whole new draft of the novel, including chapters on Pirrone and the ball, which he gave Gioacchino before leaving for Rome in May. Entitled *Il Gattopardo* (*completo*), it was written in a large, hard-backed notebook in dark blue biro; the handwriting is tiny and barely legible, many of the words running into each other. The existence of this manuscript provoked an angry dispute many years later between those who felt that this was the authentic text of *Il Gattopardo* and those who preferred Orlando's typescript (plus the extra chapters).[30] The differences between the two versions have a certain scholarly interest but they are not really important. As Gioacchino Lanza pointed out, there are hundreds of variations but all except thirty are trivial, minute changes such as *Don Fabrizio* for *il Principe* or vice versa.[31] And even those thirty are of limited importance. Two of the most significant changes are descriptive passages of a few lines: the typescript's list of various items from Don Fabrizio's bathroom, such as his soap and his sponge, has been omitted in the manuscript; and later on, the hand-written version gains a few lines in the description of the sadistic instruments found in the abandoned rooms at Donnafugata.

11

Death and Redemption

In November 1950 Lampedusa had written to his wife, who was in Rome, to tell her of a dream he had had the previous night at Capo d'Orlando. In his dream he had received a postcard announcing the hour of his execution at a barracks in Rome. So he said farewell to his parents, went to the barracks and told some soldiers that he was a condemned man who had come for his execution. They told him to wait in the corridor, so he waited for a while by himself. Then he noticed there was no one else about, realized it was pointless to stay there, and decided to escape. He descended the staircase, went out into the streets and after a long time found his father in a nightclub weeping over a bottle of champagne. He told him to inform his mother that he had escaped and then went out again, wandering through further streets until finally he arrived outside the gates of the Villa Giulia, the public gardens in Palermo where he used to play as a child.[1]

Licy specialized in the interpretation of dreams, but her husband does not appear to have written her a description of his own before. He had no desire to become one of her patients and used to joke about the impossibility of a man being psychoanalysed by his wife. But this dream, with its premonition of death, worried him and he decided to tell her about it. Later it seems to have become a recurring nightmare: several years afterwards Francesco Orlando was told of that persistent dream in which Lampedusa 'hung around the corridors of a ministry searching for the office where he would learn the date and hour of his execution'.[2]

Lampedusa had felt old some time before his sixtieth birthday.

At the age of fifty-eight he noted that his old age had begun, but even before then he had given the impression of a man much older than his years, an ill, tired, melancholic figure waiting for death. Gioacchino Lanza was eighteen when he came to know Lampedusa in 1952, but he realized even then that the older man 'found no enjoyment in life, that he was one of the defeated'.[3] The prince himself had no illusions about the impression he gave others. Orlando heard him on the telephone arranging a meeting with someone he did not know: 'You will see an old fat man at a table ...'[4] To the feeling of old age were added various ailments (emphysema, bronchitis, rheumatic pains and an operation on his nose) and repeated depressions. On two consecutive days at the beginning of 1955 he wrote in his diary the words, 'painful midday grief'. A year later he noted 'a clear feeling at home in the evening of not being able to go on. It will pass this time perhaps. But one time or another it won't go away.'[5] Later still, he confessed to Orlando 'in a phrase of the last months, brief, almost whispered, and tragic: "I can't struggle on"'.[6]

His pupil later recalled that towards the end Lampedusa 'emanated a sense of death'.[7] Describing the Palazzo Lampedusa in 1955, he had remarked that in that house he had been 'glad to feel a certainty of dying'. But like his fictional counterparts, Don Fabrizio and La Ciura, his attitude towards death was ambivalent. Before he started writing, his own view may have been even bleaker. Between them his protagonists shared the universe and the classics, and he had nothing beyond his interest in literature and history. But that late discovery of his vocation, as real and as profound as theirs, changed everything. '*The Leopard* was a preparation for a good death,' said Gioacchino many years afterwards, because it was 'a reconciliation between life and death'.[8] It gave him a purpose in living and therefore a reason to delay dying. His diaries and Orlando's memoir might sometimes suggest a slope of increasing depression, but in fact Lampedusa was less ready to die in 1957 than he had been in 1954. *The Leopard*, written throughout 1955, is a more pessimistic work than 'Lighea', which he composed a few months before his death. The tragedy of Lampedusa was the coincidence of his physical decadence with his brief period of artistic creativity.

The first indication that something was seriously wrong with his health came at the end of April 1957 when he was staying at Capo d'Orlando. One day the prince spat so much blood that he could no longer pretend it was caused by bronchitis. He thought at first that he might have tuberculosis and went to see Professor Aldo Turchetti, a leading medical figure in Palermo, for an examination. Towards the end of May Gioacchino went to Turchetti for the report and learnt that his adoptive father had lung cancer. The professor did not think there was much chance of a cure but suggested Lampedusa should consult an expert in thoracic surgery in Rome. To persuade him to go, Gioacchino decided to tell him the truth about his disease. Lampedusa's morale collapsed. He could suffer physical pain without much complaint, but when he knew he was likely to die, he lost the will to live. 'As soon as he knew the facts,' recalled Gioacchino, 'he felt much worse.'[9]

On 29 May Lampedusa left for Rome with his wife, and a few days later he moved into a clinic in Via di Trasone. On 4 June a light-hearted letter from Gioacchino and Mirella, recounting various 'motoring adventures', reached him. 'We read it together,' he wrote in his reply the following day, 'and were much amused (Licy needs very much to be amused because she is extremely depressed).' 'Amid this atmosphere of sadness, among all these doctors, these nuns, these nurses, these radiographs and these dangers, your voices reached me as those of youth and affection'. He described his X-rays and examination, and reported that Turchetti's diagnosis had been confirmed. It was necessary, however, to wait for his bronchitis to subside before the specialists 'could examine the right lung and see what really is the "problem"'. His personal view was that they would not operate but attempt a cure of 'cobalt bombs' which would be very long and boring. Licy came to see him twice a day, and her sister Lolette and his uncle Pietro also visited. There was nothing to do but read, 'yawn ceaselessly' and wait; the days were 'tedious and monotonous', without even the satisfaction of a cigarette as he had at last been made to give up smoking.[10]

The specialists did indeed decide against an operation, partly because of the persistent bronchitis and partly because the tumour on his lung, they said, was too small and recent to risk a complicated operation. In the meantime they recommended the course of 'cobalt bombs' followed by a month's rest. Afterwards he should return to Rome for Professor Valdoni to judge whether an operation was necessary. For the cobalt treatment Lampedusa was transferred to another clinic, the Villa Angela on the banks of the Tiber, which was just as boring but the food was better. The treatment was quick and painless and the equipment impressed him. By 20 June he was relatively optimistic: he was feeling less weak, he no longer coughed, and his bronchitis had almost disappeared. There would not be much to complain about, he wrote to Mirella, if he had not been so 'mortally bored'. In a letter to his Piccolo cousins he complained particularly about the nights: the intense heat and the prohibition on his smoking made it impossible to sleep. In the daytime there were visitors, including Gioacchino who came to Rome for three days and Corrado Fatta, but he was looking forward to moving to Lolette's apartment and going to the clinic daily for treatment.[11] He was also looking ahead to his month's rest. It would be wonderful, he told the Piccolos,

> to be able to send you a telegram one fine day saying, 'I will arrive on such and such a day at such and such an hour'. How lovely it would be to be able to do it (for me at least)! Let's make the young ones [Gioacchino and Mirella] come and spend some time together as in the old days before I return here for the operation.

In a letter to Mirella the following day he spoke of staying for half of his rest period at Capo d'Orlando; the remaining days, he announced surprisingly, would be spent between Bologna, Milan and Turin.[12]

A week later he was once again writing of his plans to visit Capo d'Orlando. 'It would be lovely,' he wrote to the Piccolos, 'to arrive by wagon-lit at seven in the morning, to put myself to bed in the spare room, to sleep until nine and to wake up with the illusion that nothing has happened, that everything is as it used to be'. He was still optimistic and feeling better. Giving up smoking had helped his emphysema and antibiotics had cured his bronchitis. No one seemed to know much about the state of his tumour but he felt that the treatment was going well: early each evening he was taken for his 'cobalt bombs' wearing a blue and red silk dressing-gown which Licy had given him for the occasion.

One cause for worry was his loss of weight accompanied by his lack of appetite; he felt like taking nothing but milk and tinned fruit. Writing to Mirella on 28 June, however, he said that the situation was improving and that his weight had recently increased from 79 kilos (nearly four stone less than his usual weight) to 84 kilos.[13]

His regular visitors were Licy, Lolette and Pietro della Torretta. Licy was exhausted and 'unrecognizable', he told Mirella, staying with him all day and once returning at two in the morning to make sure he was all right. Lolette brought him 'books, sweets and other trifles' and uncle Pietro arrived 'daily in his most elegant summer clothes, demonstrating an unexpected affection'. There were frequent letters from Gioacchino and Mirella and an 'affectionate postcard' from Lucio. He was particularly pleased with a 'dear, loving and witty letter' from Mirella which he answered partly in English.

> I am very pleased reading of the good progress of your relations with Giò's parents. Very pleased but not at all surprised; relating to this I have always had the strongest certitude of a final good settlement. A girl as uncommonly handsome, as uncommonly nice and as uncommonly good as you are, is sure to achieve in the long run success in this which is the simplest of the problems she will have to face.[14]

Lampedusa had been looking forward to staying at the Biancheris' apartment in the Piazza d'Indipendenza, 'eating at their table, going for short walks', and no longer feeling 'imprisoned all day' at the clinic.[15] But soon after he arrived there, at the beginning of July, his condition worsened. The cobalt treatment, which had begun to have harmful side-effects, was halted on the 12th, but by then he seems to have realized that it was after all only a palliative, offering a retardation rather than a cure.[16] Whether or not the specialists had deceived him over the extent of the cancer to begin with, it was now expanding rapidly beyond his lungs. On the final day of his cobalt treatment he spoke to Gioacchino on the telephone and then wrote him a letter: he was becoming weaker every day, he admitted, and was finding it increasingly difficult to write.[17]

During his final weeks the sick man was able to do some work. He had brought with him the manuscripts of 'Lighea' and a chapter of *The Leopard* ('A Ball'), which Licy and Lolette typed out under his direction. Tragically, Elio Vittorini chose this moment to reject the novel for the second time: his explanatory letter, written in Milan on 2 July, reached Rome via Palermo on the 17th or 18th. Lampedusa was bitter and visibly disappointed, but he was able to read out the rejection note with his customary irony during a meal at the Biancheris'.[18] Vittorini had found the novel 'very serious and honest', he read, although its tone and language were 'rather old-fashioned': its principal problem, though, was that it was 'essayish' and unbalanced. Vittorini then gave some examples of its essayishness and ended by saying that he could accept no more novels for Einaudi's *'Gettoni'* series for at least four years.[19] When Gioacchino arrived three days later, Lampedusa told him about it. 'As a review it's not bad,' he commented laconically, 'but publication no.'[20]

It is difficult to know when Lampedusa realized he was going to die. If he had known in Palermo when he learnt about the disease, did he really think that the cobalt treatment in Rome could have reprieved him? Did the optimistic bulletins and the letters about Capo d'Orlando represent genuine belief, self-delusion or the intentional deception of his friends? Such speculation is perhaps useless. By early July he certainly knew the truth and no longer bothered to pretend. 'He was waiting for death,' recalled Gioacchino, and 'he carried on with the sadness of one who knows he has to die soon, preoccupied both with leaving his wife and with the publication of his novel.' In the last days he wrote letters for Licy and Gioacchino to read after his death. Among other things he wrote to his adopted son: 'I would be pleased if the novel were published, but not at my expense.'[21] In death Lampedusa retained his innate pride. He knew *The Leopard* deserved publication but he would not countenance the humiliation of having to pay for it.

On the morning of 22 July he had severe breathing troubles. These were alleviated during the course of the day, but the patient felt a presentiment that his end was not far away. The next morning his sister-in-law found him dead. Giuseppe di Lampedusa had died in his sleep in the early hours of 23 July 1957. He was sixty years old.

A requiem mass was held on 25 July at the nearby church of the Sacred Heart of Jesus. Then his remains were taken by train to Palermo where the funeral took place at the church of Sant'Antonino close to the station.[22] Afterwards he was buried in the family tomb at the Capuchin monastery on the outskirts of Palermo.

The following January a memorial mass was held for Giuseppe a few days before the marriage of Gioacchino and Mirella. Licy remained very upset about her husband's premature death, and when she read his last diaries she was dismayed to discover how sad he had been. In her own diary she quoted Drinkwater's poem 'Who were before Me':

Now grief is in my shadow, and it seems well enough
To be there with my fathers, where neither fear nor love
Can touch me more, nor spite of men, nor my own
    teasing blame,
While the slow mosses weave an end of my forgotten
    name.

On 3 March she was telephoned by a friend, Giorgio Giargia, with the unexpected news that Feltrinelli wanted to publish *The Leopard* as one of their *Contemporanei* titles. The novelist Giorgio Bassani, who directed the series, had been very taken by the novel and wished to visit Palermo to talk about it. 'If this had only happened a year ago,' sighed Licy in her diary, it would have done much to improve Giuseppe's morale. The following day she received a letter from Bassani. 'From the first page,' declared the novelist from Ferrara, 'I realized I had found myself before the work of a real writer. Reading further, I understood that this real writer was also a real poet.'[23]

Bassani had received the typescript from Elena Croce a few days before. She had been sent one of Orlando's copies over a year earlier, with Lampedusa's permission, by Giargia. The typescript was anonymous and for some time Elena Croce did not bother to do anything with it: apparently it sat for several months in the porter's office of the Republican Party's headquarters in Rome.[24] Finally she did read it and thought it might be suitable for Bassani's new project. When he asked who the author was, she said she didn't know, but she imagined the book had been written by an old Sicilian spinster.[25]

Bassani telephoned the intermediary, Giorgio Giargia, and learnt that the author was in fact the Sicilian prince he had met several years earlier with Lucio Piccolo at the literary congress at San Pellegrino. He then wrote his eulogy of the novel to the widow and later telephoned her to discuss it.* On saying he thought the book very good except for a part towards the end, Licy asked whether he would like a chapter on a ball. Of course, replied Bassani, a ball is always a good thing, but how could one get hold of such a chapter now? Licy said that one had been written shortly before her husband's death, but she didn't know whether it was in Rome with Lolette or whether she had it in Palermo. In the last days of March she searched Giuseppe's old room and the rest of the house in the Via Butera, and even asked Francesco Orlando's mother whether her son had taken it. Then a letter from Lolette arrived announcing that she had found the chapter in her apartment.[27] On hearing of its whereabouts, Bassani went round to the Piazza d'Indipendenza and took away the chapter which Lolette had typed out the previous July. To him it seemed much less well-written than the rest and he returned to Lolette and asked if he could see the original manuscript. On comparing the two together, he realized that the problem had not been Lampedusa's writing but his sister-in-law's typing: words had been missed out and the punctuation was non-existent. Bassani therefore corrected the typescript from the original and took it away to the typesetter.[28]

Feltrinelli and Bassani were in a great hurry to have the novel published. On the last day of March, four weeks after Licy had learnt that he wished to publish it, Bassani telephoned to say he wanted *The Leopard* to come out in six weeks' time. Afterwards she noted that she had forgotten to say anything about author's royalties. Unfortunately she subsequently neglected to take professional advice on the matter and the following month signed an extremely disadvantageous contract with Feltrinelli lasting twenty years. The novel which was about to become the first

---

*Bassani's recollections of his communications with Licy conflict at several points with the evidence of her diary. Although he is in general a more reliable source than the princess, I have preferred Licy's testimony on the disputed matters because she was, after all, recording them daily while he was trying to remember them a dozen years later.[26]

'best-seller' in Italian literary history thus produced little material benefit to its author's family.

After sending the typescript and the chapter on the ball to the printer's, Bassani wondered whether there might not be further chapters lurking in unexpected places. He telephoned Licy to ask if there was a manuscript of the whole novel and she sounded so uncertain that he decided to go to Palermo to investigate. On arriving at the beginning of May, however, she told him she had searched the house and found nothing. Then they went to have coffee with Gioacchino at the Palazzo Mazzarino and Bassani remarked that it was a pity they could not find the manuscript. 'But I have the manuscript,' replied Gioacchino, and he went away to fetch the large notebook the prince had given him before his final journey to Rome. Bassani quickly leafed through its pages and saw that it did indeed contain an additional chapter, Father Pirrone's holidays, about which Lampedusa himself had had doubts.

Besides obliging him to delay publication of *The Leopard*, the discovery caused Bassani two additional problems. Licy did not want him to include the Pirrone chapter in the novel, partly because she thought it would go more suitably with the stories in a subsequent volume, and partly because her husband had not much liked it. Bassani, on the other hand, 'found it essential to the structure of the novel. This sort of descent to Hell is a fundamental clue to understanding Fabrizio and Sicily.'[29] The ensuing row caused Licy considerable anguish. On 11 May she wrote a long letter to Bassani that crossed with his 'second letter about the "holiday" [chapter] which he has unfortunately found in the manuscript Giuseppe gave to Giò'. Three days later, she drafted a long reply to Bassani, refusing him permission to publish the chapter, and then followed this with another letter on the 18th. By now poor Licy was in a terrible state, frantic and unable to sleep. Her diary entry for the 16th, written most unusually in Russian, reflects her despair: her feelings were cold and indifferent, she noted, and nothing seemed to matter any more; she was no longer excited about the book, and she was fed up with struggling against Bassani.[30] In the end she lost the argument, probably on the strength of Lampedusa's inclusion of the chapter in the 'complete' manuscript, but Licy recovered sufficiently to be able to read the proofs at the beginning of June.

Bassani's second problem was to decide whether to publish the typescript or the manuscript or a combination of the two texts. He and his secretary spent several weeks comparing both versions, each of them authoritative, and in the end decided on a synthesis. As he was not dealing with a classic requiring a critical edition, Bassani felt justified in examining the differences between the two texts and choosing whichever variant seemed better. When criticized ten years later for not having published the manuscript as it stood, he replied that he had merely done what the author would have had to do had he lived. Likewise, he had been forced to do something about Lampedusa's careless punctuation. Lampedusa was 'a great gentleman', he later said, who 'allowed himself to open a comma and not to close it. I have therefore closed all the commas.'[31]

In November 1958 the first edition of *The Leopard* was published in Milan. It was an exceptional novel, wrote Bassani in the preface, one of those works which required a lifetime's preparation. A fortnight later an enthusiastic review in *La Stampa* set the book on its path of extraordinary popularity. In July of the next year *The Leopard* won the Strega prize, Italy's leading award for fiction; by the following March, it had gone through fifty-two editions.

12

The Solitude of Don Fabrizio

During her long period of widowhood, the late Princess of Lampedusa used to insist that Don Fabrizio, the protagonist of *The Leopard*, was not an autobiographical portrait of her husband. In tastes, habits and behaviour, she once stated, he was exactly the opposite of Giuseppe.[1] All the characters of the novel were imaginary, she pointed out, except for Don Fabrizio, who was a portrait of Lampedusa's great-grandfather, and his three daughters in the final chapter, who were the great-aunts her husband had known in his childhood. If, she warned one inquirer, she read yet again that *The Leopard* had been 'reduced to the level of a *roman à clef*', she would be forced to protest to the newspapers.[2]

Lampedusa's view, however, was rather different. In a letter to Guido Lajolo, written a few weeks after he had completed the first draft of the novel, he admitted that the Prince of Salina (Don Fabrizio) was based on his great-grandfather but added: 'friends who have read it say that the Prince of Salina bears an awful resemblance to myself'. In a further letter, two months later, he announced that 'basically the protagonist is myself and the character called Tancredi is my adopted son'. Perhaps the chapters he added in the summer of 1956 convinced him that he was writing disguised autobiography because a third letter to Lajolo contains an even stronger declaration: 'Don Fabrizio expresses my ideas completely, and his nephew Tancredi is, so far as appearance and habits are concerned, a portrait of Giò; as for his morals, however, Giò is fortunately very much better than him.'[3]*

---

*These explanations are corroborated by a 'Who's Who' table of characters

Lampedusa's claims are more justifiable than Licy's, but in fact both exaggerated, as did many critics who insisted that *The Leopard* must be either an historical novel or an autobiographical work without considering that it might have been a combination of the two. Don Fabrizio and Tancredi both owe much to historical figures, Prince Giulio di Lampedusa and his nephew Corrado Valguarnera di Niscemi. They are not portraits of either of these people, because the author did not know enough about the character and personality of his relations, but some of their actions and the historical circumstances that guided them are the same. The problems of Don Fabrizio's mind may have been those which tormented Lampedusa, but his political problems, his interests and much of his property belong to Prince Giulio. Tancredi's charm and sense of humour were Gioacchino's, and the relationship he has with Don Fabrizio resembled that between the writer and his adopted son: when Lampedusa relates Salina's inability to become angry with Tancredi or the impossibility of being bored in his company, he is in fact describing his own attitude towards Gioacchino. But the conditions of the period which inspired Tancredi's behaviour are those which governed Corrado Valguarnera and his friends.

Before beginning his own book, Lampedusa read many works about Garibaldi's 'Thousand' in Sicily, one of them being the published journal of Francesco Brancaccio di Carpino, *Tre mesi nella Vicaria di Palermo nel 1860.*[4] Brancaccio was a friend of Valguarnera and his diaries record the frivolous and often ludicrous behaviour of those young Sicilian aristocrats who, like Tancredi, joined Garibaldi. Their lives before 1860 consisted largely of balls, fencing, horseplay and practical jokes: 'We did not bother much about politics and thought of nothing but enjoying life and amusing ourselves.' Then they became ballroom conspirators, plotting for the fun of it, rolling cartridges between waltzes, talking about liberty yet understanding nothing about political or social issues. While they were campaigning with Garibaldi, Brancaccio and his friends 'every night enjoyed a pillow fight for half-an-hour or so before going to sleep', and their absurd behaviour even managed to provoke a riot within the Türr division.[5]

enclosed with one of Orlando's typescripts sent by Lampedusa to his friend, Baron Enrico Merlo.

Tancredi is not Brancaccio nor Valguarnera (who was in fact a less ridiculous figure than his friends) nor Gioacchino, but a mixture of them with the addition of other characteristics invented by Lampedusa. Don Fabrizio's composition is more complicated. There are obvious similarities between him and Prince Giulio, notably their obsession with astronomy, but the author's great-grandfather seems to have been less of an autocrat than the Prince of Salina.* Fabrizio shares many of the traits of his creator, his sceptical intelligence, his intolerance, 'his mind, conditioned by long periods of solitude and abstract thought'. He shares many opinions, such as his pessimistic view of Sicily and Italian unity, and also various experiences, not of events but of feelings and attitudes. Don Fabrizio is more autobiography than invention but he is autobiography transformed into someone else, into the person the writer would have liked to have been. Lampedusa did not have Salina's arrogant confidence, his overt sensuality, his authority over others: the author's own personality, largely moulded by his mother, and his family's decadence, initiated by Prince Giulio, made him a very different person. Lampedusa shared the Leopard's ideas and reactions, had many of the inner thoughts and secret feelings, but his behaviour was that of a milder animal.

Don Fabrizio has 'an authoritarian temperament' transformed by 'the relaxing atmosphere of Palermo society ... into capricious arrogance'. Like his creator he is not interested in making money and too lazy to understand financial affairs. He has an aristocratic disdain 'about matters he considered low' and 'used to say that a house of which one knew every room wasn't worth living in'. He is both sceptical and fatalistic about the future, 'watching the ruin of his own class and his own inheritance without ever making, still less wanting to make, any move towards saving it'. When his accountant predicts that the Risorgimento will bring 'glorious new days for this Sicily of ours', Don Fabrizio remembers that 'these have been promised us on every single one of the thousand invasions we've had, by Nicias onwards, and they've never come'. Yet he is no reactionary, building Edens of the past. He is disgusted by the greed and lack of idealism of the liberal 'progressives', but he is not an apologist for the old order and the Bourbon monarchy. He ridicules much of the past and its

*See above p.12.

aristocratic survivors – 'the few hundred people who made up "the world" never tired of meeting each other ... to exchange congratulations on still existing' – but he also recognizes the good things that have gone. 'The wealth of centuries had been transmuted into ornament, luxury, pleasure; no more; the abolition of feudal rights had swept away duties with privileges.' Like Lampedusa, Don Fabrizio criticizes the past yet is himself so much a part of it that he has no illusions about the future. 'I belong to an unlucky generation, swung between the old world and the new, and I find myself ill at ease in both.'

Throughout the novel Don Fabrizio is swept by rapid gusts of sensuousness. On smelling a French rose, corrupted by Sicilian earth and the Sicilian climate, he 'seemed to be sniffing the thigh of a dancer from the Opera'; on standing before a fountain of Neptune embracing Amphitrite, he 'paused, gazed, remembered, regretted'. His moments of sensuality, however, are followed by sadness and self-disgust which fuel his 'perpetual discontent': brief moments of pleasure succeeded by long periods of reproach in continuous alternation, his rare moods of serenity disturbed by feelings of bitterness and melancholy.[6] Yet the cause of this sadness is not so much guilt as an awareness of the transience of feelings. Love never lasts – 'flames for a year, ashes for thirty' – and other feelings are even less durable. Just before dying the prince is 'making up a general balance sheet of his whole life, trying to sort out of the immense ash-heap of liabilities the golden flecks of happy moments'. Many of those flecks are no more than passing sensations, 'some moments of amorous passion', 'the exquisite feel of one or two fine silk cravats, the smell of some macerated leathers, the gay voluptuous air of a few women passed in the street'.

Fabrizio's boredom and pessimism are often relieved and then exacerbated by his sensuality. More lasting relief comes from his study of the stars, the reassurance of their permanence and reliability, the contrast with the vain and fickle preoccupations of the world. 'The soul of the prince reached out towards them, towards the intangible, the unattainable, which gives joy without laying claim to anything in return.' At the end of the ball, when as usual a brief period of happiness had been both preceded and succeeded by long, glum soliloquies, he decides to walk home.

The truth is that he wanted to draw a little comfort from gazing at the stars. There were still one or two up there, at the zenith. As always, seeing them revived him; they were distant, they were omnipotent and at the same time they were docile to his calculations; just the contrary to humans, always too near, so weak and yet so quarrelsome.

Astronomy is thus an antidote to life, a substitute in Salina's eyes for the new invention of morphia, a pastime that could 'produce serenity amid disaster'. It fulfils a similar purpose as La Ciura's classical studies and Lampedusa's own writing, providing a secret world separate from the problems of daily existence which, in the author's eyes, every civilized person needs.

In the balance sheet of Fabrizio's life, the 'many hours in the observatory, absorbed in abstract calculations and the pursuit of the unreachable', may weigh heavier than the 'amorous passion' and the brief earthly pleasures. Yet he doubts whether they should 'be really put down to the credit side of life. Were they not some sort of anticipatory gift of the beatitudes after death?' Nevertheless, they had existed for him and were a complete contrast to the rest of his life: eternity against a voluptuous moment, the immortal and incorruptible versus the corrupt and the dying. Yet the stars are not enough on their own because they satisfy only the demands of his intelligence. Sensuality and astronomy may contradict each other, but he cannot renounce one and abandon himself to the other. He is torn between the two, unable to compromise with either, finding only partial satisfaction with both.

Don Fabrizio has a family chaplain, whom he likes and to whom he confesses, and before dying he agrees to see a priest. But this is done from convention and tradition, not from religious belief. The prince swings from sybaritic pursuits to the contemplation of eternity without a personal God by whom he can regulate his ideas and his behaviour. He is a man in search of anchors for his life but he can find no anchor in the Church. The stars may provide anchorage of a sort – Venus 'always waiting for Don Fabrizio on his early-morning outings, at Donnafugata before a shoot, now after a ball' – but they have no equivalent on earth. He is reduced to clutching at old familiar things, searching for permanence in a world that is constantly changing.

Donnafugata is thus loved less for itself than for its 'sense of tradition and the perennial expressed in stone and water, of time congealed'. People, objects, institutions that he did not care for before become dear to him as they disappear. Among the uncertainties of 1860, he momentarily laments the Bourbons: 'Those Ferdinands, those Francises that had been so despised, seemed for a moment like elder brothers, trusting, just, affectionate, true kings.'

Behind the demeanour of the nineteenth-century prince, Fabrizio is a curiously modern figure, afflicted by problems which probably never disturbed his historical counterpart, Prince Giulio. The critics who dismissed *The Leopard* as an historical novel must have read it carelessly. Of course it says a good deal about Sicilian and Italian history, but it is primarily a contemporary novel about its protagonist's problems and anxieties, the problems of an outsider who has lost his way and can find no directions. The old certainties have gone, replaced by nothing substantial he can hold on to. During his dying confession he cannot even decide what were his real sins. He feels his whole life has been blameworthy rather than individual acts, and then wonders whether this consideration does not negate the whole notion of sin: 'The only real sin,' he reflects, 'is original sin.'*

Earlier in the novel Fabrizio compares the 'ghastly journey [to Donnafugata] with his own life, which had first moved over smiling level ground, then clambered up rocky mountains, slid over threatening passes, to emerge eventually into a landscape of interminable undulations, all the same colour, all bare as despair'. It could also serve as a description of Lampedusa's own life which one critic called a 'vain search for shade in a sun-parched desert'.[7] Yet if the passage is autobiographical, reflecting the writer's own disillusionment, it is also in a sense universal, expressing the alienation and restlessness of a person wandering aimlessly in a world without settled values. In a powerful essay Massimo Ganci made a similar point, comparing the 'irredeemable Sicily' of *The Leopard* to 'the sterility of modern

---

*These words appear in the final manuscript of the novel but not in the typescript made by Orlando. Bassani had both versions before him when he was preparing *The Leopard* and chose, I think wrongly in this case, the wording of the typescript.

man ... suspended in a void between a past permanently dead, though evoked in a nostalgic tone, and a future' from which he is ever more estranged.[8]

Death or oblivion provide the only release from this interminable wandering over an unmapped landscape. Fabrizio's attitude to death is naturally ambivalent: his sensual appetite for life makes him fear and dread it just as his weariness and disgust make him welcome it as a release. Death is for him two different things: he sees it as putrescence, the last stage of the corruption of living things, but also as freedom from that corruption. Much of the novel is concerned with Don Fabrizio's efforts to understand death and to come to terms with it.

Death is in the first sentence of the book and permeates the rest of the novel. It goes all the way through the first chapter, from the garden of the Villa Salina, which has 'the air of a cemetery', to the corpse of the Bourbon soldier and to Palermo itself with its 'sense of death'. Fabrizio's thoughts of his own end are accompanied throughout the novel by the deaths of animals and other people. On the way to the ball his carriage halts so that a priest bearing the Last Sacraments may pass. When he reaches the Ponteleone palace he spends much of the night reflecting on death and his contempt for the other guests gives 'way to compassion for all these ephemeral beings out to enjoy the tiny ray of light granted them between two shades, before the cradle, after the last spasms. How could one inveigh against those sure to die?' Then he goes into the library and contemplates a picture of a dying man; while wondering whether his own death will be similar, he is found by Tancredi who asks, jestingly, if he is courting death. Death follows him after the ball too, a waggon carrying quartered carcases from the slaughterhouse interrupts his walk home under the stars.

Death is a source of much of Lampedusa's imagery, frequently used in descriptions of Sicily and its 'funereal countryside', and of Sicilians themselves. The Sicilian 'sense of death' was not invented by Lampedusa. 'Death is at home in Sicily,' wrote his cousin Fulco di Verdura. 'Sicilians are used to her presence. The everlasting mournings, the continual references to dead people as if they were still alive' make the islanders familiar 'with the idea of death from earliest childhood'.[9] Don Fabrizio can thus extend some of his own attitudes to his countrymen. Sicilian behaviour, he tells the bemused Piedmontese official, reflects a hankering after death. Sicilians are interested in the artistic fashions of other countries only when these are out of date; they are attracted by the past only because it is dead. All Sicilian self-expression – the languor, the sensuality and the violence – is wish-fulfilment, demonstrating the desire for immobility and death. Like Fabrizio, Sicilians are attracted simultaneously by immortality and oblivion.

Throughout the novel Fabrizio's attitude to death remains ambivalent. In 'Lighea' La Ciura sees death as the way to immortality but the prince sometimes looks forward to it for its own sake. 'While there's death there's hope,' he thinks after hearing a funeral knell at Donnafugata. 'Nothing,' he reflects later at the ball, 'could be decently hated except eternity.' Death is therefore sought as a release rather than a promise, courted – in Tancredi's phrase – because it is an end in itself. 'As always the thought of his own death calmed him as much as that of others disturbed him: was it perhaps because, when all was said and done, his own death would in the first place mean that of the whole world?'

Yet the book is not the narrative of a single-minded courtship of death. Fabrizio's views change and so did Lampedusa's. The great death-room scene, when one not only feels for the prince but can even believe that one's own death is being described, reveals neither courtship nor rejection but merely resignation. In his last years Lampedusa too sometimes seemed to be courting death. Lacking Fabrizio's sensuality and enjoyment of life, he had fewer regrets about the past. Death must often have seemed a release, a liberation from a life that appeared wasted and aimless, and yet in the end he was not resigned to it. Death came to him later than he had once hoped but sooner than he then wanted, destroying him not after he had succumbed to despair, not at the final stage of his disillusionment with life but, tragically, at the most active and vital period of his existence.

13

The Leopard's Sicily

The publication of *The Leopard* provoked a major literary controversy in Italy, much of it centred on the historical accuracy of Lampedusa's anti-Sicilian 'polemic'. The debate was at times astonishingly intemperate. Some reviewers might claim that two pages of the novel could explain more about Sicily and its problems than volumes of learned works.[1] But others denied that Lampedusa's vision of Sicily had any validity whatever. It was 'an old and abused image', according to Enrico Falqui, the product of 'squalid ideology' and 'anti-historical conservatism'.[2] A cardinal of Palermo described *The Leopard* as one of the three factors which contributed to the dishonour of Sicily (the others being the Mafia and the social reformer Danilo Dolci),[3] a view shared by Francis Guercio who complained that 'the gloomy image of contemporary Sicily' which emerges from the works of Dolci and Lampedusa was 'one-sided and distorted': their 'combined gloom', he lamented, 'has induced a feeling in the world at large that Sicily must be the most backward and hopeless region in Italy'.[4]

Many of Lampedusa's acquaintances, who had no idea that he held such strong opinions, were shocked by the contempt and sarcasm he directed against Sicily. But his friends were well aware of his views. He used to refer to Sicily as '*questo* "backwater"'[5] and told Orlando it resembled Peru.[6] Sometimes the islanders' behaviour seemed to him uniquely ridiculous and he memorized a series of incidents which he thought could have taken place only in Sicily. Their reputed intelligence was largely mythical – 'quick wits', he alleged in *The Leopard*, which merely 'usurp the name of intelligence'. La Ciura's opinion of the Sicilians as donkeys goes beyond the views of his creator, but Lampedusa had little faith in their analytical capabilities. 'Lock five Sicilians and five Piedmontese in a room to solve a problem,' he once said. 'After a quarter of an hour all the Sicilians and none of the Piedmontese will have an answer in their heads. But after an hour all the Piedmontese and none of the Sicilians will have solved the problem.'[7] For Lampedusa the Sicilians neither created nor preserved. Goethe's view of Sicily – 'To have seen Italy without having seen Sicily is not to have seen Italy at all, for Sicily is the clue to everything'[8] – was incomprehensible to him. Ruskin was surely more justified in arguing that it was pointless to visit the island just to see buildings put up in the architectural styles of various conquerors.[9] In any case Sicily, which 'from poverty and neglect' was 'the most destructive of countries', neither understood nor attempted to preserve its monuments.[10]

The numerous targets for Lampedusa's sarcasm in Palermo included its newspapers, the stagnation of its intellectual life, and the sexual boasting of its male inhabitants, which he regarded as 'compensation for an often inhibited sex life'.[11] In his writing he was remorseless about Sicilian defects and his characters parade before the reader pursued by short, venomous phrases: Don Ciccio with his 'deluded and rapacious soul'; Russo, 'greedy eyes beneath a remorseless forehead ... a perfect specimen of a class on its way up'; Sedàra, 'all munching and grease stains', 'this little heap of cunning, ill-cut clothes, money and ignorance'; and the peasant brother-in-law of Father Pirrone: 'with his low forehead, ornamental quiffs of hair on the temples, lurching walk and perpetual swelling of the right trouser leg where he kept a knife, it was obvious at once that Vincenzino was "a man of honour", one of those violent imbeciles capable of any carnage'. Even those characters who are exempt from such remarks, like Don Onofrio or Ciccio Tumeo, serve to emphasize the deficiencies of the others. In describing Ferrara (in *I gattini ciechi*) as 'a person of sensitive feelings', we are reminded that this is 'a human species very rare in Sicily'.

But it was Lampedusa's attempt at a collective description of the Sicilian mentality that provoked the strongest criticism from reviewers, Don Fabrizio's lecture to Chevalley being singled out as especially libellous.

In Sicily it doesn't matter about doing things well or badly; the sin which we Sicilians never forgive is simply that of 'doing' at all ... Sleep, my dear Chevalley, sleep, that is what Sicilians want, and they will always hate anyone who tries to wake them, even in order to bring them the most wonderful of gifts ... your only mistake was saying 'the Sicilians must want to improve' ... the Sicilians never want to improve for the simple reason that they think themselves perfect; their vanity is stronger than their misery.

Don Fabrizio thought and said many contemptuous things about Sicilians but it was these remarks on their indolence and complacency which most enraged the critics, many of whom assumed that Lampedusa knew little about Sicilian history. According to the novelist Leonardo Sciascia, *The Leopard* was written without an 'understanding of history', whereas to Falqui it was the creature of 'an extremely retrograde conception of history' which denied the prospect of progress and liberty to Sicily.[12] The anger in these and other attacks caused Luigi Russo to complain that Lampedusa was being treated as a politician who had made a reactionary speech instead of as a novelist who had put some ideas into the mouth of one of his characters.[13] Fabrizio's views reflect many of Lampedusa's but to treat his conversation with Chevalley as if it were an historical essay was naïve and unfair. The exaggerations and generalizations should have been obvious to anyone and taken as illustrations rather than literal representations of historical truth. It was pointless to counter Fabrizio's remarks about the desire for sleep with questions such as 'What about the Vespers? What about the 1866 revolt?' Lampedusa was not discussing individual behaviour in certain periods; he was making a generalization about the behaviour of millions of people over thousands of years.

Fabrizio's ascription of Sicilian inertia to the 'cruelty of climate' and the 'violence of landscape' inspired one critic to complain that Lampedusa had reduced the 'southern question' to a matter of climatic considerations in order to justify his own laziness.[14] The sun certainly plays a dominant role in the novel, its destructive influence emphasized with a stream of adjectives – 'tyrannous', 'crude', 'implacable', 'drugging', 'savage' – and is itself seen as 'the true ruler of Sicily ... which annulled every will, kept all things in servile immobility, cradled in violence that has the arbitrariness of dreams'. There are frequent references to 'the deep gloom of Sicilian summer', 'six feverish months at a temperature of 104°', 'this summer of ours which is as long and glum as a Russian winter and against which we struggle with less success'. Anyone who visits Sicily will know that this is exaggerated – as are some of the most beautiful passages on the landscape* – but Fabrizio was not in fact claiming that the climate alone was responsible for Sicilian torpor. It was the combination of climate and landscape with 'alien pressure and varied invasions' which had shaped the island's history and formed its people's character.

Lampedusa saw Sicily as the victim of its size and geographical position. Since early classical times, Sicily has been too small and weak to defend itself, and yet too large, too strategically important and (until the later Middle Ages) too fertile to escape the interest of foreign powers. Its destiny has thus inevitably been colonial.

> We are old Chevalley, very old. For over twenty-five centuries we've been bearing the weight of superb and heterogeneous civilizations, all from outside, none made by ourselves, none that we could call our own. We're as white as you are, Chevalley, and as the Queen of England; and yet for two thousand five hundred years we've been a colony. I don't say that in complaint; it's our fault. But even so we're worn out and exhausted ... You talked to me a short while ago about a young Sicily sighting the marvels of the modern world; for my part I see instead a centenarian being dragged in a bath-chair round the Great Exhibition in London, understanding nothing and caring about nothing ...

The 'impermeability to anything new', which Lampedusa recognized as a traditionally Sicilian trait, seemed to him a

---

*e.g. '... there among the tamarisks and scattered cork trees appeared the real Sicily again, the one compared to which baroque towns and orange groves are mere trifles: aridly undulating to the horizon in hillock after hillock, comfortless and irrational, with no lines that the mind could grasp, conceived apparently in a delirious moment of creation; a sea suddenly petrified at the instant when a change of wind had flung the waves into a frenzy'.

consequence of the islands's numerous foreign conquests and the imposition of alien civilizations. There were too many monuments and too many invaders, seldom resisted and always misunderstood, which produced a sense of fatalism among Sicilians. Two and a half thousand years as a colonized people had made them incapable even of wishing to improve, so that they had turned inwards on themselves and acquired 'a terrifying insularity of mind'. Every reformer from the Arabs to the Piedmontese had been confronted and defeated by Sicilian fatalism. The island was thus irredeemable because its aspiring redeemers were always beaten. Like *The Leopard*'s cardinal, they came from outside, full of idealism and reforming zeal, and were hated, shunned and derided. 'Like everyone who in those days wanted to change anything in the Sicilian character [the cardinal] soon acquired the reputation of being a fool ... '

This pessimistic vision of Sicilian history, this view of a past consisting of recurrent themes, unexpected continuity and patterns of behaviour repeated down the centuries, is necessarily over-simplified, yet it contains essential truths that Falqui and others were unable to understand. There is a curious *déjà vu* feeling about the history of Sicily. Events from classical periods are mirrored one thousand years later under the Byzantines or two thousand years later during Spanish rule. 'So much of later Sicilian history', wrote one of the greatest of classical scholars, was 'foreshadowed' by the 'first age of tyranny' in the fifth century BC.[15] The behaviour of the conquerors, wherever they came from, and the reactions of the conquered, from whatever epoch, have so often been predictable. Except for the brief period of Norman dominion, the island's rulers tried to avoid the place – Roman emperors were as culpable as Spanish kings and Italian prime ministers of the last century – and among the feudal lords, drawing their power from the long-established latifundia, there was a millennial tradition of absenteeism.

The Sicilian response to these foreign invaders, declared Don Fabrizio, was invariably the same: they 'were at once obeyed, soon detested and always misunderstood'. This is not a libellous or even an original view. Voltaire said much the same thing when he described the Sicilians as 'nearly always hating their masters and rebelling against them, but not making any real effort worthy

of freedom'.[16] From Belisarius to the Bourbons the island had
been conquered with astonishing ease. This is partly because in
every invasion since the time of the Greeks, some Sicilian factions
have sided with the invaders, and partly because the Sicilians
have so frequently combined political intransigence with military
incompetence or even a refusal to put up a fight. In 1848, during
Prince Giulio's time, the Sicilians rebelled against the Bourbon
king, declared their independence and rejected generous
Bourbon terms for a settlement. After making this grand gesture,
however, they sat back and relaxed, and a few months later a
Bourbon army recaptured Palermo almost unopposed. It is hard
not-to agree with Sebastiano Aglianò's view of Sicilian history as
'an uninterrupted succession of desperate impulses and supine
submissions, of rapid, brightly-lit moments and zones
indeterminably dark'.[17]

Lampedusa's observations about Sicilian characteristics are
also not as outrageous or unusual as his critics seemed to think.
The islanders' complacency and their 'impermeability to anything
new' had been noticed by others before him: in the early
nineteenth century, for instance, a Lombard economist had
remarked that Sicilians had 'too high an opinion of their own
capabilities to be anxious to learn or to change'.[18] Nor is
Fabrizio's claim about 'the well-known time lag of a century in
our artistic and intellectual life' without historical foundation.
Both Sciascia and Falqui used the historian Rosario Romeo as a
witness to condemn Lampedusa's view of history and cited his *Il
Risorgimento in Sicilia*. Described as 'a rehabilitation of Sicilian
culture after Gentile ... had taught Italians to think of the island
as a cultural backwater',[19] this book certainly stresses the positive
contribution Sicily made to Italian unification. Yet it also
provides much support for Lampedusa's theory about the long
'time lag'. Acccording to Romeo, Sicily was effectively excluded
from Italian and European life for more than four centuries after
the war of the Sicilian Vespers. The Renaissance and the
Reformation passed it by, leaving the islanders to the undiluted
influence of Spain and the Counter-Reformation. Their
intellectual and moral life declined and they relapsed into a
neglected provincialism upon which even the Enlightenment
made little impact. There were virtually no political reformers
before 1780, certainly no one of the stature of Genovesi in

Naples; in any case, the few thinkers who did exist were so frightened of baronial power that they did not even advocate the abolition of feudalism.[20]

Lampedusa believed that Sicily's destiny had been determined by a combination of climate, nature, foreign invasion and indigenous folly. He has been accused of a 'vendetta' against History on account of the past's annihilation of his family,[21] but the origins of that vendetta are equally to be found in the decline of his island. The critics who were outraged by *The Leopard*'s view of Sicily were blind to the 'other' Sicily which its author loved. Like many Sicilians who live on their island, Lampedusa loved Sicily as much as he hated it, and the hatred was a direct consequence and in direct proportion to the extent of its decadence. For him it was an island of extremes which fed upon each other, the brilliance always matched in an equation with the squalor and violence. It was a country 'in which the inferno round Randazzo [was] a few miles from the beauty of Taormina Bay', a country that contained both Hell and Paradise. Those 'twenty-five centuries' of foreign invasion and neglect had destroyed most of that Paradise, that wooded land of the Greek colonists, those fertile fields of the Romans which had produced higher wheat yields than they do today. It was no coincidence that La Ciura was a Hellenist: he could understand how an incomparable island, whose fertility had enticed so many immigrants in classical times, had become the shame of southern Europe, its violence and aridity forcing millions of its people to emigrate. For La Ciura, as for his creator, no place had so much natural beauty as Sicily, and no place had been so corrupted by its people and its rulers.

'Eternal Sicily, nature's Sicily', powerfully evoked in 'Lighea', could still be found in certain places far from the chaotic towns and eroded hillsides. The 'archaic and aromatic countryside' encountered by Don Fabrizio still existed at Capo d'Orlando, which Lampedusa thought of as a sort of Arcadia that had withstood the depredations of history. It is described also in 'Lighea' during the reminiscences of Corbera and La Ciura:

> the scent of rosemary on the Nèbrodi hills, the taste of Melilli honey, the waving corn seen from Etna on a windy day in May ... the solitudes around Syracuse, the gusts of scent from

orange and lemon groves pouring over Palermo ... during
some sunsets in June ... the enchantment of certain summer
nights within sight of Castellamare bay, when stars are
mirrored in the sleeping sea and the spirit of anyone lying back
amid the lentisks is lost in a vortex of sky, while the body is
tense and alert, fearing the approach of demons.

Sicily had been perfect, had subsequently 'fallen', and was
now, in Lampedusa's word, 'irredeemable'. Yet even in its
decadence it retained in his eyes a certain corrupt greatness which
the recent centuries of degradation had not extinguished. The
critics were oblivious of this hidden pride, unaware that the
author was more sympathetic to the Sicilian's 'voluptuous torpor'
than to the zealous worthiness of Chevalley. Sicily may have been
vain and cruel but at least it was not mediocre. To Lampedusa the
north of Italy was rational but drab and he conveyed this view in
his language, his disparaging use of adjectives, his habit of using
diminutives in such a way that the Milanese count Cavriaghi
becomes a *contino* rather than a *conte*. He would never have
called a Sicilian a *contino*: in spite of the island's history, it
retained a sort of warped grandeur that could not be belittled.[22]
Lampedusa's view of Sicily as 'irredeemable' annoyed many
people who believed that technological progress and democratic
government could obliterate the legacies of centuries. In most
cases they underestimated his knowledge of Sicilian history and
misunderstood an important sentence in *The Leopard*. In his
search for a hopeful and enlightened period of the island's past,
Lampedusa went back to early classical times. By contrast with
Tuscany and the north during the Communes, the south had
enjoyed no period of cultural greatness and political liberty. Like
the Neapolitan writer Galanti, who in a similar quest had had to
go back to the Samnites, the primitive Italic tribes of Molise,[23]
Lampedusa could find nothing encouraging in subsequent eras in
Sicily except, possibly, for the century of the Norman kings. Any
attempt at any reform (political, social or economic) by any ruler
(Spanish, Piedmontese, Austrian or Bourbon) had been defeated
by Sicilian 'interests'. The 1812 constitution, established during
the brief period of British control, was fatally undermined by a
political class divided between those who thought it went too far
and those who complained it had not gone far enough. For

Lampedusa, the Sicilians' failure to support the constitution destroyed their chances of a decent future: their short-sightedness in those years ensured that the island would never experience the British form of constitutional development.[24]

The misunderstood sentence was Tancredi's famous line – 'If we want things to stay as they are, things will have to change' – which was widely seen as Lampedusa's view and even as his philosophy, although in the end it is explicitly rejected by Don Fabrizio himself. A leading historian, Francesco Renda, castigated this 'interpretation' as 'sterile' and 'distorted' without troubling to ask himself whether this really was the author's own opinion.[25] Certainly Lampedusa believed that the past was composed of endless superficial changes and a recurrent relabelling of the same object. But he also knew, as did Salina, that the era of the Risorgimento was different from its predecessors. It was not in itself a major change but it heralded real changes – in the social structure and in the economy – which paradoxically failed to alter many things or solve many of the island's problems. Sicily has obviously been transformed by the building of motorways and oil refineries and by the industrialization of the eastern seaboard. But Lampedusa would have found little evidence that it had been 'redeemed', that modern technology had been able to reduce the violence, political corruption and other evils of modern Palermo. And some of his former critics have since agreed with him. Several years after attacking him for historical ignorance, Leonardo Sciascia bravely admitted that 'Lampedusa was unfortunately right and we were wrong' about Sicilian history. After reciting the prince's chronicle of failed attempts to reform the island, he acknowledged on another occasion that Sicily had little reason to expect a 'radiant future'.[26]

Criticism of the present and pessimism about the future did not turn Lampedusa into a reactionary. Nor did his disapproval of the Piedmontese make him a Bourbon apologist. The Bourbons' spokesman in *The Leopard* is Màlvica, Don Fabrizio's brother-in-law, who argues foolishly on their behalf. The author's view of them, filtered through the reflections of the prince, is harsh and critical, though not as vituperative or as unfair as the views of Gladstone and other British liberals. Francis II is dismissed as 'only a seminarist dressed up as a general', but Ferdinand II is described during an audience with Salina: an uncouth and unattractive figure, he is nevertheless far from being Gladstone's tyrant, the 'Bomba' of traditional demonology, and his ambiguous character is well summarized in his line, 'A fine thing, science, unless it takes to attacking religion!'

Lampedusa was a monarchist capable of criticizing the monarchy when its representatives did not measure up to certain standards. In Fabrizio's words, 'kings who personify an idea should not, cannot, fall below a certain level for generations; if they do ... the idea suffers too'. Similarly, he was an aristocrat who could be ruthless about the deficiencies of his own class. It is true that Father Pirrone defends the behaviour of the nobles, their generosity as well as certain attitudes, and it is also true that Fabrizio declares it 'impossible to obtain the distinction, the delicacy, the fascination of a boy like [Tancredi] without his ancestors having romped through half-a-dozen fortunes'. But Pirrone is defending the aristocratic idea rather than individual nobles, and the prince is using that idea, with an irony lost on his listener, to impress Calogero Sedàra. Lampedusa's own views of his fellow aristocrats can be seen in his contemptuous descriptions of them at the ball and in *I gattini ciechi*. Yet, like Fabrizio, he realized that in criticizing them he was also criticizing himself:

And then these people filling the rooms [at the ball], all these faded women, all these stupid men, these two vainglorious sexes were part of his blood, part of himself; only they could really understand him, only with them could he be at ease. 'I may be more intelligent, I'm certainly more cultivated than they are, but I come from the same stock, with them I must make common cause.'

Perhaps it was this last phrase which convinced Mario Alicata of *The Leopard*'s 'ideological deficiency' and its author's reactionary views.[27] Like other critics,[28] Alicata was incensed by Lampedusa's treatment of the Risorgimento, which he considered a caricature of the Italian national struggle. Certainly, Lampedusa did not venerate the Risorgimento as the sacred event of Italian history. In his youth he had been critical of the political system produced by unification and he remained to the end of his life sceptical about the origins and achievements of united Italy. For him the Sicilian Risorgimento was little more than a change of dynasty ('Torinese instead of Neapolitan dialect') and the substitution of one class by another ('For all will be the same, just as it is now: except for an imperceptible change round of classes.') No doubt some Sicilians hoped for more: 'Afterwards,' says Russo in *The Leopard*, 'we'll have liberty, security, lighter taxes, ease, trade. Everything will be better ... ' And no doubt some Piedmontese believed, like Chevalley, that they could clean up the place in no time: 'This state of things won't last; our lively new modern administration will change it all.' But Lampedusa knew that the Sicilian 'patriots' had not wanted a real change and that in any case the Piedmontese would not have been able to achieve it.

The Leopard is in fact charitable towards the role of the Piedmontese in Sicily, satirizing their naïveté rather than their ignorance of the south* or the arrogance of their behaviour. Little is made of their politicians' high-handedness, the imposition of Piedmontese laws or the disregard of local customs and traditions. The only incident discussed at any length is the rigged plebiscite in which the Sicilians voted in favour of forming part of Italy. According to official figures, 99.8% of the voters supported unity and in more than three-quarters of the island's districts no negative votes were recorded.[30] Lampedusa was well aware of the 'deceptions of the plebiscite' and may have known that the official figures for Santa Margherita had been 993 votes in favour out of an electorate of 999.[31] His fictional returns for Donnafugata (512 positive votes and three abstentions) were thus not an exaggeration. During a morning's shooting with Ciccio Tumeo, Don Fabrizio reflects on the consequences of this deceit:

Italy was born on that sullen night at Donnafugata, born right there, in that forgotten little town, just as much as in the sloth of Palermo or the clamour of Naples ... And yet this persistent disquiet of his must mean something; during that too brief announcement of figures, just as during those too emphatic speeches, he had a feeling that something, someone had died,

---

*Count Cavour, the Italian prime minister who achieved unification in 1859–60, had never been south of Florence. He knew more about the problems of Ireland than those of southern Italy, and once said in Parliament that he thought Sicilians spoke Arabic.[29]

God only knew in what back-alley, in what corner of the popular conscience ...

At this point calm descended on Don Fabrizio, who had finally solved the enigma; now he knew who had been killed at Donnafugata, at a hundred other places, in the course of that night of dirty wind: a new-born babe: good faith; just the very child who should have been cared for most, whose strengthening would have justified all the silly vandalisms. Don Ciccio's negative vote, fifty similar votes at Donnafugata, a hundred thousand 'no's' in the whole Kingdom, would have had no effect on the result, have made it, in fact, if anything more significant; and this maiming of souls would have been avoided.

Later Lampedusa added a footnote of his own to the story of the plebiscite: 'Don Fabrizio could not have known it then, but a great deal of the slackness and acquiescence for which the people of the south were to be criticized during the following decades, was due to the stupid annulment of the first expression of liberty ever offered them.'

Perhaps Lampedusa exaggerated the consequences of the plebiscite and paid insufficient attention to the effects of the Piedmontese administration, the insensitive introduction of alien systems and institutions, the increase in taxation and, above all, the failure to attempt a solution of the social and agrarian problems. Yet there is no doubt that he knew of these and other factors that contributed to the southern question. He knew that there had been no real revolution in the south, nothing that would benefit the poorer classes. 'Everything will be better,' declares Russo, 'the only ones to lose will be the priests,' but Lampedusa knew that almost nothing got better and the only ones to win were the unscrupulous opportunists who bought up most of the Church lands at derisory prices after unification. He hated these people, 'their tenacious greed and avarice', 'their rancour and their sense of inferiority', and transformed them into Calogero Sedàra and the odious Ibba family. There may be some snobbery in his treatment of them but there is no injustice. They are the early *mafiosi*, the men who grabbed the common lands and the Church's property and held on to them by force. Sedàra is such an accurate portrait of this type that several historians of the

Mafia have described him as a prototype *mafioso*, a *'mafioso avant la lettre'*.[32] 'We were the Leopards and Lions,' reflects Don Fabrizio; 'those who'll take our place will be little jackals, hyenas.' Again this is not entirely unfair: even Romeo admitted the deficiencies of the new Sicilian ruling class which assumed many of the worst characteristics of the old.[33] Lampedusa's critic, Leonardo Sciascia, went still further, declaring that 'we must unfortunately agree' with the prince that instead of a genuine middle class Sicily had only 'a pack of jackals'.[34]

Garibaldi's triumph in 1860 had been greatly helped by an uprising of the Sicilian peasantry, but there had been little initial assistance from members of the upper and middle classes. Yet, as Denis Mack Smith has pointed out, a large majority of the peasants received no immediate benefit from the Risorgimento and, instead of the much-needed agrarian reform, the number of smallholdings decreased.[35] Nor did the situation improve. Writing in 1877, the distinguished Tuscan politician Sonnino noted that 'in Sicily our institutions are based on a merely formal liberalism and have just given the oppressing class a legal means of continuing as they always have. All power has been handed over to these people, to use or misuse as they please.'[36] Many years later, the communist intellectual Gramsci criticized the Risorgimento as a 'passive revolution' because its leaders had refused to ally themselves with the peasants; unlike the Jacobins in France, they had therefore failed to make a real revolution or create a modern national state.[37]

It could be argued that Lampedusa's criticism of the Risorgimento came from both sides, from the viewpoints of both Gramsci and the Bourbons. In his opinion it should have been a real revolution or nothing at all. If there had to be a compromise, it should have been a genuine one that merged the best things from the old regime and from the new, not one that destroyed the best in Sicilian life and preserved the worst. Lampedusa was aware of the defects of his great-grandfather's contemporaries and would not have minded so much if they had fallen to worthy opponents such as the French Jacobins or genuine revolutionary idealists like Mazzini and Garibaldi.* But to give way to a group

---

*It is significant that Garibaldi, who was after all the cause of many of Don Fabrizio's problems, is never criticized in the course of numerous references by either the author or the protagonist of *The Leopard*.

of Sedàras, scheming men of violence who cried Progress when all they wanted was Power and Profit, was too much for him. It would have been better, as well as more honourable, to have remained with the Bourbons.

These ideas may have shocked people but they were not particularly original. Many of Lampedusa's views on the Risorgimento had been held by various *meridionalisti* – experts on the southern question – and by prominent historians including Salvemini, Gobetti and Mack Smith. Gobetti's belief that fascism was made almost inevitable by the 'Risorgimento's failure to win the support of the masses or produce a responsible ruling class',[38] was shared by Lampedusa. So were many of the opinions in Mack Smith's study of Cavour and Garibaldi, a book (published a few months before *The Leopard* was begun) which may have been one of Lampedusa's historical sources.[39] 'Revisionist' views such as these, however, were attacked because they questioned the country's main national myth. In a state where almost every town has a Via Cavour, a Piazza Garibaldi or a Corso Vittorio Emanuele, Gobetti's idea of a 'Risorgimento without heroes' was a heresy which required ponderous rebuttal.[40] Mack Smith was criticized even more fatuously: the Risorgimento, he was reminded, was 'the passion of a people for its Italian identity' and he had sinned by taking away its 'soul'.[41]

These examples help explain the hostility towards Lampedusa's own comments on Italian unification. They may also explain some of *The Leopard*'s success. Many people wanted to know why an allegedly heroic national movement had led to colonial disaster, the depopulation of the south, Mussolini and involvement in two world wars. Lampedusa gave them a partial answer: in his pages they could read how unification was a flawed movement which had been imposed upon the south in such a way as to produce long-lasting resentment and prevent the emergence of a sense of national identity. In short, by deflating past heroes, *The Leopard* was able to explain the emergence of more recent villains.

14

Il caso Lampedusa

No novel in Italian literature has caused so much argument, aroused so much passion and begun so many quarrels as *The Leopard*. About 400 articles in Italian have been written about this single work, many of them shrill denunciations of other people's views on the subject. The early reviewers debated at length whether *The Leopard* was or was not an historical novel, whether its author was very knowledgeable or entirely ignorant of Sicilian history, and which writers could be regarded as Lampedusa's mentors or antecedents.* Later arguments became more recondite and an entire book was written in an attempt to prove the superiority of the prince's typescript over his final manuscript.[1] More recently, one has been devoted to the imagery of *The Leopard*[2] and another to a Jungian analysis of 'Lighea'.[3]

The Leopard's first review, written by Carlo Bo in *La Stampa*, appeared at the end of November 1958. 'I opened the book with suspicion,' he recalled several years afterwards. 'I opened it with the certainty that by the fiftieth page I would have nothing more to do with it, but it was not like that. I needed only a few pages ... to understand that this Sicilian gentleman was a real writer.'[4] Bo's eulogy was followed by enthusiastic reviews from some of Italy's leading literary figures. Eugenio Montale, who in his youth had been the first Italian critic to recognize the talent of Svevo, was among the first to see the merits of *The Leopard*. Recalling his one meeting with Lampedusa, he said he had never suspected

---

*Four reviewers between them concocted a list of 'influences' of such diversity as to include Stendhal, Tolstoy, Proust, Ariosto, Leopardi, Verga, De Roberto, Pirandello and Brancati. Other critics found traces of many others, including Gogol, Balzac, Flaubert, Maupassant, Zola and D'Annunzio.

that the prince could become 'a writer second to none of the literati' present at the conference of San Pellegrino.[5] Geno Pampaloni stressed the writer's poetic gifts and his handling of an 'epoch of transition' during which precious things are inevitably thrown out with the old.[6] The liberal politician and writer, Luigi Barzini, agreed with him, arguing that The Leopard's theme was

> the inevitable decline, which cannot be halted, of the old virtues and graces that have grown useless but made life human even for humble people; the triumph of other qualities, rougher but essential in the modern world, which do not correct the old injustices but often merely show them up, make them unbearable, and replace them with others that are sometimes crueler and worse.[7]

As the favourable reviews multiplied and the novel's popularity increased, Lampedusa came under attack from several directions. His critics can be roughly divided into four categories: fervent Catholics who disliked his pessimism; the literary Left which thought novels ought to be avant-garde and 'committed'; marxists who attacked his view of history and apparent denial of progress; and Sicilian apologists who were outraged by his portrait of Sicily and who argued that Sicilians were no more violent and irrational than other peoples. The accusations of the last two groups were discussed in the last chapter. Those of the first were generally predictable, Catholic reviewers usually recognizing the book's artistic merits while lamenting its 'distressing spiritual emptiness'.[8] To Giuseppe de Rosa, who found many things to admire in the novel, its 'gravest defect' was 'its pessimism with no way out and no hope'. 'The sense of death and destruction' which permeated the book was 'morally unacceptable' but the real tragedy of The Leopard was this: 'There is no God, or if there is, he is a being far from the world and from the heart of man.'[9]

Much of the strongest and most puzzling criticism came from Italy's radical intelligentsia which had acquired a virtual monopoly of the country's literary output after the Second World War. For over ten years it had been sponsoring 'neo-realist' fiction, but now it was pursuing other things: 'commitment' and 'progressiveness' were still important, but so were innovation and avant-garde 'experimentalism'. The late fifties were years of agonized debates: what future was there for the novel? Which direction should it take? Literary journals sent questionnaires to various writers and printed their answers to questions about the place of 'social realism' in contemporary fiction.[10] Intellectuals tried to work out new roles for writers and new 'paths' for their writing. Pasolini even tried to formulate rules for writing poetry which should be 'radically innovative but regulated by an awareness of political and social realities'.[11]

In this climate it was hardly surprising that *The Leopard* should find detractors. A novel that was easy to read, with well-drawn characters and conventional syntax, written by someone who awarded no roles to socialist realism or avant-garde experimentalism, was bound to be anathema to many intellectuals. They saw it merely as a reactionary book which did not help them solve 'the crisis of the novel', pointed out no new directions and ignored the problems which tormented the modernists. Worse still, it seemed to threaten the literary structure which these people had laboriously put together since the war. 'For the last thirty years,' complained the Tuscan novelist Pratolini, 'we have strained to advance our literature. Lampedusa has put us back sixty years.'[12]

The intellectual most discomfited by *The Leopard*'s success was Elio Vittorini. Not only did it publicize his own misjudgement in rejecting the book for publication, it also jeopardized his principal project – described by him as the 'modern renovation of literature'[13] but regarded by others as the megalomaniac imposition of a certain brand of writing by a 'publishing pontifex'.[14] Embarrassed by the affair, Vittorini tried to justify his rejections with some peculiar arguments. He could not force himself, he explained, 'to love writers who express themselves within traditional patterns' and therefore he could only have loved *The Leopard* if it had been written a long time ago and recently 'discovered in some archive'.[15] Elsewhere he declared that if it had 'come out around 1930 its place in the history of Italian literature would be a little above (but also far to the right) of the efforts of Nino Savarese. But published today it will end up beneath them.' Anyway, he added, Lampedusa's 'conception of death (that is the fear and acceptance of it)' was 'old-fashioned and discounted': today people thought about death in a quite different way.[16]

Vittorini's rather fatuous claim that *The Leopard* was 'right-wing' was made by other writers such as Alberto Moravia and Franco Fortini and by the heavy guns of the Communist Party press. Perhaps the nadir of left-wing criticism was reached in the party's journal *Rinascita* which found the novel without literary merit: the public had read the book with boredom, it announced against all the evidence, and then added patronizingly that most people had probably not got beyond the first few pages.[17] Given all this, it was highly disconcerting for the Italian Left to discover that the French writer Louis Aragon, one of the leading marxist intellectuals in Europe, considered *The Leopard* to be 'one of the great novels of this century, one of the great novels of all time, and perhaps ... the only Italian novel'. In his opinion it was 'absolutely senseless' to call it a right-wing book. Far from being, in Moravia's curious notion, a novel which expressed 'the ideas and view of life' of the ruling class,[18] Aragon saw *The Leopard* as a criticism of Lampedusa's own class that was not only 'merciless' but also 'left-wing'. The Italian response altogether bewildered the French critic who related a conversation in which Moravia had grumbled that *The Leopard* was 'a right-wing book', a 'success for the right' apparently decreed by unspecified 'right-wing people'. Aragon also reported encounters with other Italians who complained that the book ignored modern techniques, that it owed nothing to Joyce or Proust and, most heretical of all, that it was not 'committed literature'.[19]

The Leopard was published in France in 1959 and had an enthusiastic reception. As in Italy there was much debate about whether or not it was an historical novel and much searching for Lampedusa's literary ancestors. Stendhal and Proust were naturally prominent among these, but the more cosmopolitan critics discerned traces of Huxley and García Lorca and some emphasized that it was a very 'Mediterranean' book.[20] One noted with relief that it was 'a long way from the little "Parisian" novels which have been raining upon us for some years from the vicinity of the church tower of Saint-Germain-des-Prés'.[21] In general the French admired the descriptions of the Sicilian landscape and *Le Monde*'s critic praised certain scenes which gave 'a perfectly just idea of the social state of Sicily and the relations between the classes' in 1860.[22] Another reviewer concluded that the book had 'the density, the gravity and the breadth that one can expect in a solitary work, meditated upon for an entire life, of which it expresses the essence'.[23]

The English edition was published a few months later and extensively praised by the most prominent British reviewers. Almost all of them suggested that it was a very 'Stendhalian' novel, that the author wrote with 'Stendhalian subtlety' or that Tancredi was 'a Stendhal figure ... a sort of Sicilian and aristocratic Julien Sorel'[24] – statements that are all highly questionable and may be attributed to the fact that the cover mentioned Stendhal as the author's favourite novelist. Lampedusa was praised for his 'Mediterranean pessimism and cynicism', for his 'symbolism and urbane irony' and for his 'rich but never decadent style'.[25] Don Fabrizio himself was a masterly character, 'presented with a subtlety of understanding which Stendhal would have comprehended and admired'.[26] There was a little adverse criticism of minor details which was not always intelligible. Raymond Mortimer, who thought *The Leopard* had 'extraordinary merit' even though it was 'imperfect as a novel', claimed that 'the two worst passages in the book – descriptions of the scent in a garden and of the food at a ball – resemble bad patches in Zola'.[27] Harold Nicolson also thought that the book had 'great intrinsic merit' but complained that Lampedusa was 'stupid about animals' and had no 'real knowledge of canine nature' – an eccentric opinion of someone who had spent his life surrounded by dogs and one not justified by a reading of the novel. One of the most sensible remarks, in any language, came from the elderly E.M. Forster who said in the *Spectator* that this 'noble book' was 'not a historical novel' but 'a novel which happens to take place in history'.[28]

The French and British reviews, especially those by Aragon and Forster, had a sobering effect on *The Leopard*'s Italian critics. Most of them gave up discussing it, though one, Leonardo Sciascia, began a lengthy public retraction. Although literary critics had encouraged people to think that he and Lampedusa were at opposite poles in their views on Sicily, Sciascia himself started to have doubts about this in the late sixties. Favourable references to *The Leopard* began to appear in his articles and admiration of Lampedusa's historical views increased to such an extent that Sciascia used him as an authority at almost every

opportunity. By 1979 he was even quoting with approval passages
he had denounced twenty years earlier.[29] When asked why he had
changed his mind, Sciascia admitted that various factors had
prevented him from appreciating *The Leopard* at the time of its
publication. Shortly before writing his review, he had read an
account of the craven Sicilian noblemen who, after deposing the
Bourbon king in 1848, had retracted and begged his forgiveness
the year after. As Lampedusa's great-grandfather had been
among them, this had encouraged Sciascia to see the novel as an
apology for a worthless class of people. Furthermore, he was
annoyed by the attitude of many of the Sicilian Left: recalling
someone else's remark that 'there is no communist sitting beside
a duke who doesn't feel shivers of pleasure', he was irritated by
the sight of Palermo's communists apparently 'shivering with
pleasure' over *The Leopard* because it had been written by a
prince.[30]

Gradually the polemics died down, though some of the lesser
arguments continued, augmented from time to time by fresh
debates. The novel had caused much consternation in Palermo
among the surviving nobility, but Sicilian aristocrats moved in a
closed circle and this seldom reached the press. Gioacchino
Lanza later recalled the 'amazement' of these people in the face
of such 'impropriety'; certain things, they felt, should have been
allowed to disappear silently without being recorded in a novel.[31]
They were particularly horrified by the characters of Tancredi
and Angelica, whom they took to be portraits of Corrado
Valguarnera and his wife Maria Favara, revered ancestors of
many of them. One of this couple's descendants, Fulco di
Verdura, complained that he had 'found many discrepancies'
between his grandparents and their supposed fictional
counterparts,[32] which was not surprising because Lampedusa had
not tried to make them very similar.

Over the years several people appeared with theories that
Lampedusa had plagiarized, or at least borrowed heavily from,
other writers. One claim, that *The Leopard* was based on
Giuseppe Maggiore's *Sette e mezzo*, was effectively demolished
by the historian Virgilio Titone.[33] A more persistent accusation
was that Lampedusa had lifted much of his work from De
Roberto's *The Viceroys*, a novel he knew but did not much care
for, dismissing it as a 'picture of the Sicilian aristocracy seen from

the servants' hall'.[34] Various critics have claimed that Lampedusa took themes, ideology, ambience and even characters and conversations from De Roberto.[35] There are certainly some surface similarities – with two novels about Sicilian noble families during the Risorgimento there are bound to be – but the style, approach and treatment of the protagonists could hardly be more dissimilar.[36] As Archibald Colquhoun, the translator of both works, pointed out in his introduction to *The Viceroys*, *The Leopard* was a 'very different book with a similar plot'.[37]

In 1968 Carlo Muscetta, who taught literature at Catania University, reopened *il caso Lampedusa* with a dramatic announcement to a press agency. The published text of *The Leopard*, he claimed, was not the 'real' one and must be substituted at once by the manuscript version: it was necessary to publish a new text and to retranslate the foreign editions. This piece of sensationalism caused an uproar, as Muscetta had intended, and the following year Gioacchino Lanza felt obliged to publish an edition of the novel based on Lampedusa's final manuscript. He added a preface, however, quietly showing that Muscetta had greatly exaggerated the differences between the texts and adding that it was impossible to consider one superior to the other; as we have seen, Bassani had produced a synthesis between the two different versions and could not have been expected to do anything else. The matter might have ended there had it not been for another critic, Antonio Dipace, who in 1971 tried to prove that Muscetta's thesis was completely wrong: in his view the typescript was far better and more authentic than the manuscript. Dipace's case relied on the supposition that Lampedusa had not transcribed his manuscript from the typescript (because all of Orlando's copies had been sent to other people) but from an earlier, less polished manuscript. Unfortunately for Dipace, however, his hypothesis was rebutted by the two people who saw Lampedusa daily during the relevant period, his wife and his adopted son. Although this put an end to the controversy, it leaves unexplained the curious fact that some obtrusive and amateurish alliterations occur in the manuscript but not in the earlier typescript.[38]

Licy's declaration on this issue was one of many similar interventions. She survived her husband for twenty-five years, spiritedly guarding his reputation, and died in 1982 at the age of eighty-seven. Her old age was magisterial and eccentric, nourished by memories of her Baltic origins and upbringing: one of her nephews remembers her arriving in Rome, very old and slow-moving, intent only on reciting Russian poetry to her sister Lolette, who was by then also very old and almost entirely deaf.[39] Throughout the quarter-century of her widowhood, she was ready to embroil herself in argument with anyone who disputed her view of Lampedusa's character and several people were threatened with litigation. She gave interviews reluctantly, remaining suspicious of journalists or anyone who wanted to write about her husband. Aspiring biographers were turned away with uncompromising refusals to help. One of them, Andrea Vitello, persevered in his research regardless, but he was never allowed to see the hundreds of letters and other documents in the Via Butera dealing with Lampedusa's life.

Her husband's reputation did not in fact need such tenacious custodianship. *The Leopard*'s success was unprecedented in Italy: twenty years after its publication, it had sold over a million copies, had gone through 121 editions, and been translated twenty-three times.[40] In a 'referendum' held by an Italian literary weekly in 1985, it was voted 'the most loved' as well as one of the two 'most important' Italian novels of the twentieth century.[41] It was also the subject of a famous and beautiful film by Visconti.

Carlo Bo regarded *The Leopard* as a 'miracle' because it was a work 'rich with literary culture' which had succeeded 'in reaching the popular mind'.[42] Montale held a similar view, pointing out that Lampedusa had managed to have his book read 'by people who had sworn never again to open an Italian novel'.[43] This may be partly ascribed to Barzini's belief that it was the 'book that made all us Italians understand our life and history to the depths. (Only Sicilians think they are different from the rest of their fellow countrymen. We in the rest of Italy know that the island is like one of those concave shaving mirrors, in which we see our image pitilessly enlarged, both faults and virtues.)'[44]

Yet this explains only a fraction of *The Leopard*'s enduring appeal. It is strange now to read all those criticisms of the late fifties, especially those accusations that the book was old-fashioned. *The Leopard* has weathered better than its detractors and it is the neo-realists and experimentalists themselves who now seem out-of-date. The principal reason for the work's success lies ultimately in its timelessness. It is not the book of a certain period or a particular fashion, nor does it depend on the linguistic or other props of this or that era. *The Leopard* is a classic because it ignored the fads of a literary generation and concentrated on perennial concerns. Lampedusa once said that London would never die because Dickens had made it immortal, and to many people he has done the same for Sicily. Yet his own immortality will not rest on the evocation of a certain place in a certain epoch – memorable though that is – but on the sensibility and experience he distilled in his writing. Lampedusa's work will survive, long after the last palaces of Palermo have gone, because he wrote about the central problems of the human experience.

Notes

Abbreviations

1. Diaries	The diaries of Giuseppe di Lampedusa
2. Licy's diaries	The diaries of Alessandra di Lampedusa
3. Palazzo Lampedusa	The Lampedusa palace in Via Lampedusa where Giuseppe lived from birth until its destruction in 1943
4. Via Butera	The house where Lampedusa lived for the last ten years of his life
5. *Letteratura Inglese I–V*	The manuscripts of Lampedusa's courses in English literature 1953–5
6. *Lettere Francesi*	Lampedusa's *Invito alle lettere francesi del Cinquecento*
7. 'Lezioni . . .'	Lampedusa's *Lezioni su Stendhal*
8. 'Places . . .'	Archibald Colquhoun's translation of Lampedusa's *I luoghi della mia prima infanzia*
9. 'Ricordi . . .'	*Ricordi di Infanzia.* Lampedusa's original manuscript of *I luoghi della mia prima infanzia*, later altered by his widow

1:   The Inheritance (pp. 5–14)
  1. Caterina Cardona, *Lettere a Licy* (1987) p.62.
  2. Andrea Vitello, *Giuseppe Tomasi di Lampedusa* (1987) p.73.
  3. Fulco di Verdura, *The Happy Summer Days* (1976) p.51.
  4. Andrea Vitello, *I Gattopardi di Donnafugata* (1963) pp.35–9 and table 1.
  5. Information from Sir Steven Runciman to the author.
  6. Vitello, *op.cit.* (1963) pp.41–5.
  7. Francesco Palazzolo Drago, *Famiglie nobili siciliane* (1927).
  8. Denis Mack Smith, *Medieval Sicily* (1969) p.157.
  9. Vitello, *op.cit.* (1963) p.120.
  10. Anthony Blunt, *Sicilian Baroque* (1968) p.149.
  11. Vitello, *op.cit.* (1963) pp.92–7.
  12. J. Wickham Legg, *The Reformed Breviary of Cardinal Tomasi* (1904) pp.7–14.
  13. *Ibid.* pp.5–6.
  14. *Letteratura Inglese II*.
  15. Vitello, *op.cit.* (1963) pp.124–5.
  16. Denis Mack Smith, *Modern Sicily* (1968) p.308.
  17. Rosario La Duca, *Cercare Palermo* (1985) p.32.
  18. The document has been signed Epifanio M. Turrisi but the date has been obscured except for the year 1801.
  19. Letters found in the Palazzo Lampedusa, one undated, the other of 1849.
  20. Vitello, *op.cit.* (1963) pp.259–60.
  21. The character and achievements of Prince Giulio are discussed at length in Vitello, *op.cit.* (1963) pp.147–63 and Vitello, *op.cit.* (1987) pp.254–65.
  22. Gioacchino Lanza Tomasi, 'Pubblicatelo ma non a mie spese', *La Fiera Letteraria* 4 January 1968.
  23. Raleigh Trevelyan, *Princes under the Volcano* (1972) pp.147,173.
  24. Denis Mack Smith, *Victor Emanuel, Cavour and the Risorgimento* (1971) p.191.
  25. Unpublished document from Via Butera. 'Estremi degli atti più importanti riguardanti Casa Lampedusa', 28 August 1938.
  26. The matter is discussed at length by Vitello *op.cit.* (1963) pp.164–9.
  27. See note 25.
  28. *Ibid.*
  29. Francesco Caravita di Sirignano, *Memorie di un uomo inutile* (1981) p.16.

2:   A Sicilian Childhood (pp. 15–30)
  1. 'Places ...' pp.29–30.
  2. *Ibid.* pp.32–3.
  3. *Ibid.* p.34 and ms. of *'Ricordi ...'*.
  4. *Ibid.* p.36.
  5. *Ibid.* pp.39–40.
  6. Tina Whitaker's diary 5 July 1908. Quoted in Raleigh Trevelyan, *Princes under the Volcano* (1972) p.346.
  7. Unpublished diaries in the Via Butera.
  8. Letter from Giulia Trigona to Beatrice Palma, 17 October 1910. Via

Butera.

9. R. Giuffrida and R. Lentini, *L'Età dei Florio* (1986).

10. Pietro Nicolosi, *Palermo Fin de Siècle* (1979) p.11.

11. Unpublished diaries at the Via Butera.

12. G. P. Samonà, *Il Gattopardo, i Racconti, Lampedusa* (1974) p.285.

13. Anna Pomar, *Donna Franca Florio* (1985) p.128.

14. Undated letters found in the ruins of the Palazzo Lampedusa, May 1985.

15. Fulco di Verdura, *The Happy Summer Days* (1976) p.149.

16. 'Places ...' p.48.

17. Gioacchino Lanza Tomasi, 'Un tramonto dorato' in Giuffrida and Lentini, *op.cit.* p.155.

18. Trevelyan, *op.cit.* p.326.

19. Pomar, *op.cit.* p.136.

20. Verdura, *op.cit* p.134.

21. Nicolosi, *op.cit.* p.18.

22. Denis Mack Smith, *Modern Sicily* (1968) p.266.

23. Verdura, *op.cit.* p.112.

24. Mack Smith, *op.cit.* p.290.

25. Verdura, *op.cit.* p.138.

26. Pomar, *op.cit.* p.134.

27. Trevelyan, *op.cit.* p.326.

28. Samonà, *op.cit.* p.431.

29. Luigi Barzini, *From Caesar to the Mafia* (1971) p.210.

30. 'Places ...' p.68.

31. Information from Sir Steven Runciman to the author.

32. 'Places ...' pp.42–3.

33. *Ibid.* pp.44–5.

34. *Ibid.* pp.46, 73–4 and ms. of '*Ricordi* ...'.

35. Ms. of 'Ricordi ...'.

36. *Letteratura Inglese I*.

37. 'Places ...' p.55.

38. Francesco Orlando, *Ricordo di Lampedusa* (1963) pp.68–9.

39. 'Places ...' pp.64–5.

40. *Ibid.* p.67.

41. *Ibid.* p.31 and ms. of 'Ricordi ...'.

42. Trevelyan, *op.cit.* p.358.

43. See note 8.

44. Andrea Vitello, *Giuseppe Tomasi di Lampedusa* (1987) p.51.

45. Pomar, *op.cit.* pp.188–90.

46. Vitello, *op.cit.* p.56.

3: The War and Fascism (pp. 31–44)

1. Document from the Via Butera. Stamped 1915, but dated 12 May 1917, it refers to the year 1913–14.

2. G. P. Samonà, *Il Gattopardo, i Racconti, Lampedusa* (1974) p.435.

3. Document dated July 1915 and signed by il Direttore della Segreteria of the Università degli Studi di Roma.

4. Document dated 7 February 1916. Via Butera.

5. Andrea Vitello, *Giuseppe Tomasi di Lampedusa* (1987) p.62.

6. Document from the Via Butera. He was made a reserve major in November 1917.

7. Three letters found in the rubble of the Palazzo Lampedusa. Two of them seem to have been written in May 1916, the third in the following autumn.

8. *Ibid.*

9. Information from Giuseppe Biancheri.

10. Vitello, *op.cit.* p.66.

11. Information from Francesco Agnello and Giuseppe Biancheri.

12. Information from Giuseppe Biancheri.

13. Luigi Barzini, *From Caesar to the Mafia* (1971) p.204.

14. Information from Gioacchino Lanza Tomasi.

15. Gaspare Giudice, *Pirandello* (1975) p.149.

16. Samonà, *op.cit.* p.439.

17. *Ibid.*

18. *Ibid.* p.441. See also Gaetano Falzone, 'Il "mio" Gattopardo', *Giornale di Sicilia* 13 June 1962.

19. Samonà, *op.cit.* p.438.

20. Several albums of 1925 and 1926 from the Via Butera.

21. *Letteratura Inglese I.*

22. *Letteratura Inglese V.*

23. *Letteratura Inglese II.*

24. *Letteratura Inglese V.*

25. *Letteratura Inglese II.*

26. *Le Opere e i Giorni*, May 1926, November 1926 and March–April 1927.

27. *Letteratura Inglese III.*

28. Francesco Orlando, *Ricordo di Lampedusa* (1963) p.18.

29. *Letteratura Inglese I.*

30. *Letteratura Inglese II.*

31. 'Places ...' p.33.

32. Samonà, *op.cit.* p.353.

33. Undated. Via Butera.

34. From the remains of books and card catalogues found in the Palazzo Lampedusa.

35. Untitled and undated four-page manuscript from the Via Butera.

36. See note 26.

37. Vitello, *op.cit.* p.76.

38. Letter dated 8 September 1927. The signature is unclear but may be Raffaele Calgini.

4:   The Wanderer in England (pp. 45–58)

1. Francesco Orlando, *Ricordo di Lampedusa* (1963) p.42.

2. Photograph album from the Via Butera.

3. Orlando, *op.cit.* p.41.

4. *Ibid.*

5. *Lettere Francesi* p.56.

6. Information from Gioacchino Lanza Tomasi. See also *The Times* 16 November 1922.

7. Raleigh Trevelyan, *Princes under the Volcano* (1972) p.398.

8. Documents from the Via Butera.

9. *Ibid.*

10. Letters from Sir Steven Runciman to the author, 1986.

11. *Letteratura Inglese II.*

12. *Letteratura Inglese IV.*

13. *Letteratura Inglese I.*

14. *Letteratura Inglese II.*

15. *Letteratura Inglese III.*

16. *Ibid.*

17. *Letteratura Inglese IV.*

18. Andrea Vitello, *Giuseppe Tomasi di Lampedusa* (1987) p.91.

19. Story told by Lampedusa to Gioacchino Lanza Tomasi.

20. *Letteratura Inglese IV.*

21. *Letteratura Inglese II.*

22. Orlando, *op.cit.* p.36.

23. *Letteratura Inglese IV.*

24. *Letteratura Inglese I.*

25. *Letteratura Inglese IV.*

26. *Letteratura Inglese I.*

27. *Ibid.*

28. Letters from Lady Hermione della Grazia to the author, 1986.

29. Archibald Colquhoun in *Two Stories* ... p.19.

30. Gioacchino Lanza Tomasi to the author.

31. Vitello, *op.cit.* p.96.

32. Orlando, *op.cit.* p.38.

33. *Ibid.* pp.38–9.

34. *Letteratura Inglese I.*

35. *Letteratura Inglese V.*

36. *Letteratura Inglese III.*

37. *Letteratura Inglese II.*

38. *Letteratura Inglese IV.*

39. *Letteratura Inglese V.*

40. Lampedusa's commonplace book. Via Butera.

41. *Letteratura Inglese II.*

42. *Ibid.*

43. *Letteratura Inglese IV.*

44. Orlando, *op.cit.* p.37.

45. *Ibid.*

46. *Ibid.* p.39.

47. *Letteratura Inglese II.*

48. *Ibid.* Also Orlando, *op.cit.* pp.39–40, 68-9.

49. Library in the Via Butera.

5:   A Baltic Marriage (pp. 59–72)

1. *Letteratura Inglese I.*
2. Library in the Via Butera.
3. Andrea Vitello, *Giuseppe Tomasi di Lampedusa* ('1987) pp.74–5, 101.
4. *L'Espresso* 19 July 1987.
5. Archibald Colquhoun's introduction to 'Places ...' p.16.
6. Caterina Cardona, *Lettere a Licy* (1987) pp.30–3.
7. *Ibid.* p.46.
8. *Ibid.* pp.46–7.
9. Vitello, *op.cit.* pp.123–4.
10. Letter dated 17 August 1932, Munich.
11. Letter to Giulio di Lampedusa, dated 24 August 1932, Riga.
12. Letter to Beatrice Lampedusa, 24 August 1932, Riga.
13. Letter to Beatrice Lampedusa, 29 August 1932, Riga.
14. *Ibid.*
15. Letter from Alessandra Palma to Beatrice Lampedusa, postmarked 6 September 1932, Riga.
16. From the diary of the Marchesa della Torrettà.
17. Interview with Francesco Orlando in *Il Messaggero,* 23 July 1987.
18. See the article by Stefano Malatesta in *La Repubblica* 5 June 1987, and the coverage by *L'Espresso* 19 July 1987. The denials come, with unquestionable authority, from Boris Biancheri and Gioacchino Lanza Tomasi in *La Repubblica* 13 June 1987.
19. Undated letter, Via Butera.
20. *Letteratura Inglese III.*
21. Cardona, *op.cit.* pp.40–5.
22. From various letters in the Via Butera by Alessandra di Lampedusa, Giuseppe di Lampedusa, André Pilar and Lila Iljascenko, 1935–8.
23. Letter from André Pilar to Lampedusa, Château Vuippens, 23 September 1942.
24. Cardona, *op.cit.* pp.40–5.
25. Found in the Palazzo Lampedusa May 1985.
26. Under various headings, *Storia Genealogica, Morti e Testamenti, Estremi di atti di Casa Lampedusa* and *Indirizzi Eredi.*
27. *Letteratura Inglese I.*
28. Vences Lanza to the author, May 1987.
29. G. Falzone, *Storia della Mafia* (1975) p.13
30. G. Falzone, 'Il "mio" Gattopardo', *Giornale di Sicilia* 13 June 1962.

6:   The Troubles of Don Giuseppe (pp. 73–88)

1. Andrea Vitello, *Giuseppe Tomasi di Lampedusa* (1987) p.132.
2. *Lettere Francesi* p.103.
3. Francesco Orlando, *Ricordo di Lampedusa* (1963) p.68.
4. Document from Via Butera.
5. Vitello, *op.cit.* pp.131–3.
6. Caterina Cardona, *Lettere a Licy* (1987) p.77.

7. From an English translation of a letter Licy wrote in October 1939, probably to her mother.

8. Cardona, *op.cit.* pp.51–6.

9. *Letteratura Inglese I.*

10. Cardona, *op.cit.* pp.56–8.

11. *Ibid.* p.60.

12. Vitello, *op.cit.* p.134.

13. Cardona, *op.cit.* p.64.

14. *Ibid.* p.59.

15. For information on the Piccolo family I am grateful to several people including Vences Lanza and Gioacchino Lanza Tomasi.

16. From Eugenio Montale's afterword to Lucio Piccolo's *Canti Barocchi e altre liriche*, translated and reproduced in Brian Swann and Ruth Feldman (eds), *Collected Poems of Lucio Piccolo* (1972) p.202.

17. *Letteratura Inglese IV.*

18. *Lettere Francesi* p.42.

19. Orlando, *op.cit.* p.72.

20. Gioacchino Lanza Tomasi's introduction to the Duke of Salaparuta's *Cucina Vegeteriana* (1971) p.vii.

21. V. Consolo, V. Roncisvalle, J. Tognelli (eds), *Lucio Piccolo* (1979) pp.94–5.

22. Gioacchino Lanza Tomasi, *op.cit.* p.vii.

23. Cardona, *op.cit.* pp.64–6.

24. *Ibid.* pp.71–2.

25. *Ibid.* pp.73–5.

26. *Ibid.* p.83.

27. *Ibid.* p.76.

28. 'Places...' p.37.

29. *Ibid.* p.35.

30. Cardona, *op.cit.* p.81.

31. Count Giuseppe di Sarzana to the author.

32. Vitello, *op.cit.* p.135.

33. *Letteratura Inglese II.*

34. Vitello, *op.cit.* pp.139–42.

35. Interview with Francesco Orlando, *Il Messaggero* 23 July 1987.

36. Cardona, *op.cit.* p.83.

37. Michel David, *La Psicoanalisi nella cultura Italiana* (1966) p.540.

38. From Lampedusa's Red Cross files in Via Butera.

39. Letter from Lampedusa to il Presidente del Comitato Centrale della Croce Rossa Italiana, 4 May 1946.

40. Letter from Lampedusa to Umberto Zanotti-Bianco, Presidente Generale della Croce Rossa Italiana, 1 August 1946.

41. Letter from G. B. Vicentini to Lampedusa, 5 May 1947.

42. Vitello, *op.cit.* p.154.

43. Interview with Antonio Curatolo, *Dimensione Sicilia* September 1987.

44. 'Places ...' pp.56–7.

45. Gioacchino Lanza Tomasi to the author.

46. Guidebook to La Fondazione Piccolo, Capo d'Orlando. See also Vitello, *op.cit.* pp.336–8.

7:   At Home in the Via Butera (pp. 89–105)
    1. Letter from Derek Hill to the author, July 1985.
    2. Giuseppe Biancheri to the author.
    3. Francesco Corrao in *Dimensione Sicilia* September 1987.
    4. Francesco Orlando, *Ricordo di Lampedusa* (1963) p.16.
    5. Derek Hill, *op.cit.*
    6. Francesco Caravita di Sirignano, *Memorie di un uomo inutile* (1981) p.14.
    7. Descriptions from, respectively, Giorgio Bassani, Vences Lanza and Luigi Barzini.
    8. Caravita di Sirignano, *op.cit.* p.14.
    9. Diaries, 1955–6.
    10. Licy's Diary, 1952.
    11. Hill, *op.cit.*
    12. *Ibid.*
    13. Caravita di Sirignano, *op.cit.* pp.14–15.
    14. Bernard Berenson, *Sunset and Twilight* (1964) p.313.
    15. Vences Lanza's anecdote to the author is corroborated by Lampedusa's diary, 27–8 January 1956.
    16. Caravita di Sirignano, *op.cit.* p.14.
    17. Orlando, *op.cit.* p.9.
    18. Ms of 'Ricordi ...'
    19. Interview with Francesco Orlando, *Il Messaggero* 23 July 1987.
    20. Caterina Cardona, *Lettere a Licy* (1987) p.86.
    21. Gioacchino Lanza Tomasi to the author.
    22. Orlando, *op.cit.* p.11.
    23. Giancarlo Buzzi, *Invito alla lettura di Tomasi di Lampedusa* (1976) p.21.
    24. Letter from Alfonso de Otazu to the author, February 1988.
    25. Gaetano Falzone, 'La Sicilia de "Il Gattopardo" ' in *Vie Mediterranee* (1959) No.19.
    26. Gaetano Falzone, *Storia della Mafia* (1975) p.12.
    27. Orlando, *op.cit.* pp.75–6.
    28. *Ibid.* pp.76–7.
    29. Interview with Gioacchino Lanza Tomasi, *Famiglia Cristiana* 7 May 1986.
    30. Falzone (1975), *op.cit.* p.13.
    31. *Letteratura Inglese II.*
    32. Andrea Vitello, *Giuseppe Tomasi di Lampedusa* (1987) p.192.
    33. Gaetano Falzone, 'Il "mio" Gattopardo', *Giornale di Sicilia* 13 June 1962.
    34. Interview with F. Pavone, *Humanitas* 11 February 1960.
    35. Orlando, *op.cit.* p.72.
    36. *Ibid.* p.86.
    37. *Letteratura Inglese V.*
    38. Orlando, *op.cit.* p.70.
    39. *Letteratura Inglese V.*
    40. Vitello, *op.cit.* p.129.

41. Hill, *op.cit.*
42. Gioacchino Lanza Tomasi to the author.
43. Orlando, *op.cit.* p.10.
44. *Ibid.* pp.13–15.
45. Via Butera.
46. Interview in *Weekend Telegraph,* 4 February 1966.
47. Interview with Francesco Orlando, *Il Messaggero* 23 July 1987.
48. Gioacchino Lanza Tomasi to the author. See also his article, 'Il sacrificio di Concetta', *La Fiera Letteraria* 4 January 1968.
49. *Ibid.*
50. Diaries 1955–6.
51. 'Lezioni ...' p.17.
52. 'Places ...' p.40.
53. Orlando, *op.cit.* p.45.
54. 'Lighea', p.96.
55. *Letteratura Inglese IV.*
56. Orlando, *op.cit.* p.45.
57. Lanza Tomasi, *op.cit.* (1968).
58. *Letteratura Inglese I.*
59. *Ibid.*
60. *Letteratura Inglese III.*
61. *Letteratura Inglese I.*
62. Information from Giuseppe and Boris Biancheri to the author.
63. Licy's diary, 1956.
64. Gioacchino Lanza Tomasi to the author.
65. Francesco Agnello to the author.
66. Vences Lanza to the author.

8:   The Consolation of Literature (pp. 106–24)
1. *Letteratura Inglese III.*
2. Francesco Orlando, *Ricordo di Lampedusa* (1963) p.15.
3. Interview in *Weekend Telegraph* 4 February 1966.
4. Luigi Barzini, *From Caesar to the Mafia* (1971) p.216.
5. *Ibid.* p.215.
6. Orlando, *op.cit.* p.17.
7. *Ibid.* p.22.
8. Giuseppe Paolo Samonà, *Il Gattopardo, i Racconti, Lampedusa* (1974) pp.454–7.
9. Orlando, *op.cit.* p.20.
10. *Letteratura Inglese III.*
11. *Letteratura Inglese IV.*
12. *Letteratura Inglese II.*
13. 'Lezioni ...' p.49.
14. *Lettere Francesi* p.5.
15. Orlando, *op.cit.* pp.10–12, 16, 22–4.
16. *Letteratura Inglese I.*
17. *Ibid.*

18. *Ibid.*

19. *Ibid.*

20. Orlando, *op.cit.* p.27.

21. *Letteratura Inglese I.*

22. *Ibid.*

23. *Letteratura Inglese II.*

24. *Letteratura Inglese III.*

25. *Letteratura Inglese II and III.*

26. *Letteratura Inglese IV.*

27. Manuscript headed *Le solite premesse inutili* at the beginning of *Letteratura Inglese V.*

28. *Ibid.*

29. *Letteratura Inglese V.*

30. *Ibid.*

31. *Letteratura Inglese III and V.*

32. Orlando, *op.cit.* pp.28–9.

33. *Ibid.* pp.26–7.

34. *Lettere Francesi*, pp.7, 18–19, 22, 25, 33.

35. *Ibid.* pp.50–6.

36. *Ibid.* pp.95–6.

37. *Ibid.* p.103.

38. *Ibid.* pp.53, 101, 112.

39. 'Lezioni ...' pp.3, 18, 19, 24, 31–2, 61.

40. *Ibid.* pp.64–7, 82–3.

41. *Ibid.* pp.12–16, 51–6, 60–1.

42. Orlando, *op.cit.* pp.50–5. *Lettere Francesi*, p.21.

43. Diaries, 1955–6.

44. Caterina Cardona, *Lettere a Licy* (1987) pp.86–7.

45. *Ibid.*

46. Orlando, *op.cit.* p.58.

47. *Ibid.* p.43.

48. *Letteratura Inglese I and V.*

49. *Letteratura Inglese IV.*

50. Orlando, *op.cit.* p.43, Samonà, *op.cit.* pp.453–4.

51. *Letteratura Inglese I and III.*

52. *Letteratura Inglese III and IV.*

53. *Letteratura Inglese V.*

54. *Letteratura Inglese IV.*

55. *Letteratura Inglese V.*

56. *Ibid.*

57. *Letteratura Inglese IV.*

9:   The Reluctant Writer (pp.125–39)

1. Quoted by Eugenio Montale in his afterword to Lucio Piccolo's *Canti Barocchi e altre liriche*, translated and reproduced in Brian Swann and Ruth Feldman (eds), *Collected Poems of Lucio Piccolo* (1972) p.197.

2. Leonardo Sciascia, *La corda pazza* (1982) p.178.

3. Swann and Feldman, *op.cit.* p.204.

4. *Ibid.* p.202.

5. Giorgio Bassani, preface to *Il Gattopardo*.

6. Swann and Feldman, *op.cit.* p.202.

7. Bassani, *op.cit.*

8. *Letteratura Inglese IV*.

9. Ferdinando Scianna, Dominique Fernandez and Leonardo Sciascia, *I Siciliani* (1977) p.xviii.

10. Simonetta Salvestroni, *Tomasi di Lampedusa* (1979) p.25.

11. Gioacchino Lanza Tomasi, preface to *Il Gattopardo* (1969) p.vii.

12. Francesco Orlando, *Ricordo di Lampedusa* (1963) pp.89–90.

13. Letter to Guido Lajolo, 31 March 1956.

14. Gioacchino Lanza Tomasi, 'Donnafugata non c'è più', *La Fiera Letteraria* 8 February 1968.

15. Luigi Barzini, *From Caesar to the Mafia* (1971) p.204.

16. Archibald Colquhoun, translator's note to *The Leopard* (1961).

17. Bassani, *op.cit.*

18. Gioacchino Lanza Tomasi, 'Pubblicatelo ma non a mie spese', *La Fiera Letteraria* 21 March 1968.

19. Lanza Tomasi, *op.cit.* (1969) p.x.

20. Lanza Tomasi, 'Pubblicatelo ...' *op.cit.*

21. Giorgio Bassani, *Le parole preparate* (1966), p.178.

22. Ms of 'Ricordi ...'

23. Orlando, *op.cit.* pp.59–61.

24. Diary, 1955.

25. Orlando, *op.cit.* p.61.

26. *Ibid.* pp.61–3.

27. Diary, 1955.

28. *Ibid.*

29. *Ibid.*

30. Freya Stark, *Some Talk of Alexander* (1982) p.132.

31. Diary, 1955.

32. Lanza Tomasi, 'Donnafugata ...' *op.cit.*

33. From the library, Via Butera.

34. For the Palma visits I have used the 1955 diary and the evidence of Francesco Agnello and Gioacchino Lanza Tomasi. Andrea Vitello discusses the visits at length in *Giuseppe Tomasi di Lampedusa* (1987) pp.219–24, but his account is sometimes contradicted by the diary. He insists, for example, that Lampedusa did not see the archpriest on this occasion.

35. Diary, 1955.

36. *Ibid.* Also evidence from Agnello and Lanza Tomasi.

37. Diary, 1955.

38. Diary, 1956.

39. *Ibid.*

40. *Ibid.* Also Orlando, *op.cit.* pp.79–80.

41. Orlando, *op.cit.* pp.80–2.

42. *Ibid.* p.89.

43. Lanza Tomasi, 'Pubblicatelo ...' *op.cit.*
44. Letter to Lajolo, *op.cit.*

10:   Vocation and Commitment (pp. 140–52)

1. Andrea Vitello, *I Gattopardi di Donnafugata* (1963) pp.22–31.
2. Quoted in Andrea Vitello, *Giuseppe Tomasi di Lampedusa* (1987) p.234.
3. Letter from Mondadori, 10 December 1956.
4. Gioacchino Lanza Tomasi, 'Pubblicatelo ma non a mie spese', *La Fiera Letteraria* 21 March 1968.
5. Letter to Guido Lajolo, 2 January 1957.
6. Licy's diary, 18 December 1956.
7. Basilio Reale, *Sirene siciliane* (1986) p.89.
8. Vitello (1987) *op.cit.* pp.240–2.
9. Information from Francesco Agnello to the author. See also Reale's remarks in an article by Stefano Malatesta in *La Repubblica* 15 October 1986.
10. Leonardo Sciascia, *La corda pazza* (1982) p.177.
11. Luigi Barzini, *From Caesar to the Mafia* (1971) p.90.
12. Francesco Caravita di Sirignano, *Memorie de un uomo inutile* (1981) p.15.
13. Letter to Lajolo, *op.cit.*
14. *Ibid.*
15. *Ibid.*
16. Diaries, 1955–6.
17. Letter to Lajolo, *op.cit.*
18. Diary, 1956.
19. Letter to Lajolo, *op.cit.*
20. Giuseppe Paolo Samonà, *Il Gattopardo, i Racconti, Lampedusa* (1974) p.298.
21. Extracts taken from Alfred Alexander's *Stories of Sicily* (1975).
22. Via Butera.
23. Norman Douglas, *Siren Land* (1983) pp.4, 15.
24. Translations by Archibald Colquhoun in Lampedusa's *Two Stories and a Memory* (1961).
25. *Ibid.* From E.M.Forster's introduction.
26. Information from Gioacchino Lanza Tomasi.
27. Lanza Tomasi (1968) *op.cit.*
28. Gioacchino Lanza Tomasi, preface to *Il Gattopardo* (1969) p.xii.
29. Francesco Orlando, *Ricordo di Lampedusa* (1963) p.82.
30. See notes 1 and 38 in Chapter 14.
31. Lanza Tomasi (1969) *op.cit.* pp.xiii–xviii.

11:   Death and Redemption (pp. 153–62)

1. Caterina Cardona, *Lettere a Licy* (1987) p.15.
2. Francesco Orlando, *Ricordo di Lampedusa* (1963) p.79.
3. *Dimensione Sicilia* September 1987.
4. Orlando, *op.cit.* p.78.
5. Diary, 1956.
6. Orlando, *op.cit.* p.79.

7. *Ibid.* p.78.

8. Gioacchino Lanza Tomasi, unpublished paper read in Austin 1986.

9. Gioacchino Lanza Tomasi, 'Pubblicatelo ma non a mie spese', *La Fiera Letteraria* 21 March 1968. Andrea Vitello, *Giuseppe Tomasi di Lampedusa* (1987) pp.314–15.

10. Letter to Mirella Radice, 5 June 1957.

11. Two letters to Mirella Radice, one 20 June 1957, the other undated. Letter to the Piccolos reproduced in Vitello, *op.cit.* pp.316–17.

12. *Ibid.*

13. Letter to Mirella Radice, 28 June 1957. Letter to the Piccolos of 27 June reproduced in Vitello, *op.cit.* pp.317–18.

14. Letter to Mirella Radice, 28 June 1957.

15. *Ibid.*

16. Vitello, *op.cit.* p.319.

17. Letter to Gioacchino Lanza Tomasi, 12 July 1957.

18. Information from Boris Biancheri.

19. Reproduced in Vitello, *op.cit.* pp.249–50.

20. Gioacchino Lanza Tomasi, preface to *Il Gattopardo* (1969) p.x.

21. Lanza Tomasi, *op.cit.* (1968).

22. Vitello, *op.cit.* pp.321–2.

23. Licy's diary 4 March 1958.

24. Giuseppe Paolo Samonà, *Il Gattopardo, i Racconti, Lampedusa* (1974) p.214.

25. *Ibid.* p.361.

26. See Bassani's interview in *Giornale di Sicilia* 13 January 1970.

27. Licy's diary, 1958.

28. Bassani, *op.cit.*

29. Olga Ragusa, *Narrative and Drama* (1976) p.16.

30. Licy's diary, 1958.

31. Bassani, *op.cit.*

12:   The Solitude of Don Fabrizio (pp.163–70)

1. Andrea Vitello, *I Gattopardi di Donnafugata* (1963) p.215.

2. Andrea Vitello, *Giuseppe Tomasi di Lampedusa* (1987) p.332.

3. Letters to Guido Lajolo, 31 March 1956, 7 June 1956 and 2 January 1957.

4. Translated into English as *The Fight for Freedom: Palermo 1860* (1968).

5. *Ibid.* pp.46–51, 72–4, 189–94.

6. See Simonetta Salvestroni, *Tomasi di Lampedusa* (1979) pp.68–9, 74, and Maria Pagliara-Giacovazzo, *Il "Gattopardo" o la metafora decadente dell'esistenza* (n.d.) pp.31, 34.

7. Ferdinando Castelli, *Letteratura dell'Inquietudine* (1963) p.304.

8. Massimo Ganci, 'La Sicilia del Gattopardo': introduction to a special numbered edition of *Il Gattopardo* (1969).

9. Fulco di Verdura, *The Happy Summer Days* (1976) p.102.

13:   The Leopard's Sicily (pp.171–84)

1. See, for example, Giorgio Pullini's review in *Letterature Moderne* March–

April 1960.

2. Enrico Falqui, *Tempo* 30 May 1959. Also published in his *Novecento Letterario* (1961).

3. Gaia Servadio, *Luchino Visconti* (1981) p.175.

4. Francis M. Guercio, *Sicily* (1968) p.67.

5. *Letteratura Inglese IV.*

6. Francesco Orlando, *Ricordo di Lampedusa* (1963) p.33.

7. *Ibid.* p.32.

8. J.W. Goethe, *Italian Journey* (1982) p.246.

9. *Letteratura Inglese IV.*

10. 'Places ...' p.73.

11. Orlando, *op.cit.* p.33.

12. Leonardo Sciascia, *Pirandello e la Sicilia* (1983) p.130. Falqui, *op.cit.*

13. Luigi Russo, 'Analisi del Gattopardo' in *Belfagor* 30 September 1960.

14. Giuseppe Stammati refers to this in '"Gattopardeschi" e no' in *Belfagor* 31 March 1960.

15. M.I. Finley, *Ancient Sicily* (1979) p.45.

16. *Ibid.* pp.56–7. Quoted from Voltaire's *Le Siècle de Louis le Grand.*

17. Sebastiano Aglianò, *Cos'è questa Sicilia* (1945).

18. Denis Mack Smith, *Modern Sicily* (1969) p.400.

19. Agatha Ramm, 'The Risorgimento in Sicily' in *English Historical Review* vol LXXXVII (1972). Walter Maturi, *Interpretazioni del Risorgimento* (1962) pp.666–72.

20. Rosario Romeo, *Il Risorgimento in Sicilia* (1982) pp.12–15, 40–52.

21. Andrea Vitello, *I Gattopardi di Donnafugata* (1963) p.246.

22. Sergio Zatti, *Tomasi di Lampedusa* (1972) p.36.

23. Franco Venturi, *Italy and the Enlightenment* (1972) p.221.

24. Information on Lampedusa's views from Francesco Agnello.

25. Francesco Renda, *Storia della Sicilia dal 1860 al 1970* (1984) p.14.

26. Leonardo Sciascia, *La Sicilia come metafora* (1979) p.52. Andrea Vitello, *Giuseppe Tomasi di Lampedusa* (1987) p.370.

27. Mario Alicata in *Il Contemporaneo* April 1959.

28. E.g. Renda, *op.cit.* Falqui, *op.cit.* and Giuliano Manacorda, *Storia della Letteratura Italiana (1940–65)* (1967) p.305.

29. Denis Mack Smith, *Cavour* (1985) p.216.

30. Denis Mack Smith, *Cavour and Garibaldi 1860* (1954) pp.389–90.

31. Vitello, *op.cit.* (1963) p.308.

32. Anton Blok, *The Mafia of a Sicilian Village 1860–1960* (1974) p.11. Norman Lewis, *The Honoured Society* (1984) p.14. Leonardo Sciascia, 'Mafia', reprinted in Fabrizio Calvi, *La vita quotidiana della Mafia dal 1950 a oggi* (1986) p.11.

33. Romeo, *op.cit.* p.385.

34. Leonardo Sciascia, *La corda pazza* (1982) p.179.

35. Denis Mack Smith, 'The Peasants' Revolt in Sicily, 1860' in *Victor Emanuel, Cavour and the Risorgimento* (1971).

36. Quoted in Denis Mack Smith, *The Making of Italy, 1796–1866* (1968) p.379.

37. Antonio Gramsci, *Sul Risorgimento* (1959).

38. S.J. Woolf, *The Italian Risorgimento* (1969) pp.95–6.

39. This was the opinion of *The Leopard*'s translator, Archibald Colquhoun.

40. E.g. Adolfo Omodeo, *Difesa del Risorgimento* (1955) pp.444–6.

41. N. Rodolico. Cited in Derek Beales, *The Risorgimento and the Unification of Italy* (1981) p.19.

14: *Il caso Lampedusa* (pp. 185–93)

1. Antonio Dipace, *Questione delle varianti del Gattopardo* (1971).

2. Maria Pagliara-Giacovazzo, *Il "Gattopardo" o la metafora decadente dell'esistenza* (n.d.).

3. Basilio Reale, *Sirene siciliane* (1986).

4. Carlo Bo, *L'eredità di Leopardi e altri saggi* (1964) p.304.

5. Eugenio Montale, *Corriere della Sera* 12 December 1958.

6. Geno Pampaloni, 'Il Gattopardo' in A.Moravia and E.Zolla, *Saggi Italiani 1959* (1960) p.134.

7. Luigi Barzini, *From Caesar to the Mafia* (1971) p.221.

8. From a review in *Etudes*. See Ivos Margoni, '"Il Gattopardo" in Francia' in *Belfagor* 30 September 1960.

9. Giuseppe de Rosa in *La Civiltà Cattolica* April 1959.

10. See, for example, *Nuovi Argomenti* May–August 1959.

11. See M.Caesar and P.Hainsworth, *Writers and Society in Contemporary Italy* (1984) p.26.

12. See Margoni, *op.cit.*

13. Andrea Vitello, *Giuseppe Tomasi di Lampedusa* (1987) p.238.

14. Giuseppe Paolo Samonà, *Il Gattopardo, i Racconti, Lampedusa* (1974) p.215. See also Giancarlo Buzzi, *Invito alla lettura di Tomasi di Lampedusa* (1976).

15. Vitello, *op.cit.* p.238.

16. Interview in *Il giorno* 24 February 1959.

17. *Rinascita* March 1959 p.219.

18. Alberto Moravia, *L'Espresso* 7 April 1963.

19. Aragon wrote two articles on Lampedusa in *Lettres françaises* 23 December 1959 and 18 February 1960.

20. Margoni, *op.cit.*

21. Jean Prasteau in *Le Figaro* 18 November 1959.

22. Maurice Vaussard in *Le Monde* 1 December 1959.

23. Jean Blanzat, *Le Figaro Litteraire* 18 November 1959.

24. See, for example, Harold Nicolson in the *Observer* 8 May 1960.

25. *The Times* 12 May 1960. Raymond Mortimer in *The Sunday Times* 8 May 1960.

26. Nicolson, *op.cit.*

27. Mortimer, *op.cit.*

28. *Spectator* 13 May 1960.

29. Leonardo Sciascia, *La Sicilia come metafora* (1979) p.52.

30. See Sciascia's letter in Samonà, *op.cit.* p.412.

31. Gioacchino Lanza Tomasi's introduction to the Duca di Salaparuta,

Cucina vegetariana (1971) p.v.

32. Fulco di Verdura, *The Happy Summer Days* (1976) p.149.

33. *Corriere della Sera* 12 December 1958.

34. See Barzini, *op.cit.* p.213. Also Archibald Colquhoun's introduction to Federico De Roberto, *The Viceroys* (1962) p.13.

35. Vittorio Spinazzola, *Federico De Roberto e il verismo* (1961) p.215. See also Buzzi, *op.cit.* pp.53–60.

36. See the article by T.O'Neill, 'Lampedusa and De Roberto' in *Italica* vol. 47 no.2 1970.

37. Colquhoun, *op.cit.* p.11.

38. Dipace, *op.cit.* and Samonà *op.cit.* pp.216–31. See also Gioacchino Lanza Tomasi, 'Pubblicatelo ma non a mie spese' in *La Fiera Letteraria* 21 March 1968, and his preface to the 1969 edition of *Il Gattopardo*.

39. Information from Giuseppe Biancheri.

40. Vitello, *op.cit.* p.350.

41. *Ibid.* p.351.

42. *Ibid.* p.352.

43. Eugenio Montale, *Corriere della Sera* 6 October 1963.

44. Barzini, *op.cit.* p.203.

Bibliography

List of books cited in the Notes

Addamo, Sebastiano, *Vittorini e la narrativa Siciliana contemporanea*, Sciascia (Caltanisetta) 1962.

Aglianò, Sebastiano, *Cos'è questa Sicilia*, Mascali (Syracuse) 1954.

Alexander, Alfred, *Stories of Sicily*, Elek Books (London) 1975.

Barzini, Luigi, *From Caesar to the Mafia*, Hamish Hamilton (London) 1971.

Bassani, Giorgio, *Le parole preparate*, Einaudi (Turin) 1966.

Beales, Derek, *The Risorgimento and the Unification of Italy*, Longman (London) 1981.

Berenson, Bernard, *Sunset and Twilight*, Hamish Hamilton (London) 1964.

Blok, Anton, *The Mafia of a Sicilian Village 1860-1960*, Blackwell (Oxford) 1974.

Blunt, Anthony, *Sicilian Baroque*, Weidenfeld and Nicolson (London) 1968.

Bo, Carlo, *L'eredità di Leopardi e altri saggi*, Valecchi (Florence) 1964.

Brancaccio di Carpino, F., *Tre mesi nella Vicaria di Palermo nel 1860*, (Napoli) 1900.

Buzzi, Giancarlo, *Invito alla lettura di Tomasi di Lampedusa*, Mursia (Milan) 1976.

Caesar, M. and Hainsworth, P., *Writers and Society in Contemporary Italy*, Berg (Leamington Spa) 1984.

Calvi, Francesco, *La vita quotidiana della Mafia dal 1950 al oggi*, Rizzoli (Milan) 1986.

Caravita di Sirignano, Francesco, *Memorie di un uomo inutile*, Mondadori (Milan) 1981.

Cardona, Caterina, *Lettere a Licy*, Sellerio (Palermo) 1987.

Castelli, Ferdinando, *Letteratura dell'Inquietudine*, Massimo (Milan) 1963.

Consolo, V., Roncisvalle, V., Tognelli, J. (eds), *Lucio Piccolo*, Sciascia (Caltanisetta) 1979.

David, Michel, *La Psicoanalisi nella cultura Italiana*, Boringhieri (Turin) 1966.

De Robertis, Giuseppe, *Altro Novecento*, Le Monnier (Florence) 1962.

De Roberto, Federico, *The Viceroys*, Harcourt (New York) 1962.

Dipace, Antonio, *Questione delle varianti del Gattopardo*, Di Mambra (Latina) 1971.

Douglas, Norman, *Siren Land*, Penguin (London) 1983.

Falqui, Enrico, *Novecento letterario*, Valecchi (Florence) 1961.

Falzone, G., *Storia della Mafia*, Pan (Milan) 1975.

Finley, M.I., *Ancient Sicily*, Chatto and Windus (London) 1979.

Giudice, Gaspare, *Pirandello*, Oxford University Press 1975.

Giuffrida, R. and Lentini, R., *L'età dei Florio*, Sellerio (Palermo) 1986.

Goethe, J.W., *Italian Journey*, Penguin (London) 1982.

Gramsci, Antonio, *Sul Risorgimento*, Riuniti (Rome) 1959.

Grana, Gianni (ed), *Novecento* (vol.3), Marzorati (Milan) 1980.

Guercio, Francis, *Sicily*, Faber (London) 1968.

La Duca, Rosario, *Cercare Palermo*, La Bottega di Hefesto (Palermo) 1985.

Lewis, Norman, *The Honoured Society*, Eland Books (London) 1984.

Mack Smith, Denis, *Cavour*, Weidenfeld and Nicolson (London) 1985.

—— *Cavour and Garibaldi 1860*, Cambridge University Press 1954.

—— *The Making of Modern Italy 1796–1866*, Macmillan (London) 1968.

—— *Modern Sicily*, Chatto and Windus (London) 1969.

—— *Victor Emanuel, Cavour and the Risorgimento*, Oxford University Press 1971.

Manacorda, Giulio, *Storia delle Letteratura Italiana (1940–65)*, Riuniti (Rome) 1967.

Maturi, Walter, *Interpretazioni del Risorgimento*, Einaudi

(Turin) 1962.

Moravia, A. and Zolla, E., *Saggi Italiani 1959*, Bompiani (Milan) 1960.

Nicolosi, Pietro, *Palermo Fin de Siècle*, Mursia (Milan) 1979.

Omodeo, Adolfo, *Difesa del Risorgimento*, Einaudi (Turin) 1951.

Orlando, Francesco, *Ricordo di Lampedusa*, Vanni Scheiwiller (Milan) 1963.

Pagliara-Giacovazzo, Maria, *Il "Gattopardo" o la metafora decadente dell'esistenza*, Milella (Lecce) n.d.

Palazzolo Drago, Francesco, *Famiglie nobili siciliane*, Arnaldo Forni (Palermo) 1927.

Parris, John (ed), *The Fight for Freedom: Palermo, 1860*, Folio Society (London) 1968.

Piccioni, Leone, *La narrativa Italiana tra romanzo e racconti*, Mondadori (Milan) 1959.

Piccolo, Lucio, *Canti Barocchi e altre liriche*, Mondadori (Milan) 1954.

Pomar, Anna, *Donna Franca Florio*, Valecchi (Florence) 1985.

Ragusa, Olga, *Narrative and Drama*, Mouton (The Hague) 1976.

Reale, Basilio, *Sirene siciliane*, Sellerio (Palermo) 1986.

Renda, Francesco, *Storia della Sicilia dal 1860 al 1970*, Sellerio (Palermo) 1984.

Romeo, Rosario, *Il Risorgimento in Sicilia*, Laterza (Bari) 1982.

Runciman, Steven, *The Sicilian Vespers*, Cambridge University Press 1984.

Salaparuta, Duke of, *Cucina vegetariana*, Esse (Palermo) 1971.

Salvestroni, Simonetta, *Tomasi di Lampedusa*, La Nuova Italia (Florence) 1979.

Samonà, G.P., *Il Gattopardo, i Racconti, Lampedusa*, La Nuova Italia (Florence) 1974.

Scianna, F., Fernandez, D. and Sciascia, L., *I Siciliani*, Einaudi (Turin) 1977.

Sciascia, Leonardo, *La corda pazza*, Einaudi (Turin) 1982.

——— *Pirandello e la Sicilia*, Sciascia (Caltanisetta)1983.

——— *La Sicilia come metafora*, Mondadori (Milan) 1979.

Servadio, Gaia, *Luchino Visconti*, Weidenfeld and Nicolson (London) 1981.

Spinazzola, Vittorio, *Federico De Roberto e il verismo*, Feltrinelli (Milan) 1961.

Stark, Freya, *Some Talk of Alexander*, Michael Russell

(Salisbury) 1982.

Stirati, Arnaldo, *Il Gattopardo*, Le Muse (Rome) 1966.

Swann, B. and Feldman, R. (eds), *Collected Poems of Lucio Piccolo*, Princeton University Press 1972.

Tomasi di Lampedusa, *Il Gattopardo*, Feltrinelli (Milan) 1960.

———— *Il Gattopardo (edizione conforme al manoscritto de 1957)*, Feltrinelli (Milan) 1986.

———— *Invito alle lettere francesci del Cinquecento*, Feltrinelli (Milan) 1979.

———— *The Leopard*, Collins (London) 1961.

———— *Lezioni su Stendhal*, Sellerio (Palermo) 1978.

———— *I Racconti*, Feltrinelli (Milan) 1976.

———— *Two Stories and a Memory*, Collins (London) 1962.

Trevelyan, Raleigh, *Princes under the Volcano*, Macmillan (London) 1972.

Venturi, Franco, *Italy and the Enlightenment*, Longman (London) 1972.

Verdura, Fulco di, *The Happy Summer Days*, Weidenfeld and Nicolson (London) 1976.

Vitello, Andrea, *I Gattopardi di Donnafugata*, Flaccovio (Palermo) 1963.

———— *Giuseppe Tomasi di Lampedusa*, Sellerio (Palermo) 1987.

Wickham Legg, J., *The Reformed Breviary of Cardinal Tomasi*, Church Historical Society (London) 1904.

Woolf, S.J., *The Italian Risorgimento*, Longman (London) 1969.

Zatti, Sergio, *Tomasi di Lampedusa*, Cetim Bresso (Milan) 1972.

Index